Travelling light

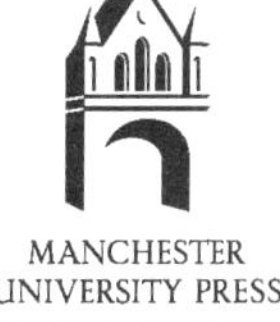

The Critical Image

This series explores the historical and contemporary uses of photography. It aims to develop photographic history and criticism and investigates practice. The publications draw on methods and theories widely used in art history, literature, film and cultural studies.

Series editor John Taylor
Department of History of Art and Design
Manchester Metropolitan University

Already published

Jane Brettle and Sally Rice (eds) *Public bodies – private states: new views on photography, representaion and gender*

David Brittain *Creative Camera: thirty years of writing*

Sarah Kember *Virtual anxiety: photography, new technologies and subjectivity*

John Roberts *The art of interruption: realism, photography and the everyday*

Lindsay Smith *The politics of focus: women, children and nineteenth-century photography*

John Taylor *A dream of England: landscape, photography and the tourist's imagination*

John Taylor *Body horror: photojournalism, catastrophe and war*

Travelling light

photography, travel and visual culture

Peter D. Osborne

MANCHESTER UNIVERSITY PRESS
Manchester and New York

distributed exclusively in the USA by St. Martin's Press

Published by Manchester University Press
Oxford Road, Manchester M13 9NR, UK
and Room 400, 175 Fifth Avenue, New York, NY 10010, USA
http://www.man.ac.uk/mup

Distributed exclusively in the USA by
St. Martin's Press, Inc., 175 Fifth Avenue, New York,
NY 10010, USA

Distributed exclusively in Canada by
UBC Press, University of British Columbia, 6344 Memorial Road,
Vancouver, BC, Canada V6T 1Z2

British Library Cataloguing-in-Publication Data
A catalogue record for this book is available from the British Library

Library of Congress Cataloging-in-Publication Data applied for

ISBN 0 7190 4400 6 *hardback*
0 7190 4401 4 *paperback*

First published 2000

06 05 04 03 02 01 00 10 9 8 7 6 5 4 3 2 1

Typeset by Lionart, Birmingham
Printed in Great Britain by Bell & Bain Ltd, Glasgow

Contents

List of figures and plates

Figures

Plates

The plates will be found between pages 116 and 117.

Illustrations not otherwise credited are by the author or from the author's collection.

Acknowledgements

The use of the visual material in this book was made possible through the generous support of the Krazna-Krausz Foundation and the London Institute.

For their influence or for their advice and expertise offered recently or in the past and bearing both directly and indirectly on the development of this book, I'd like to express my gratitude to the following: John Allen, Allen Abramson, Stevie Bezencenet, Zarina Bhimji, Shirley Eber, Jon Gooding, Dick Hebdige, Steve Heyman, Neil Mathesson, Colin Osman, Jorma Puranen, Mark Read, Colonel Redpen, Bill Schwarz, Les Shackell, Mike Stanhope, Denys Watkins, and to my colleague Anne Williams.

Thanks also to John Taylor, the series editor, and to Lauren McAllister and Matthew Frost of the Manchester University Press editorial staff for their hard work and forbearance.

For both their enthusiasm and scepticism I'd also like to thank past and present BA (Hons) Photography students at the London Institute's London College of Printing.

For practical and logistical support sometimes given at critical moments, my thanks to: Andrea Livingstone at Kraszna-Krausz, Frank Holmes, Fotini Papatheodorou, Fivos Spathopoulos, Steve Engelhart, and to Simon Lyes and Debbie Roland in the LCP School of Media library; and above all to Marion Scott for her time and patience.

Peter D. Osborne 2000

To Bethany and Marion
and
to the memory of Joanne Temple
who would have travelled further

Part I

Before photography

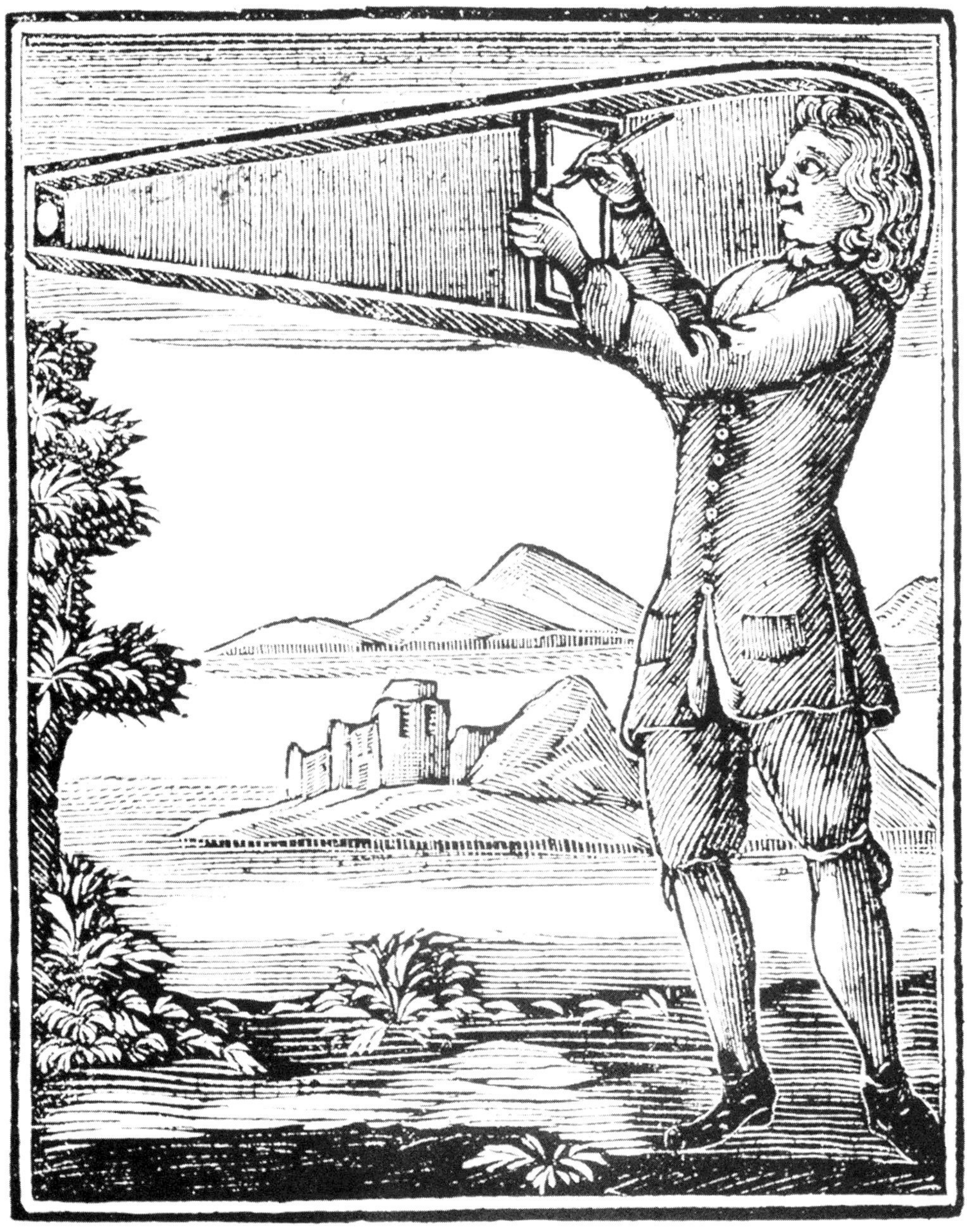

Camera obscura to demonstrate the workings of the eye: 'a darkened room, or perspective Box, in which all the Appearances that are made in the Eye are in some manner represented'. From The Posthumous Works of Robert Hooke, London, 1705. p. 126. (Courtesy of the British Museum (Natural History)).

Fig. 1 Portable camera obscura in use. See Wees (1980).

1
Camera portabilis: god, space and optics – the visualisation of mobility before 1840

> First god invented the voyage – then came doubt – then nostalgia. (*Ulysses' Gaze*, directed by Theodore Angelopoulos)

> The Renaissance ... [brought] forth the kind of consciousness that provides the cosmological foundation for tourism: the idea that truth lay outside the mind and spirit ... this urge to explore and understand. (Nelson Graburn, *Tourism: The Sacred Journey*)

> To travel is to see – travel is essentially a way of seeing, a mode of seeing: it is grounded in the eye, in our visual capacity. (Bernard McGrane, *Beyond Anthropology*)

As soon as there was photography there was travel photography. In October 1839 the Frenchman (it seems precipitate to describe him as a *photographer*) Pierre-Gustave Joly de Lotbinière was making daguerreotypes on the Acropolis in Athens. It was barely nine months since the French Academy of Sciences had reported on Daguerre's invention, and less than eight weeks since it had been 'solemnly revealed' to the world at the Institut de France on 29 August, and already the supposed roots of European civilisation were being gathered up by the new mechanism (Lemagny and Rouillé 1987: 20).

Clearly the medium was the product of a need. But its unhesitating lift-off was not due to an instant convergence between itself and the culture of travel, for they were not separate. The invention of photography was a leap in the evolution of types of image-making long associated with travelling. Indeed travel and the making of visual images have always cohabited at the core of the general process of modernity. Photographs superseded earlier forms of graphic imaging, whose role in the construction of the taste and desire for travel, of the objects and goals of travel and of the portrayal of the range of travelling subjects themselves had been important. The contribution of the photographic image to these processes soon became indispensable. But the causes of its appearance lie in a far broader set of developments than one of visual culture's lines of descent.

Photography is a social machine, an 'assemblage' of technical procedures, signifying effects and economic functions (Deleuze 1988: 13). These derive from a conjunction of movements and transformations taking shape during the

Renaissance of the sixteenth century and the social and scientific revolutions of the period that followed. All would supply part of photography's basic programme, and photography would in turn furnish part of modernity's as they developed within and alongside each other across the nineteenth century. The most significant elements within the conjunction were: the rise of market society and the beginnings of modern individualism; the overseas expansion of Europe; the appearance of a conception of space as deep, continuous and based in a particular understanding of human eye-vision; the rise of observational science and its use of optical devices; the use of the same devices in surveying, cartography and picture-making; the associated valorisation of the cognitive importance of seeing and travelling; the establishment of spatial realism and naturalism in the visual arts; the linking of travelling with education, personal development and pleasure; the increasing application of rules to all kinds of travel (how to prepare, what to see, what to learn and so on); the conceiving of travel as a way of discovering, even imposing order in and on the world; and the development of travel as a source of material for the expanding markets in literary and visual goods.

While competitive self-interest and the force of social change continually ignited the vigour and cruelty of the Renaissance and its aftermath, what also drove its people to explore in every direction was the need to fill a great emptiness that had opened up in the cosmology and the sense of self of many Europeans – the lack at the heart of modernity, the origin of its anxiety but also a source of its dynamism and creativity. This emptiness induced the urge to travel, to fill the spatial void with human presence, or to find whatever was imagined to have been lost. It impelled the creation of images to fill the vacant spaces with human features and meanings or to draw the dreamer or traveller towards a world that might be repossessed.

In essence the emptiness remains with us at the beginning of the twenty-first century and still underlies our need to travel and to picture our journeys. In the early modern period it was manifested in three ways: as a consequence of new observations and theories of the material universe; in the unappeasable hunger of market society's acquisitive subject; and in the fear of the complete loss of order, communication and coherence which was threatened by the fading away of medieval Christianity's 'shared symbolic order' and the theological schisms and protracted religious wars of the seventeenth century. These states of mind were immanent in the period's ideas and practices concerning space, mobility and visual representation and will be identified here as part of them.

Copernicus in 1543 and Galileo in 1610 and 1632 displaced humanity from its traditional position at the centre of a fixed and finite universe by proposing a heliocentric system with a mobile earth travelling through infinite space. Discussing the evolution of the modern psyche from this intellectual revolution Paul Oppenheimer argues that it left the human race abandoned without an address in an uninhabited, endless and possibly godless space – in a cosmos with no centre and no edge. In Seamus Heaney's words, 'everywhere being nowhere / who can prove / one place more than another?' (*The Birthplace*). Homesick, filled with a desire equivalent to its loss, humanity was now seen as fated to search for a way home or for a way of accommodating to its situation or for a means of signifying it (Oppenheimer 1997: iv). From this time space would be linked not only to power and wealth but also to uncertainty and longing – and to representation.

There is no doubt that from the sixteenth century Europe witnessed an 'explosion of geography' involving a 'multiplication of images' such as maps, topographical pictures and the countless images in which Europe dreamed the strangeness of distant regions and their peoples and now additionally the strangeness of the world in general and the cold space above it (Alpers 1989: 134; Wittkower 1987). Out of its concern to measure, survey and navigate through the widening material world they sought to know and control, Europe's unsettled and expansionist cultures came to rely on a knowledge gathered by optically based observational and measuring techniques such as the telescope and the microscope. The Italians revived and improved on another device, the camera obscura, employing it in the surveying and mapping of land and urban planning and in the visualisation for painting of spatial depth and structure (Crary 1990; Marbot in Lemgany and Rouillé 1987; Wees 1980; Wheelock 1977; White 1987). In the seventeenth century the mercantile Dutch were able to manufacture a more mobile version of the camera obscura which incorporated lenses. Other visualising mechanisms appeared over the next two hundred years. Two prominent examples of these were the claude glass and the camera lucida, each designed to organise and magnify the visual pleasure of landscape. They re-established the connection with what was thought of as nature's most essential form, refined viewers' aesthetic evaluations and served as drawing aids – the means of producing images.

Through these mechanisms the world was becoming represented as a picture – a framed visual display laid out for a spectator. Heidegger famously described this reconfiguring of the world through the human *perspective* as a founding act of modernity, an era he named the 'age of the world [as] picture' (Heidegger 1977: 128–30). Copernicus may have cost humanity its home in the universe but this kind of picturing offered it accommodation at the centre of its own world. The classical mode of this picturing was 'linear perspective' or 'quattrocento perspectiva' developed by Italian architectural theory and adapted for use in painting. In some degree the expression of the effects of the camera obscura, linear perspective creates a spatial architecture constructed through human single-eye vision by organising its depiction of space by means of 'projective geometry' which retains the eye at a still point – the picture's origin and conclusion – while launching the look outwards into the picture space.

By centring the visualisation of space in the human eye the world is re-staged as though it was founded in the human, as if the human was the ground of all being – 'the relational centre of that which is as such' (Heidegger 1977: 128). Space is shown as continuous and unified. Its integrity is confirmed by being arranged around the pivotal human subject. Space then becomes an effect of the human look which bestows on it a sovereignty and a kind of ownership. Space transforms into place and place into property – 'man's estate'. For this reason some have seen linear perspective as the visual ideology of mercantile capitalism, part of the cultural apparatus of its 'space-economy' (Certeau 1984: 92; Jay in Foster 1988; McQuire 1998: chapters 2 and 4; Smith and Katz in Keith and Pile 1993: 75, 80; Virilio 1994: 64 and chapter 1). Viewed in this light, the visual taking *in* of the world can be seen as an act that precedes action – that of actually taking it *over* (Virilio 1994: 61; McQuire 1998: 22). Projective geometry gives to space the thrusting form and vertiginous dynamic of expansionist, acquisitive ambition. It produces a way of seeing expressive of a subjectivity the American filmmaker Stan Brakhage once called 'westward ho-ing man ... a form of sight which is aggressive and which seeks to make any landscape a piece of real-estate' (Brakhage in Wees 1980: 32). For this subjectivity the world must remain remote and empty until it can be acquired as property and suffused with exchange value and the projected personality of an owner.

In the northern Renaissance the pictorial representation of space underwent further development. Dutch painting took over Italian art's commitment to the rendering of objects and figures in three-dimensional space. But where Italian painting *revealed* the world as the revelation of an *idealised* human eye at rest, Dutch artists attempted to show how a picture of the world is something made and made out there in the physical world. In her study of Holland's visual culture in the seventeenth century, Svetlana Alpers shows how, through their application of the camera obscura and its principles, the Dutch produced aspects or views without a static or single viewer – the results of an observer moving through actual space (Alpers 1989: 51–2). A painting such as Vermeer's *View of Delft* does not replicate a single eye view but an 'aggregate of views made possible by a *mobile* eye' (Alpers 1989: 27, my italics).

As concept and practice the Dutch 'mobile eye' reflected a much wider movement in empirical approaches to the nature of space which informed the prehistory of photography and modern travel. For example, in his work on geometry Descartes, whose contemporary influence on thought was enormous and who also produced treatises on the nature of eye vision, approached the subject not as if it was a question of '"pure" (that is, formal) mathematics alone, but a science of spatial relations dealing with space *encountered in experience*' (Toulimin 1990: 171; Descartes 1965: especially 90 and passim). However, with its emphasis on travelling and direct observation based on acknowledging the material world's independence of observers and on their need to immerse themselves in it, the 'mobile eye' remains one of seventeenth-century Holland's most abiding contributions to early modern visual culture.

Dutch confidence in its own empiricism was underwritten by its alliance with the ordering activity of optical systems – with, above all, the camera obscura. Dutch acceptance of the mediation of the lens in the production of images was as important a contribution to early modern visual culture as the 'mobile eye'.

From Kepler they had learned that seeing is itself a picture-making process, and Dutch painters were able both to admit the constructed nature of their representations and at the same time to claim their art as being objective – commensurate with the workings of the human eye and informed by the spatial structures of the real world. Their approach is demonstrated in the use they made of the camera obscura. They resolved the instrument's ordering function – the construction of perspectival images – with its facility for giving apparently direct access to an objective reality, albeit one rendered luminous and concentrated by lens and frame (Alpers 1989: 32). Dutch art was as concerned to create its own order as any other. Its difference lay in including in its practice an opening up of perception and representation to the effects of an objective material reality. In this formal sense it was an art of travelling.

Of course the historical realities of travel and trade shaped Dutch aesthetic theory and dominated much of its subject matter. Holland was, after all, Europe's major seaborne trading power at this time. Dutch artists routinely produced maps or topographical views, or featured ships in their work. Others composed *still lifes* incorporating navigational devices, or objects and fruits from faraway places, themselves the signifiers of the remote and of the longing to own objects made precious by the spell of distance. Where religious art had proclaimed the Other Place of the Divine, these works contained a yearning for the transforming intensities of what was geographically out of reach and perhaps for the possession of space itself. They are also the celebrations of their society's ability to achieve it. A new metaphysics was being created no longer from the still point at which God was contemplated, but in movement, out there in a dynamic world.

The co-presence of visual representation and travelling was determined most powerfully by the general project of European expansion. Of this, Dutch enterprise was a pioneering example. By the eighteenth century the project's aims had become enlarged. It sought not only to collect the world but to arrange it into European classifications (Boorstin 1985: 433; Foucault 1974: 132–8; Pratt 1992: 27). Yet the process stimulated greater self-consciousness in many Europeans as they encountered wildly different cultural systems. The intellectual as well as the economic effects of the European voyages of discovery in the Renaissance and early modern period brought, in David Livingstone's words, 'an immense cognitive and cultural challenge to tradition' (quoted in Gregory 1994: 17). This encouraged less a relativist tolerance than a desire to establish the new modes of observation and interpretation which would impose order on experience as well as infuse order with experience. While the spectacular and frequently spurious tales of seafarers continued to evoke worlds of wonder and abomination beyond the boundaries of Christendom, the increasingly pragmatic ends of the expeditions were at the same time beginning to generate more accurate descriptions if not comprehensions of the new worlds and cut the mariners' tall stories down to size. What is notable is how a visual sense transformed by the visual theories and optical devices we have been discussing was increasingly promoted as the means, supposedly, of escaping the limitations of traditional modes of description before the oceans of unfamiliar phenomena. In the methods and expectations of the new visual-observational approaches the features of linear perspective and the camera obscura are plain to see. The world was made to appear not simply visible but visually ordered, embedded in unified space by an observation free of the distortions of the observer's subjectivity. The world was spread out before the observer, separate from the mind but available for intellectual, aesthetic and economic possession – Heidegger's world picture (Gregory 1994: 34).

Alongside the force of history and the pragmatics of exploration, spurring the dependence on the assumed certainties of optically structured observation lay the continuing fear of social chaos and the disintegration of pan-continental systems of knowledge, communication and diplomacy. The fear first arose as the feudal system began to fail. It was inherited most immediately, though, from the immensely destructive religious conflicts of the seventeenth century. The Reformation radically and violently divided Europe. The Thirty Years War killed as much as a third of the population of the German regions. In his discussion of the intellectual responses to this crisis Stephen Toulimin identifies the urgency with which thinkers embraced a shared and communicable description of reason and rational enquiry. Descartes's '*rational method*', he argues, was intended to provide 'a certainty that circumvented religious oppositions' (Toulimin 1990: 99). Leibnitz, he notes, 'dreamed of an ideal *language* that could be learned and understood by people of any country, culture or religion', one based on mathematical symbols (Toulimin 1990: 99 and passim; see also Eco 1997: chapter 7). The context also explains the ready and widespread cultural acceptance of Newton's cosmology by Europe's intellectual classes. The Newtonian principle of absolute and continuous space contrasted Europe's broken landscapes and shattered social geographies and opened up the prospect of future re-integration.

Throughout the period similar expectations were being raised by the re-orderings of visual perception and representation we have encountered. In addition to knowledge based in mathematics it was hoped that a direct yet optically disciplined visualisation of the real combined with the systematic naming of everything in it might also provide the basis of a universally shared method of understanding. The visual theory of Kepler and Descartes pictured the eye as a pure disembodied mechanism. The camera obscura produced a simplified mono-vision. All seemed to reflect the 'clean', uncorporeal and decontextualised character of rationalist philosophy. In turn, rationality aspired to equal the clarity of a flawless lens as if, like the optically refined brilliance gathering into a camera obscura, reasoning and observation could transcend the partisanship of society and history, the importunings of the body and the instability of all interpretations based in human language. As Jonathan Crary writes, 'the camera, in a sense, was a metaphor for the most rational possibilities of a perceiver within the increasingly dynamic disorder of the world' (Crary 1990: 53).

The sixteenth and seventeenth centuries transformed how subjectivity in general was produced in relation to space and representation (McQuire 1998: 22). Throughout the same period the connection between travelling and the development of the particular individual was also confirmed. On the evidence of the picaresque novel or the *Bildungsroman* the importance of the journey of personal discovery for the evolution of the modern self was fundamental. The self was unfinished, no longer given but something to be made. Unlike the heroic or tragic journeys of self-discovery in premodern cultures those of the modern self did not seek to discover who one is but what one could become. By definition, the modern self was a journey. But the journey functioned more than metaphorically. In the seventeenth and eighteenth centuries actual journeys and the *visual* experience they entailed were considered essential for the nurturing education and taste of the person (Wilton and Bignamini 1996; Cardinal in Porter 1997; Elsner and Rubiés 1999). But most importantly, given that the cluster of sights and encounters that constitute any particular journey belong to the traveller alone, travelling and its visual epiphanies became linked to the actual *formation* of the individual. The Renaissance and European expansion required a 'self-fashioning' mobile individual, whose improvised personality could adapt to changing situations (Greenblatt 1980: 227). By the seventeenth century individualism was rejecting traditional authority (usually Classical and literary) as the traveller's guide in favour of the 'truth of one's eyes' (Adler 1989). By the eighteenth century the journey and the eye's experience had become twin testaments of evolving individuality, and currencies in the status war-of-position being waged in an emergent consumer culture.

At the turn of the nineteenth century a complex of significant meanings and practices had become gathered around travel and visual representation. When combined with later technical advances and pressed by the economic demands and social needs of the new century, the cultural energy generated would actuate the formation of photography.

The immediate application of photography to the depiction of travel is explained by the fact that it was, on the one hand, a crystallisation of three hundred years of culture and science preoccupied with space and mobility and, on the other, the expression of its own time – the epoch of capitalist globalisation, the construction of a new middle-class identity and the dramatic speeding-up of transportation and communication. Photography was a representational tool refined in the service of these processes. It was also the perfect product of its economic culture – a commodity in its own right. It lowered the price of images and thus increased their consumption. It introduced a mobile visual system whose realism met the demand for what was considered to be scientific objectivity, and whose ability to fascinate produced visual objects of reverie, fantasy and idealisation, effects equally valued by the ruling aesthetics and popular spirituality of the time.

Certain characteristics of the medium in itself specially befitted it for the needs of the age. One of these was the degree of kinship between qualities peculiar to the photographic image and the condition of travelling. Realism is habitually taken to be the single key to photography's nature and purpose. But distance, movement and travelling can also be adduced as parts of its essence. For sure, photography traded on its claim to optical truth. But unlike its predecessor, the camera obscura, the photograph separates the viewer in time and space from the guarantors of this truth – the events and objects that had generated the image.[1] Where the camera obscura engaged the viewer in an apprehension of a visible world that was mediated but co-present, the photograph brought to a multitude of viewers a secondary image – the fragmentary trace of a forsaken event. Like starlight photographs are transmitted through time and space from sources often long extinguished. Their shadow-presences in the image deepen the sense of absolute distance from these origins. Hence, photography requires from its viewers an imaginary travelling through the traces of actual space towards an unreachable beginning in the pro-photographic event; and a phenomenological travelling between existence, the image and non-existence, the absent object. 'Photography', writes Christian Metz, 'is a cut inside the referent, it cuts off a piece of it, a fragment, a part object, for a *long immobile travel of no return*' (Metz in Squiers 1990, my italics).

As a cultural practice, Victorian photography's relationship with travel was inseparable from its identity as a commodity. The characteristic that most made its commodification so successful was most obviously the infinite reproducibility of its images. In spite of the Daguerreotype's precise and finessed realism, the lack of this facility led to its supersession by systems evolving from its reproducible rival, the Talbotype. But the conditions for commodification were also laid down by this relocation of the viewer's involvement from actuality to representation. Unmoored from the precise locations of its origin, the photograph is transported into an independent dimension made up of circulating and interacting images in which the photograph's informational, aesthetic or monetary values are generated. It is significant that some of the earliest reflections on photography as a commodity-form cite not only portraiture but also travel and tourism imagery. For example, writing in 1859 the American Oliver Wendell Holmes noted that:

> There is only one Coliseum or Pantheon but how many millions of potential negatives have they shed – representatives of billions of pictures – since they were erected? Matter in large masses must always be fixed and dear: form is cheap and transportable. (Holmes (1859) in Newhall 1981: 60)

Holmes's language soon transmutes into a monetary register. He refers to the popular photographs of 'foreign views' (and carte-de-visite sized portraits) as 'the sentimental greenbacks of civilisation' (Holmes in Newhall 1981: 69). He forsees photography forming a global economy of visual knowledge made up of libraries exchanging stereoscopic images. To achieve this Holmes called for the universal standardisation of formats, use of shot scales and so forth, so that comparisons could be made between compatible images: 'There may grow up something like a universal currency of these banknotes, or promises to pay in solid substance, which the sun has engraved for the bank of nature' (Holmes in Newhall 1981: 69).

As the 'promise to pay in solid substance' the photographic image becomes an enticement to visit the site of its origins, the referent, the gold standard of realism. It offers the incitement to travel, to purchase the real in the form of visual consumption. It becomes the promise to exchange the representation for the real, the copy for the original, the simulacrum for the authentic. It promises to remunerate the bearer of the paper currency of photography with the gold coin of the tourist's 'experience' and the traveller's rapture. In this complex of travel, global distribution of imagery and circulation of money much of the reality of nineteenth-century capitalist culture was being manufactured. In time it would grow into the hyper-complex world system of late twentieth-century neo-capitalism with its 'abstract space' made up of countless variegated pathways from roads and air routes to fibre-optic cabling and wave frequencies along which flow commodities, people, information, digitalised finance, political instructions and images (Lefebvre 1991: 53).

In this globalising economy the image becomes what Stephen Greenblatt has called 'mimetic capital'. Greenblatt underlines the 'crucial' connection between mimesis and capitalism arguing that under the domination of capitalism 'the proliferation and circulation of representations (and devices for the generation and transmission of representations) achieved a spectacular and virtually inescapable global magnitude' (Greenblatt 1991: 6).

In the nineteenth century photography's contribution to the elaboration of this image-economy was critical. Echoing Holmes somewhat, Walter Benjamin regarded it as a considerable force in extending the sphere of the market economy in general by offering 'in limitless quantities, figures, landscapes, events which had previously been utilised either not at all, or only as pictures for one customer (Benjamin 1973: 163). But photography was not merely a passive, reflective process. Like other forms of 'mimetic capital', the activity of the photographic image broke beyond the forces that produced it to become itself the cause of effects in the social and cultural worlds. As capital was for Marx a relation of production, so representation is for Greenblatt 'not only the reflection or product of social relations but ... is in itself a social relation'. 'Representations', he adds, 'are not only products but producers, capable of decisively altering the very forces that brought them into being' (Greenblatt 1991: 6).

Throughout the nineteenth century the function of the photograph was strongly determined by its part in the process of unifying the geographical, economic, ideological and, indeed, imaginary territory across which capitalism was being extended. This process combined brute force with the logic of the market, and the efficacy of technology with the allure and cultural violence of representation. Modes of industrialised travel, communication and representation appeared with each other and as part of each other. Mechanised transportation, serial production processes and the new techniques of graphic reproduction brought about transforming consequences for both economy and culture.[2] Increases in production rates and speed of travel were hallucinatory. World trade doubled between 1800 and 1840 and increased by a further two hundred per cent in the next fifty years (Lemagny and Rouillé 1987: chapter 4; Hobsbawm 1977: chapter 3). With the coming of the steam locomotive land journeys could be completed in one-tenth of the time required for the horse-drawn coach. The steamship increased sailing speeds by three hundred per cent (Harvey 1989: 241).

From the same dynamic ecology issued the application of steam-driven technology to newspaper and periodical production, Morse's telegraph, the rotary press and, in the 1860s, the typewriter. Economy, technology and culture meshed as transportation and communications systems were worked in tandem towards the same end – the creation of integrated national and global political-economic orders. Trains, passing through several time zones, began to run according to a single, central 'train-time'. Press distribution was vastly extended and the telegraphic network cast over more and more territory. One major effect of these developments was to turn the United States and the British and French Empires, to take the most powerful and influential examples, into cohesive informational and spatial entities.

Shaped by these actualities photography imposed its own effects. Though implicated by its realism in the material world the absence in the photograph of the objectifying referent left the image open to the roamings of the imagination and to the all-important identification processes. Through this duality travel photography acted to bind the viewer psychically into the reality of the global system it pictured. The whole universe of travel photography was evoked in each individual image, as though it formed part of a single vast photograph. And collectively travel photographs pictured the global system as though it was truly a single, continuous space. They displayed it as a chain of appearances, the manifestations of a unified order whose absorbing eye and identifying consciousness was situated in the imperial centres of Western Europe and North America and whose representative was the eye and subjectivity of the viewer. Thereby the global system acquired global visibility, and as the trade in travel photographs flourished the visibility acquired both its commodity form and its consuming subject.

As we saw earlier, the photograph has been thought of as a type of currency, a sign of possession, as the imaginary purchase of and on places and even peoples. Jonathan Crary compares directly the function of nineteenth-century photography with that of money. He ties both into the process that fused identity with the capitalist world order. 'Photography and money', he writes, 'become homologous forms of social power in the nineteenth century. They are equally totalising systems for binding and unifying all subjects within a single global network of valuation and desire' (Crary 1990: 13).

In the nineteenth century photography purchased, promoted and circulated an identity for the middle class and its emulators, one established on the full investment of subjectivity in the market and in the life of commodities (the basis of its social and material existence). It was an identity located in a world space, a system of places, which it also regarded as extensions of itself. This activity of the photograph was common to both the travel and topographical image and the middle-class portrait. In fact the function of travel photography was not so different from that of portraiture – the sustaining of the objective egoism of the middle class. This clientele was regaled with its own features, its own interests and identifications, in the image of the world which the travel photograph conveyed to it. Its class power, cultural and religious preoccupations, its confusion of allure and anxiety before the bodies of ethnic strangers, were all present in the images soon flowing like money into the metropolitan centres.

From its first appearance photography articulated a relationship between identity, space, mobility, the market economy and representation – a set of connections at the base of the capitalist modernity which has until now governed the course of the modern world. Throughout its history, in all the variations and applications of travel photography (or the photography of travel), the same connections appear again and again. In the chapters which follow they will be encountered in relation to the colonial photograph, the Victorian domestic consumption of travel imagery, in relation to tourism, in the photography of twentieth-century exiles and in the actual and aesthetic journeyings of modern and postmodern art photographers. This itinerary represents a journey through images by means of the images and a listening in to one of the conversations that modern culture endlessly holds with itself and only now may be coming to an end – or moving on to something else.

Notes

1. For a full and very impressive discussion of this issue see Crary 1990; for a critique of Crary see Mitchell 1994: 19–24.
2. In 1803 mechanised paper-making introduced into England; 1814 steam-powered press; 1827 multiple-cylinder stereotype printing. All of these were high-speed, low-cost techniques which made cheap, good-quality reproduction and printing of images possible. See Anderson 1991.

Part II

The nineteenth century

2
The reverie of power: Victorian travel photography and the depiction of Egypt, the Holy Land and India

Making things available

Early on in Luis Buñuel's film *The Phantom of Liberty* a sexually aroused couple from the French upper middle class are shown looking at postcards. As each image is turned up one or other of them expresses shock and disapproval while clearly growing more excited. 'Disgusting!' exclaims one, 'Obscene!' cries the other, 'that's going *too* far!' Clearly the audience is encouraged to assume they are viewing pornography.

We soon discover that the pair are handling depictions of long-established nineteenth-century touristic sites: the Sacré Coeur, the Arc de Triomphe, the column in the Place Vendôme, maybe the Paris Opera House, a number of bourgeois-imperial buildings – and a sunset, which somehow also manages to appear both French and bourgeois.

The satirical conflation of two normally segregated modes of representation and experience – pornography and tourism – hints at an unconscious intimacy between them. It is a trope familiar to viewers of Buñuel's comic and 'tender subversions'. However, his lightness of touch covers a serious intent and the scene brings to mind a number of themes at the centre of this study's concerns.

Buñuel teases into the open the long association between travel and sexual adventure. But the film's comic turn achieves a more radical defamiliarising effect through replacing pornography by the monuments and sacred sites of bourgeois civilisation and making them the cause of moral outrage. Official and honoured objects are thus reclassified as taboo and morally defiled. Famous sites are shown as if they are the shameless celebrations of some crime or degradation. Indeed, given their origins in the cruelties of colonialism and warfare, so many can be viewed only with ambivalence. For this reason the sequence calls to mind Walter Benjamin's words, 'There is no document of civilisation which is not at the same time a document of barbarism' (Benjamin

1973: 25). The Sacré Coeur, after all, was built in thanksgiving for the crushing of the Paris Commune.

The sequence also reminds us of how tourism's sites and monuments are at once actual places and objects and symbolic forms and states of mind: entities often constituted and experienced entirely by means of images and signs, evoking and evoked by reverie and desire. They form part of what Dean MacCannell in his study of tourism has called 'the system of attractions', a cultural process extending far wider than the activities of the tourism business (MacCannell 1976). Buñuel's couple consume and are consumed by the products of this system. Dependent since the 1840s on photography, it has promoted the products of power as the objects of desire. The first decades of this system and the place of photography within it will be the subject of this chapter and the one that follows. They will concentrate on both the spaces and places depicted and on the mental and social spaces from which they were viewed.

In 1859 the self-styled 'men of science' of the Photographic Society of Ireland, then of course a British colony with an Anglo-Irish ascendant class, were treated to a report on a photographic trip through Spain conducted by one of its members, Sir J. J. Coghill. He presented a number of his stereographs which he describes in the paper later published in the *Journal of the Photographic Society* (*JPS*) in London. One shows, 'strange sea rocks, fantastically grouped', pictured less for their romantic qualities than for having been the site of a British naval disaster in the sixteenth century. Another image records a monument to the English hero Sir John Moore. Coruna provides a few 'street scenes' but Guadalquivir is a disappointment and the unvarying landscape is blamed for failing to conform to Coghill's taste for the picturesque. (Coghill 1859: 249 and passim).

However, his enthusiasm is fully restored on arriving in Gibraltar where without hesitation he makes 'a few negatives of a place no true Briton can contemplate without pride and intent' *(JPS* 1859: 254). The presentation is rounded off with some reflections on the continuing decline of Spanish power and the irresistible rise of Britain.

Coghill's Spain is merely a place where British history is staged, where British taste is serviced and assessed accordingly. The Spain which obeys other rules, which tells other narratives, is all but blinded out, judged to be, as Mary Louise Pratt has put it, 'aesthetically underdeveloped' (Pratt 1992: 218). Travel here is a ritual of self-affirmation in which the world in general is presented as little more than the projection of the traveller's mentality, in which the traveller's standards are the only arbiters of discrimination, in which the world photographed is the only world thought worth seeing.

This account affords an example of how self-enclosed travel photography could be in a mentality so evidently convinced of the rightfulness of its supremacy. It demonstrates how the travel photograph mediates the world not only through the procedures of the medium but also by means of the shared assumptions about the world of photographers and viewers. Bakhtin spoke of language as a 'communal engagement'. He maintained that the word has two faces: one formed by those whose word it is, the other by those for whom it is intended (Bakhtin 1973: chapter 1 and in Clark and Holquist 1984: 232–7). Photography, too, is a 'communal engagement', its meanings and applications produced by the activities of both maker and viewer. All the images discussed in this chapter were visual commodities made with the viewer in mind. The selection of subject matter and the formation of visual styles would have been shaped by nineteenth-century viewers' assumed ideological needs, their cultural competence and what they expected of photography.

In his study of the colonising of Australia Paul Carter writes, 'there is no non-directional, unimplicated point of view from which the traveller can describe the facts of the journey' (Carter 1987: 31). Shaping all tastes and preconceptions concerning travel photography were the values and consequences of colonial expansion. All forms of travel, and therefore all travel photography outside the metropolitan centres, was in some way touched by colonialism. The subject matter and the visual structure of the photographs established for the viewer a relationship to the world that was more than perceptual or aesthetic. It staked out what Edward Said has called a '*strategic location*' (Said 1991: 20). A photograph is a representation whose meanings and applications derive from its position in a signifying ecology made up of other representations – other photographs, related forms of representation, critical writings, general cultural knowledge and belief and so on. For this reason Said's reflections on the discourses of imperialism apply with as much force to travel photography as they do to the more traditional scholarly and literary forms he studied for their production of colonising knowledge.

> Everyone who writes about the orient must locate himself vis-a-vis the orient; translated into his text, this location includes the kind of narrative voice he adopts, the type of structure he builds, the kinds of images, themes, motifs that circulate in his text – all of which add up to deliberate ways of addressing the reader, containing the orient, and finally, representing or speaking in its behalf. (Said 1991: 20; see also Mills 1991: 48 and passim)

Said speaks of the European soldier, scholar, missionary, trader or scientist thinking of the 'Orient' simply, 'because he *could be there*, or could think about it, with very little resistance on the Orient's part' (Said 1991: 7; Alloula 1987). For the coloniser, the world takes on what Mary Louise Pratt has termed, 'the colonized quality of *disponibilité*', viewed as though being at the disposal of the coloniser was the foundation and purpose of its existence (Pratt 1992: 163).

Making things available (*disponible*), putting them at the disposal of the viewer, is one of basic effects of the photographic medium. 'In the photograph', writes Barthes, 'something has posed in front of the tiny hole and has remained there forever' (Barthes 1982: 78). The phenomenon made possible Victorian travel photography's primary imperial role of naturalising the 'quality of *disponibilité*' by giving it 'objective' visual form. Another characteristic deepened its impact. Detached from its objects in time and space, the photograph equips its viewers with the Classic visual morphology of power – a seeing which remains itself unseen.

Commercial travel photography was also governed by clients' expectations of the medium itself. They were almost impossibly mixed. Photographs were required to provide equally the neutral accuracy of the photographic trace, the shop-window spectacle of the exotic, and the epiphanous engagement with the sacred. Each of these effects was expected to carry viewers beyond their everyday existences and yet confirm their most central assumptions concerning the world in general and the non-European world in particular.

The importance of a site in the viewer's cultural order determined the intensity of the viewing experience. In the minds of many Victorians certain places had a quasi-mystical status. For the religiously devout or the enthusiast for imperialism, images of the Holy Land or of colonial India could hold prodigious power. Therefore, before everything else, the photograph was expected to furnish proof of a site's existence and recreate something of its presence. As one might expect from this, the early history of travel photography reveals how photographers returned again and again to the same significant locations.

Travel books based on the photographic image had been in existence since 1842 when the Parisian optician Lerebours produced a collection of lithographs by a number of photographers. Titled *Excursions Daguérrienes: villes et monuments les plus remarquable du monde*, it included three lithographs based on Pierre-Gustave Joly de Lotbinière's Daguerreotypes made almost three years before on the Acropolis. Only technical reasons delayed for a further ten years the appearance of a travel book featuring actual photographic prints. The first was probably Maxime du Camp's *Egypte, Palestine et Syrie* published in 1852 and sponsored by the French state. But volumes of photographs were extremely expensive and it was more common to encounter such images in other modes of display and distribution: as published in part series, sold loose by print dealers, featured in exhibitions and world fairs, and graphically reproduced in the illustrated journals. But there was another limitation to the use of the photographic print. It lacked the impact of the stereoscope.

Prior to the Kodak revolution of the late 1880s and the rise to mass popularity of the postcard from around 1900, the most common way of looking at travel photography for much of the nineteenth century was by means of the stereoscope (Kyro 1966; Woody in Geary and Webb 1998). Its associated viewers and image cabinets were common furnishings in the Victorian culture of home education and entertainment. While it's hard for us now to comprehend how astonishing photographs of distant sites were to the fresh and relatively unsceptical Victorian eye, we need to understand that the most seductive of photographic formats was the stereoscope, which even today, after a century of cinema, retains some of its power to amaze. Part of the seduction of photography lay in its naturalism and the fineness and multiplicity of its detail. In the more complete illusion of the stereoscope they could become overwhelming. For the American author Oliver Wendell Holmes, the stereoscope transformed such qualities into a sublimity of the real. He was amazed at seeing objects, 'as large as they are seen in nature' and so realistic they threatened to touch him, even to do him injury. He was struck by the fact that distant objects were rendered as sharply as foreground surface textures, that is by the illusion of deep space. Above all, Holmes was overcome by inexhaustible details so numerous 'that we have the same sense of infinite complexity which nature gives us' (Holmes 1859 in Newhall 1981: 58).

The stereoscope viewing device masks out the distracting environment and the viewer is drawn into the intensified illusion of all-round, deep and receding space. Different planes emerge within the image, like layers of cut-out theatre scenery. Together they create for the viewer the sensation of being in a miniaturised optical theatre full of presences given an uncanny realism by the viewer's sense of being immersed in the same space as the representation, participating in it like a theatre audience sharing the space of the performance. The human figures in the stereoscope, in biblical sites for example, seem to be have been rescued from the past by the image's power to replicate space – brought closer to the 'here and now'. At the same time they seem unreal, like actors preserved in an ancient hologram, performing in some allegorical piece endlessly re-enacted. By its assembly of effects the stereoscope provided for its clients the most vivid imaginary transportation and the continuous dramatisation of what they believed to be eternal truths.

Evidently photography held an enviable enchantment for the Victorians. Judging by their rhetoric some experienced a photographic ecstasy, an ecstasy of looking; and ecstasy, as we know, is a form of 'stepping out' – of which the travel photograph must have offered a double helping.

The ruins of Egypt

By the middle of the nineteenth century European tourism with its infrastructure of communications, hotels, sites, guides, dragomans and itineraries, was relatively well established in the Middle East, or Near East as it was then more commonly known. Photography was introduced into this 'system of attractions' as a standardising mechanism fixing sites and viewpoints, guiding tourist behaviour, establishing visual lexicons and grammars for particular sites, acting as conventional and objectified memory, and becoming in general the indispensable ritual and token of the trip. Soon tourism was unimaginable without photography.

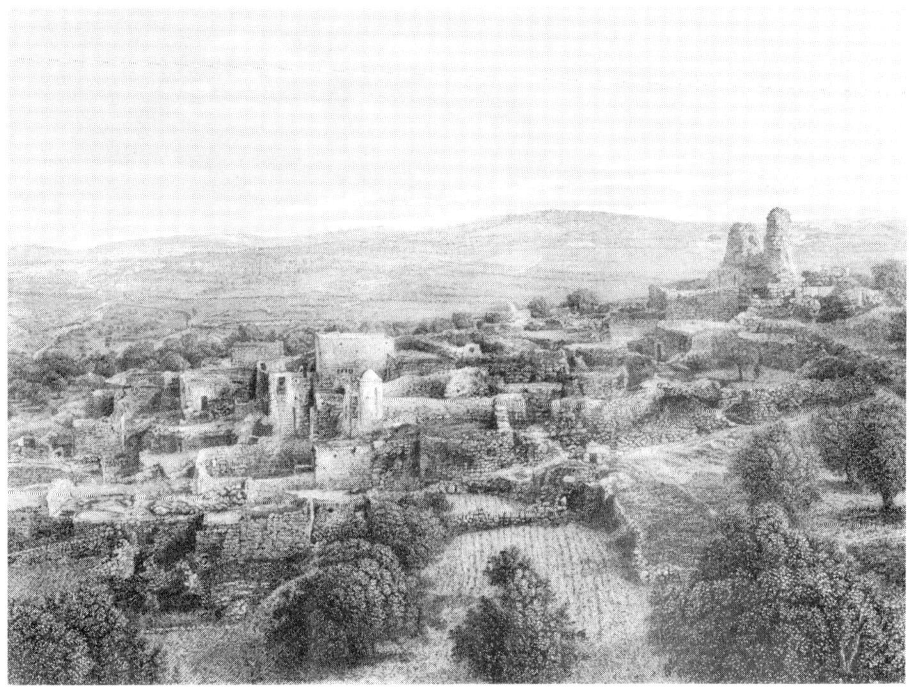

Fig. 2 Francis Frith, 'View of the Village of Bethany in Palestine', n.d., photograph 1857–60. Engraving from a photograph by Frith.

Many European photographers established themselves in the region. The French Bonfils family was based in Beirut, with outlets in Europe and North America. Work by them appeared in the Baedeker guide, another crucial standardising influence on tourism for many years. James Robertson, who worked with Félice Beato, sold prints of Jerusalem direct to tourists in the hotels. Work by him was also exhibited at the 1855 *Exposition Universal* in Paris. In Europe such work was readily available in book form and as folios of prints (figure 2) or albums from dealers such as the London based P. and D. Colnaghi and Scott & Co. Also in London studies of the Middle East were viewable in frequent exhibitions at the Photographic Society (Henisch & Henisch 1990).

An exemplary figure of the 1850s and 1860s was the English photographer Francis Frith. His production levels and mode of working were near industrial. His operation was integrated with the requirements of his backers and distributors, such as the publishers of stereoscopic images, Negretti and Zambra. Output was set in ratio to demand. Highly productive working methods and the use of diverse formats and modes of display were used. A series of visits to the Middle East extracted thousands of images. Studies of the same place were made in three different formats: the stereoscope and two plate sizes (8×10 inches and 16×20 inches). The products came available to the public in gallery shows, expositions, laid into books, as loose prints, stereo photographs, magic lantern slides and in the form of a number of special luxury products such as large prints (21×29 inches), and a limited-edition volume retailing at 150 guineas (Gernsheim 1988; Perez 1988: 163).

The majority of Frith's images were purchased by those who would never travel far. They were promoted as standing in for immediate experience by conveying the viewer to the scene by the power of the image. One of the texts which accompanied his photographs makes this clear: 'The value of a photograph – its principal charm at least – is its infallible truthfulness. We may have long revelled in the poetry of the east; but this work enables us to look, as it were, upon its realities' (Mrs Sophia Poole quoted in Van Haaften 1980: xvii, cited in Perez 1988: 84). Consequently much of Frith's work is distant, panoramic and literal. It proposes itself as honest, unembellished Quaker photography from a photographer of Quaker origins, offering viewers truthful transmissions of what they were unable to see for themselves. Certainly, his stereoscopic *Views in Egypt and Nubia* (figure 3) stand out from the typical stereo images of the period. Most of these were little more than optical entertainments exploiting the sensational effects of the stereoscope for their own sake.

Frith's images draw on the power of the stereoscope to intensify the viewer's wonder for the subjects rather than the effects. His studies of the Egyptian palaces and temples are simple and deeply focused. The foreground space remains uncluttered. Here the stereoscope's combination of spatial realism and theatricality heightens the viewer's sense of moving into, of sharing the same space as the objects. Through the stereo-viewer the disposition of and the relations between architectural elements are magnified; and the weight of the structures is apprehended so powerfully that Frith's images can still give up authentic scientific insights as well as creating the more touristic sensation of '*being there*'.

Many in the nineteenth century may have lauded the naturalism of the photographic apparatus. But even if it had been possible to sustain the proposition that photographs did not interpret but merely reproduced objectively the visual experience of places such as Egypt, in the minds of European photographers and spectators alike the country was already a set of myths and meanings awaiting evocation. Egypt was, as Barthes might have put it, *Egypticity* – the signifier of mythical values, already a sign of itself. It was already representation.

For visitors of the 1850s and after Egypt was less a contemporaneous political entity than a stone theatre of frozen time arranged to instigate reverie and wonder. Such presentations of the country were entirely consonant with Europe's colonising impulses. Egypt's strangeness – its difference – represented a challenge to Europe's post-Enlightenment mentality with its claim to universality and to its self-awarded licence to decode and subordinate the cultural systems of others.

Wonder, perhaps the most favoured form of response to the Egyptian sites

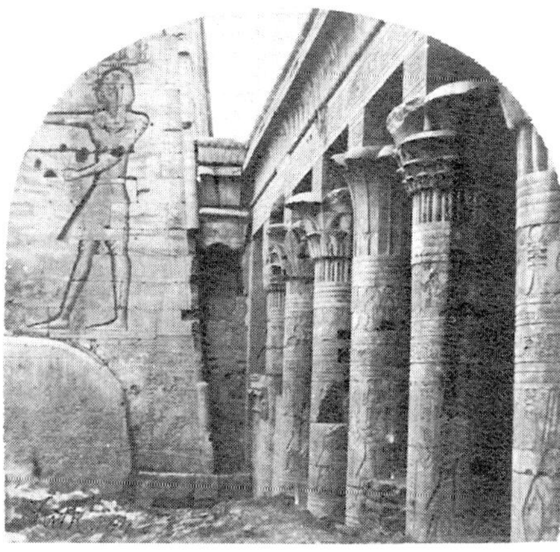
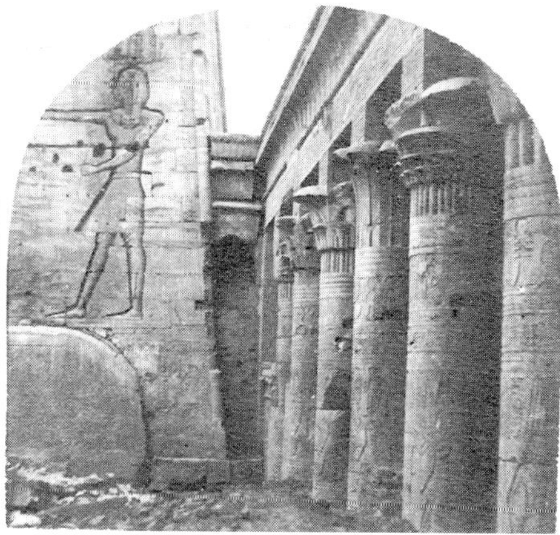

Fig. 3 Francis Frith, 'The principal Court of the Large Temple at Philae' (stereograph). From *Views in Egypt and Nubia*, *c.* 1860.

and their meanings, functioned to meet this challenge by negating their difference, their autonomy, and thereby taking possession of them. Stephen Greenblatt has shown how, within the colonising mind, wonder deprives its object of its own meanings and prepares it for take-over. Posing as simple astonishment, as no more than the expression of an honest inability to comprehend the unfamiliar, the 'speechlessness' of wonder is saying that its object lies below the horizon of possible representation. To become comprehensible it must be overtaken by the coloniser's cultural categories (Greenblatt 1991: 15–25).

It might be argued that wonder in this context is an historically specific instance of the activity of all cultural systems in the face of the Real in the sense understood by Lacan. He took the Real to be whatever escapes and therefore defies the symbolic order, whatever lies beyond meaning and indicates the possibility of its negation. Ultimately the Real is death, the threat to all orders, and is therefore the ultimate otherness. To preserve the stability and coherence of the cultural order, death, the Real, and all forms of difference must be transformed into representations – icons, signs – and in this way safely re-absorbed into the order of the Symbolic (Bronfen 1992: 46).

Certainly in the years before photography Europeans had transformed Egypt into picture and text. The numerous scholars and picture-makers who accompanied the Napoleonic invasion of 1798 produced the encyclopedic *Description de l'Egypte*, a vast conspectus of Egyptian life which included almost three thousand illustrations featuring many of the ruins and artefacts of the ancient kingdoms. In the *Description* and in subsequent developments such as the evolution of Egyptology, a mostly French, German and British affair, and the founding of the Cairo Museum by a Frenchman, Auguste Mariette, Egypt became 'rediscovered'. Egypt was recreated in terms of the European view of world history and arranged into a repertoire of items, themes and sites, upon which future writers, painters and travellers drew deeply (Said 1991: 86 and 176). Egypt was to be understood by means of knowledge refined from the outside. It became a place to be looked upon, contemplated, represented. In short, Egypt was laid out for inspection, then further reduced by popular imagery and tourism to little more than the archaeology and mystique of the Pharoaonic centuries plus a few touristic images of contemporary characters and activities of interest for confirming Egypt's degraded location in premodernity – desert folk, masked women, water carriers and the like.

Egypt was imprisoned for ever in the past, seized in the amber of European iconising. Long before disembarking European travellers knew what had to be seen and how it was to be interpreted. One wonders if the visitor's direct encounter with, say, the Sphinx – Auden's 'Presence in the hot invaded land' – soon came to function as the confirmation of its own images.

In much of the work of Frith, Arnoux, Bonfils and others the essence of Egypt is the ruin and the archaeological site. To the nineteenth-century viewer this preponderance of ruins conveyed a number of meanings. Emblems of lost times, they have long featured in tourism's itineraries expressing, as Dean MacCannell has demonstrated, modern society's desire to recover, in the cultures of other places and other epochs, the authenticity it imagines it has lost in its own (MacCannell 1976: introduction). In the nineteenth century the European desire to connect with lost authenticity had more to do with the necessity of establishing foundations and traditions which would legitimate Europe's claims to moral and cultural superiority. For the European elites the selective tracing of their cultural descent from certain adopted parent societies such as ancient Egypt, was the expression of this necessity. Their ability to uncover and interpret Egypt's lost *imperium* gave Europeans possession of what they regarded as a greatness with which might infuse their own. At the same time by restoring and decoding its fragments, by re-inventing Egypt, Europe had made itself both Egypt's originator and its inheritor. More than this, European archaeology signified and proclaimed its capacity for disinterring truth itself. For the function of ruins, as Derrida has noted, is to indicate the existence of truth by standing as the traces of its disappearance (see Dews 1987: 9).

The cultural interest of Europeans in Egypt grew alongside their political engagement. This had extended from Napoleon's campaigns through de Lessep's canal-building and the British occupation of 1882. The perceived political instability of this zone of the flaking Ottoman Empire was mirrored in the often-expressed belief that the Egyptians were incapable of caring for the ancient monuments. Their assumed incompetence was used to justify intervention. At the very beginning of the medium's history Arago claimed for photography the role of maintaining this vanishing patrimony as, with the support of the great explorer von Humboldt, he introduced the Daguerreotype to the French Assembly:

> Everybody will realise that had we had photography in 1798 we would possess today faithful pictorial records of that which the

> unlearned world is forever deprived of by the greed of the Arabs and the vandalism of certain travellers. (quoted in Glasser 1992)

From the start photography was mobilised against the dying of the light. Not only would the photographic trace bring off a small triumph over personal oblivion, it would also salvage the products of human civilisation in general. Of course this was not a neutral role. For Arago the facility of the new 'European' medium for making such visual records further legitimated the rights of Europeans to penetrate all regions of the world. In the earliest moments of its inception photography was nominated a cultural tool of Europe's *civilising mission*.

Yet, ruins were educational. There were lessons in the stones for a middle class both genuinely curious and eager for self-improvement through knowledge. This class was concerned also with its relationship to the Other experienced across both geographical space and historical time. Travel photography condensed them together: the otherness present in the contemporary space of the colonial 'contact zone' and the otherness of a profound past whose traces littered the desert. Furthermore, acquaintance with the decline of ancient empires was of special importance to an imperialist Europe. For such a culture ruins inevitably carried a monitory weight, signifying, as Edward Said puts it, 'the fall from classical greatness' (Said 1991: 233). Whether experienced directly or mediated by engravings and photographs, the prospect of ruins in the desert will have conjured up this theme in the Victorian traveller's or viewer's mind. Surfacing in the English imagination will have been Shelley's 1817 poem 'Ozymandias' with its central image of the enormous broken statue of a forgotten ruler, the personification of cold, remorseless yet transient power now prostrated in the desert sands.

The informational use of the photograph would have become coupled here with its power to trigger reverie, turning the represented world into rather loose and inexact metaphors. The photograph's ambiguity of meaning encourages this. Peter Wollen speaks of the photograph as 'free writing time', distinct from the 'imposed reading time', of the narrative-bound film (see Metz in Squiers 1990). In the nineteenth century the particular association between ruins and reverie soon became such a cliché that Flaubert applied his specialised mockery to the word by including it in his compendium of dead thinking, *The Dictionary of Received Ideas*: '"Ruins" Induce reverie; make a landscape poetic' (Flaubert 1976: 324).

Reverie remains a key pleasure in travelling's confection of pleasures. The freedom to daydream, to lose oneself in reverie, is part of travel's promise of freedom, part of the traveller's privilege. For those who travelled in the nineteenth century such a non-utilitarian surrendering to subjectivity or 'sensibility' for its own sake, such pleasure taken in purposelessness, was indeed a holiday from the system. They belonged to a society marked for those outside the aristocracy by its relentless promotion of diligence and self-denial. And for that reason travel and the traveller's reverie were enjoyments for ever tinged with a guilt to be assuaged only by the educational or religious gains of travelling.

Reverie held a further attraction for the ordinary traveller or would-be traveller. It was an activity requiring no deep knowledge of the object that stimulated it. Anyone could have a reverie – it was democratic. Flaubert's Bouvard and Pécuchet come to mind; those bourgeois buffoons who possessed a million facts but little wisdom who 'conjured up visions of lands all the more beautiful for being totally imprecise' (Flaubert 1976: 29).

But reverie also had philosophical and literary significances inherited from one of the key cultural influences on travel and tourism: Romanticism, a movement which continued to inform the sensibilities of the literate middle class throughout the whole of the nineteenth century.

Linked to Romantic theories of imagination, the reverie was a form of guided daydream in which, excited by a particular stimulus such as a landscape, the mind gave in to the drift of thought, fantasy and memory. Although it was the apotheosis of subjectivity, reverie was also seen to have a religious dimension as a means of connecting the individual with the '*world soul*' (Abrams 1971: 431–62). Romanticism saw the human subject as exiled from its objects, from nature in particular, by over-individuation and by a disastrous commitment to analytical reason. Through the associative power and the affective-sympathetic logic of the imagination this exile might be overcome; the subject might reintegrate with the external entitites and bring about a sensuous comprehension of the world. The homeless spirit might find its dwelling. In a voice still inflecting this tradition Oliver Wendell Holmes, in his 1859 essay on the stereograph speaks of the mind that '*feels* its way into the very depths of the picture' (Holmes in Newhall 1981: 57, my italics).

Twentieth-century reflections on reverie have associated the activity with the mind's capacity for freeing itself from present reality in order to imagine the world as other than it is. The power to imagine lies at the heart of Sartre's theory of human freedom (Sartre 1972: 217). For Bachelard the imagination is a permanent challenge to what exists, the beginning of a 'surpassing' of reality. In the *rêverie* the imagination continuously re-creates reality as 'the guardian of the emergence of being ... the purest expression of human freedom' (Kearney 1991: 93).

But can we speak of the reveries brought about by travel imagery either as the expression of such freedom or as the means of Romantic reintegration with the world? In the 1850s the photograph, and the travel photograph in particular, provides the homebound Holmes with the vehicle for mental travelling. The photographically induced reverie delivers him a freedom over space:

> Oh, infinite volumes of poems that I treasure in this small library of glass and pasteboard! I creep over the vast features of Ramses, on the face of his rock hewn Nubian temple; I scale the huge mountain

> crystal that calls itself the pyramid of Cheops, I pace the length of the three titanic stones of the wall of Baalbec ... I pass, in a moment, from the banks of the Charles to the ford of Jordan, and leave my outward frame in the arm-chair at my table, while in spirit I am looking down upon Jerusalem from the Mount of Olives. (Holmes in Newhall 1980: 59)

Furthermore it gives him freedom over time when, gazing into some photographs of Anne Hathaway's cottage, he is struck by hand marks left on the door and wonders if it is possible that

> scales from the epidermis of the trembling hand of Anne Hathaway's young suitor, Will Shakespeare, are still adhering about the old latch and door, and that they contribute to the stains we see in our picture. (Holmes in Newhall 1980: 59)

These rhetorical invocations of sacred presences have become too familiar in the banalities of the tour guide, whether mouthed before the holy places of Jerusalem, at the bardolatrous shrines of Stratford-upon-Avon or in the texts and titles accompanying touristic photographs in general. Holmes's reveries may demonstrate the mind's freedom to wander, to recompose absent times and locations. But they also show how the reveries of tourists are likely to be the reveries determined by tourism and its imagery. As with advertising, the freedom to dream is the freedom to dream on tourism's terms. What might be a basis of the mental freedom of human beings – the imagination – can also become the means by which they are more thoroughly organised. What we see developing in the travel culture of the nineteenth century is, perhaps, less the liberator of the imagination than its trainer. C. Campbell has identified what he calls 'the great divide' in bourgeois culture between, on the one hand the attractions of hedonism and fantasy, shaped by a diluted Romanticism, and on the other by the calculations of the economic machine which make the former possible (Campbell 1987). One needs to balance the appreciation of the pleasure and release offered to viewers by the travel photograph with the understanding that it functioned equally as a means of disciplining the desires of consumers and of structuring their perceptions of the world of others.

And yet the experience of travel and tourism has always included the elation of 'getting out of oneself' – if only temporarily and within secure and organised boundaries. Of course, such experience in transient self-estrangement is more thoroughly distanced in the form of photographs viewed at home. Returning to the photography of the Egyptian ruins, they offered – continue to offer – metaphysical entertainment as well as imaginary translocation. For, however practised, to gaze on those dead signs, the fossils of voided cultures, is to look down into the 'deep time' of an immense human past. It is to stare into an impenetrable otherness. The hooded, zoomorphic figures seem to belong to a

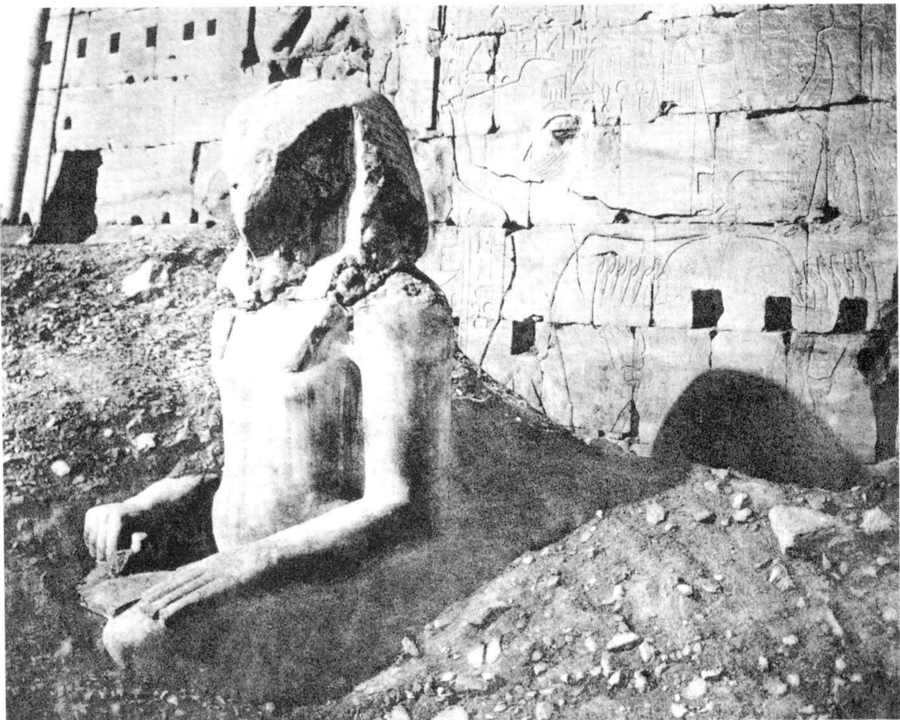

Fig. 4 Félix Teynard, 'Colossus at Karnak', 1851–2. From *Calotypes of Egypt*. Courtesy the publishers Hans B. Krauss Junior and Robert Herschowitz and the Weston Gallery, Carmel, California.

time just prior to the onset of any human narrative; the obliterated faces bear no personality; the gelid, hieratic entities betray no awareness of any humanistic sentiment, promise no warm psychology.

While Frith's commitment to a descriptive style tended to depress such unnerving effects, they are encouraged in the work of Félix Teynard, whose calotypes of Egypt, made in the 1850s (figure 4), employ the sculptural effects of light and shade to make palpable the presences of the sphinxes and colossi, and a framing which pushes the eye towards their silent strangeness, a strangeness deepened by the silence of photography (see Teynard 1992).

However, certain of Frith's photographs do escape being mere replications of the scene. For example, in the 1857 study *Colossil and Sphynx Nubia* (figure 5) the simplicity of form and the absolute remoteness of the figures stranded in time give the photograph the condensed energies of the poetic image. The nineteenth-century English viewer is unlikely to have resisted the urge to translate the experience into literature, recalling again the closing lines of 'Ozymandias': 'Nothing beside remains, round the decay / Of that colossal wreck, boundless and bare / The lone and level sands stretch far away.'

Another inheritance which tourism had accepted from Romanticism was the sublime, the grail of the Romantic journey. The sublime experience was a

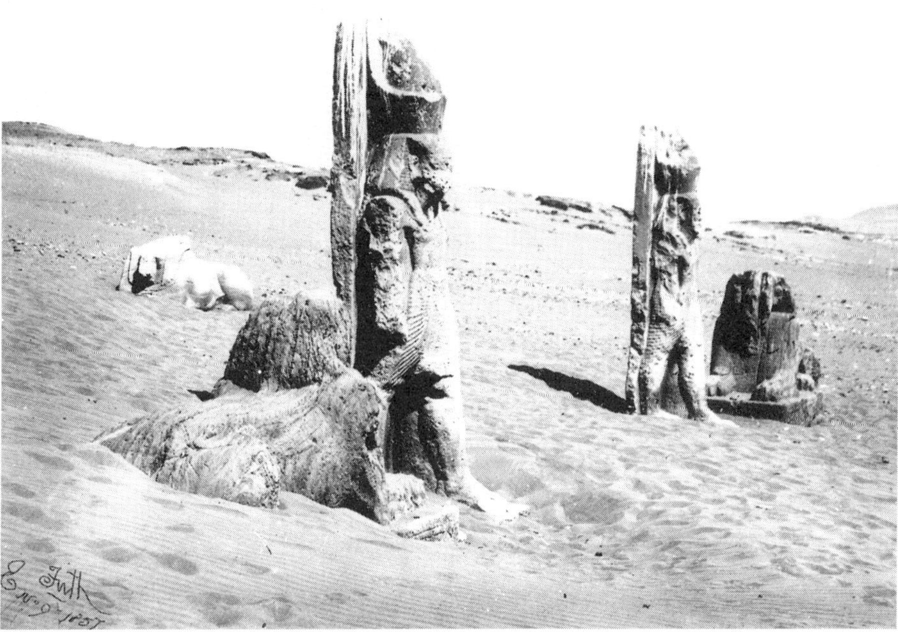

Fig. 5 Francis Frith, 'Colossil and Sphynx, Nubia', 1860s.

radically intensified state of mind and emotion brought about by certain objects and events located beyond the borders of the familiar. Stood before them, the perceiver's psyche would be stretched beyond its habitual bounds by a sense of awe and a feeling of estrangement. 'Terror' was the emotion identified by both Kant and Edmund Burke as the sublime's key sentiment (Kant 1960; Burke 1998). The sublime, with its experiences of self-displacement, extreme fear or pleasure which shocked the individual out of his or her familiar selfhood, might, it was thought, be capable of bringing about self-knowledge and enhancement, even self-transformation.

Typically, the sublime was thought to lie in the rapt apprehension of the immense and powerful qualities of certain natural phenomena, such as limitless space, height or depth or the convulsive energies of storms and quakes. But it was manifested in other kinds of experience. Extreme aesthetic beauty could generate the effects of the sublime; as too could the meeting with the wild authenticity of cultures or individuals imagined to be uncorrupted or undiminished by over-civilisation. Such encounters might immerse the traveller in the sublimity of dangerous and seductive otherness.

Ruins were commonly associated with the sublime for their monumentalism, their vertigo-inducing age, the immense solitude of the wildernesses from which they were so often disinterred. In his essay on the sublime, Kant makes direct reference to the Egyptian sites and the oceanic wastes of the desert (Kant 1960: 48–9).

The discriminations of neo-Classical taste alighted upon the mathematical and social order embodied in the architectures of Egypt, Classical Greece and Rome. Neo-Classicism aspired to reconstruct the lost or ruined whole, if only in the mind. On the other hand, Romantic travellers were often more exalted by the beauty of the destruction itself (Lister 1973: chapter 4). On visiting the ruins of Petra in the 1840s Augustus Hare wrote:

> Surely no picture that the world can offer of the sudden destruction of human power can be more appalling than fallen Poblet, beautiful still, but most awful in the agony of its destruction. (quoted in Macauly 1964: 50–64)

In such accounts of Romantic travelling it remains unclear whether the sublime experience affords travellers a deeper comprehension of their object through sympathy and identification, or merely incorporates the world into the interior topography of the traveller's sensibility, uses the world as entertainment. Victor Burgin, for one, is unconvinced of the former claims made for the sublime. He unleashes all his rationalist – and reductionist – scorn on to the concept, regarding it as 'simple displacement, a banal metaphorical transference of affect from the woman's body to these caverns and chasms' (Burgin 1986b: 117).

Yet, at its most revolutionary, Romantic travel and its Symbolist, Surrealist and proto-Surrealist offspring could be open to both the being and the topography of the Other in which terror or love might represent a means to a transformatory end. If necessary the most radical journey might conclude in a dying into otherness, metamorphosis or disappearance. 'O que ma quille éclat! O que j'aille à la mer!', cried the occupant of Arthur Rimbaud's *Le Bateau Ivre* (1871), 'O let my keel burst! O let me go into the sea!'

The Romantic traveller and image-maker may have dreamed of liquidating the distances between subject and object. However, Romanticism was tied to a difficult twin, exoticism, a way of seeing and mode of knowledge concerned with the maintenance of distance. Whatever its qualities, repellent or fascinating – or naive – the exoticised place, object or person exists as something to be looked on, as eternally strange and impenetrable. It is an aesthetic rather than an historical entity. It is produced as an endless run of repeat performances. It becomes fixed in the limitations of the viewer's interest, deprived of its own significations, denied the history of its own becoming. Further to the repertoire of types and specimens of the carte-de-visite and album prints, contemporary Egyptians appeared among the ruins as nameless guides or porters, or as figures establishing the scale of the monuments. They attended on the thing that diminished them (figure 6).

As a mode mediating the Other, the exotic exerted a far greater force on the development of at least commercial tourism than Romanticism. Together, the

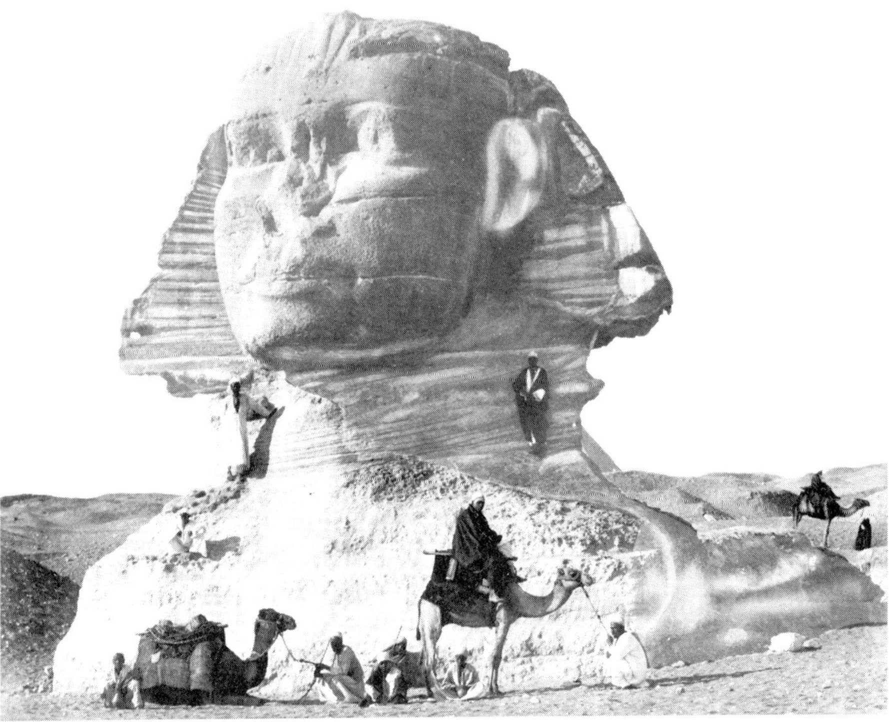

Fig. 6 Hyppolite Arnoux, 'The Sphynx', *c.* 1868.

Cheops Pyramid, the Sphinx, the ruins of Karnak, the great temple of Abu Simbel and the rest formed an ensemble of exotic attractions signifying an 'authentic' Egypt which deferred, even erased, the actual contemporary society. The ancient ruins signified (still signify) the absence of all modern Egypts. The Egypt of the present was complex, difficult, probably unhealthy and threatened to stare back from the independence of its own ontological space. It was also the material basis for the European presence, a colonial possession – and colonialism was a project from which tourism was inseparable but of which it has always been inclined to claim innocence.

The following photograph (figure 7) possibly made by Arnoux as well, was collated into an album devoted to Egypt but its provenance or subject is unclear. It was pasted on the reverse side of the Sphinx photograph (figure 6). Although Arnoux worked out of Port Said from the 1860s it could have been purchased as easily from a dealer in Europe where it was certainly kept and viewed.

Here exoticism consigns its subject to the state of abjection.[1] The unkempt hair, the enlarged hands, the beads, the loose clothing together constitute a hopelessly premodern humanity which must have appeared to the middle-class Europeans who once owned and peered at this picture as almost hostile in its unabsorbable difference; a humanity as ruined and far-off as the ancient stone figures themselves.

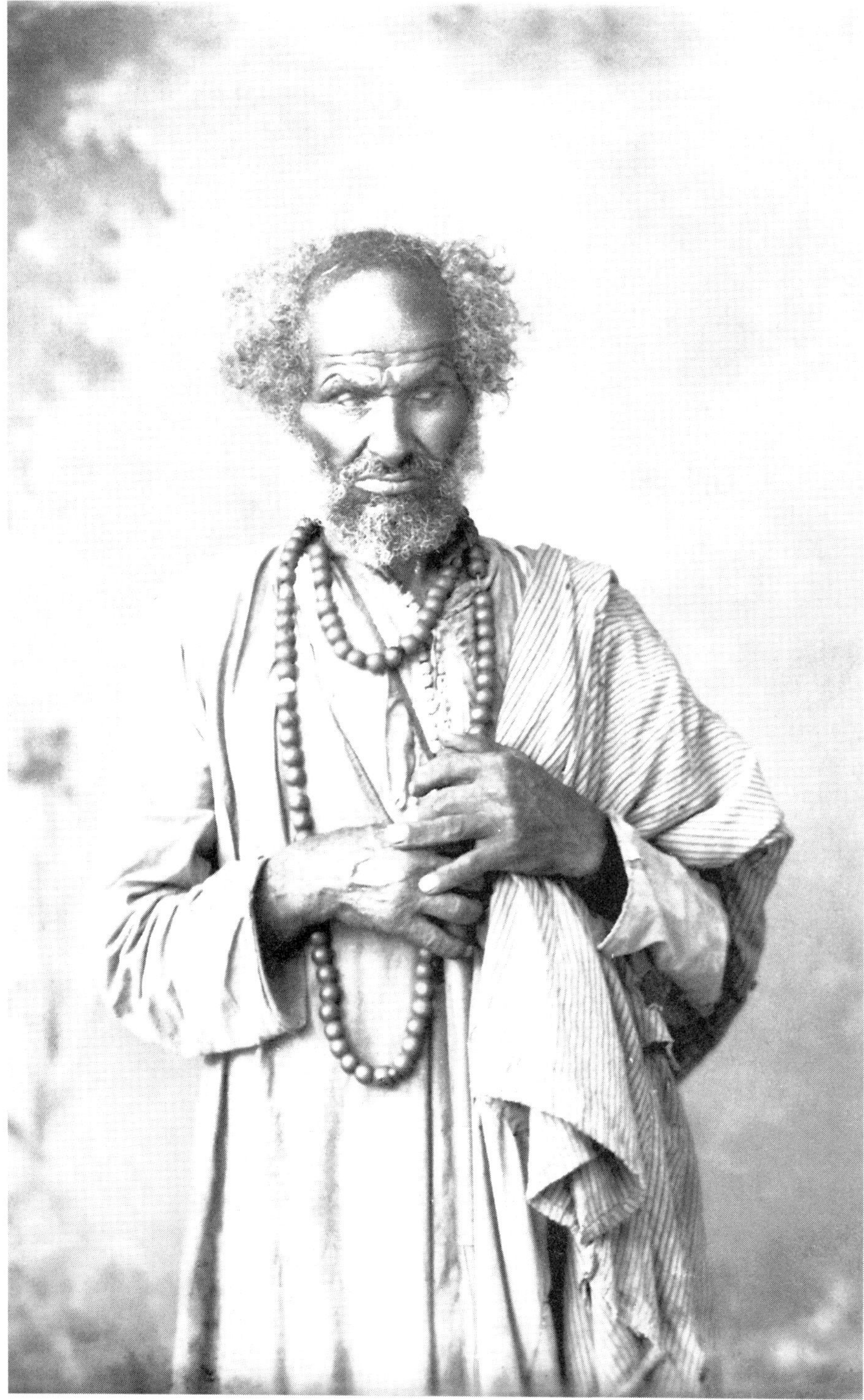

Fig. 7 Hyppolite Arnoux (?), subject unknown. From *An Album of Egypt*, 1860s.

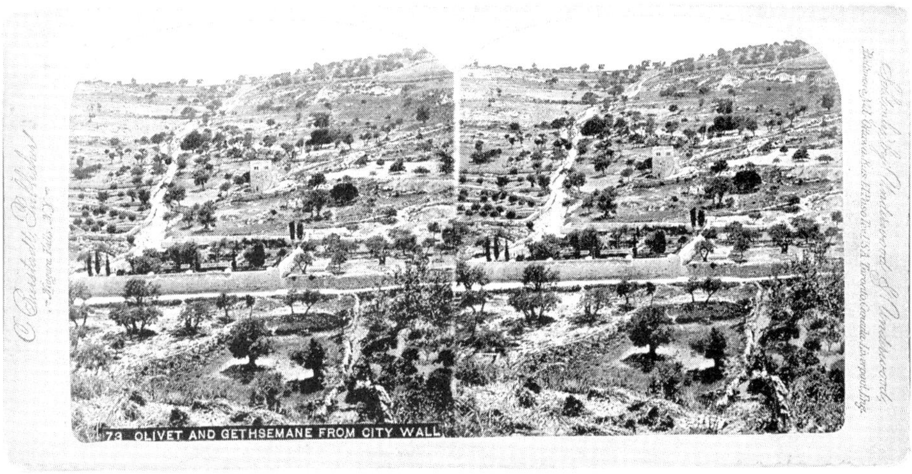

Fig. 8 Underwood and Underwood Ltd, 'Olivet and Gethsemane from City Walls' (stereoscope), n.d.

Above all the man is blind – stone blind. This fact completes the voyeurism the photograph is servicing; a voyeurism in which the colonial theme within tourism's visual culture is clear. This is the 'seeing that proceeds unseen' (Mitchell 1991: 24; Alloula 1987). The man's visual incapacity renders him entirely available to the visual tourist whose look cannot be returned. The photograph compounds this. As photographic object he is a man, *pace* Barthes, who will always be the man who cannot see our seeing of him. Here the visual connotes understanding and domination. If the man represented a threat to the European viewer, it is this that would have made him harmless, uncomprehending, and thus without power. Whatever his cultural origins, in an album devoted to Egypt, his blindness becomes the blindness of Egypt, representing ultimately colonialism's production of an Orient incapable of self-development and change. It expresses the tourist's desire to fix as well as fix on the object of his or her fascination.

Spirit photographs: the Holy Land

In the nineteenth century photographs made or purchased on a journey to Palestine indicated two kinds of distance: the physical distance between points of departure in Europe or North America and Jerusalem, and the distance between the material world and a spiritual one. Photography seemed to reduce both kinds; bringing the geographical and the theological equally within reach, making them tangible – touching the eyes, touching the rock.

If a major purpose of travel is to make contact with significance and authenticity, the Middle East offered the Christian believer the most powerful contact available. MacCannell notes how all tourist sites come into being through a process of 'site-sacralisation' (MacCannell 1976: chapter 5). The River Jordan, Bethlehem, the Mount of Olives, the village of Bethany, indeed the whole city of Jerusalem and the dozens of other biblically important places and traces which made up the territories known as the 'Holy Land' were already established as sacred sites in text, tradition and pilgrimage long before modern tourism appeared. However the trip to Jerusalem in the nineteenth century had additional qualities and purposes expressive of the historical period and its European and North American middle class.

Those most shaped by Protestantism were ambivalent towards their own wealth and the enjoyments it made possible. Contentment struggled with the fear of corruptibility. However, travelling in the Holy Land offered escape from the dilemma by balancing the pleasures and the wasteful expense of tourism against the spiritual capital raised through the self-denying hardships of negotiating hot and uneven roads and by placing oneself where the divine had once entered the world. As the journey crossed sacred as well as actual distance it could be represented as a passage through suffering to spiritual fulfilment. Although nineteenth-century travellers sometimes compared themselves to the pilgrims of old, if they were Protestant they would have shared the confessional suspicion of pilgrimage for being too close to Popery and magic. However, the technical rationality of the photograph appears to have reassured them. Photographs of such travellers before the holy places were proofs of real and righteous endeavour and celebrations of the power and mechanisms that made these spaces *available* to the travellers. For a culture dominated by industrial production, the journey generated not only spiritual capital but a tangible product – the photograph. Photography was a species of work, whether carried out by oneself or purchased from a professional. Susan Sontag has noted how in the twentieth century the highest numbers of tourist photographs appear to be taken by those from people 'most handicapped by the work ethic' (Sontag 1978: 10). Their need to maintain productivity even while on holiday marks them as descendants of the Victorian puritan traveller.

Travel is often a form of reaffirmation. This is especially so in the case of the religious journey which, as well as reviving a faith grown enfeebled, often aims to reaffirm a whole system of belief. In the mid nineteenth century, assailed by powerful intellectual and social challenges, Christianity was certainly in need of reconfirmation. Science, rationalist philosophy, Darwinian evolutionism and scientific socialism all served to increase the pressure on the foundations of religious orthodoxies which had been building up since the Enlightenment. If sermonising and traditional authority could no longer confound sceptic or secularist then religious faith had to be reinforced by recourse to direct witness which simply disavowed scientific method or observable evidence. Another solution was somehow to acquire for religion some scientific method. Jerusalem remained the legitimating source of meaning, the 'centre Out There' in Victor

Turner's phrase. Perhaps, in the age of observational science, Middle Eastern archaeology could provide at least the High Church believer with concrete evidence of biblical truth (an approach that began to be shaped by new methods of Bible study in the eighteenth century). Touching the actual rocks might even deepen the ardour of the evangelists' uncomplicated faith; though, given evangelism's association with the less wealthy, they were unlikely to travel so far.

Secure religious faith was regarded by many in the dominant classes as the essential underpinning of the social order itself. Its absence most likely would erode acceptance of social hierarchies and bring about the collapse of authority. Taking his cue from Carlyle's description of the age as one 'destitute of faith, but terrified at scepticism', John Stuart Mill observed how many of his contemporaries preferred to keep any serious religious doubts to themselves fearing that the weakening of religious belief would destabilise society. From this perspective, says Mill, a doctrine is judged not so much on its truth as on its usefulness (Mill 1968: 140–1).

Whether in the minds of the pragmatist or the devout, the interdependence of Christian belief and the survival of the social order continued to be assumed into the next century. One notably feverish example is the highly successful 1903 novel *When It Was Dark* by Guy Thorne (the pseudonym of Rayner-Gull) disinterred by Claude Cockburn in his study of ideology and popular fiction, *Bestsellers*. Powered by antisemitic hysteria, it relates the blackmailing by Jews of the British Museum's greatest expert on Palestinian archaeology, a dissolute and morally compromised Welshman who is induced to fabricate evidence proving that the resurrection of Christ never took place. By destroying its deepest foundation the blackmailers aim to bring down both Christian religion and Christian society. When the plot's details are learned by one of the book's heroes its consequences are obvious to him – instant social disorder, war, crime and the collapse of all sexual restraints (Cockburn 1972: 35). A muscular Christian hero appears, unmasks the plot and saves Western civilisation. The blackmailer ends his days a lunatic in Manchester; the archaeologist is lynched before his own house.

When It Was Dark is a book obsessed by threats to the internal social order and by the question of 'true' Englishness – the villains are not quite English enough, they are Jews or Celts. And yet it places the ultimate foundation of social unity and national identity elsewhere, in the 'Holy Land'. As the 'centre, Out There', the 'Holy Land' represents the origin of both a metaphysics and a social reality. The book speaks of a system almost undone by outsiders, yet whose own foundation lay outside itself.

This mentality was not confined to popular fiction. The trip to the 'Holy Land', itself already laden with centuries of narrative and imagery, functioned as a rite of passage. It involved travellers passing out from and passing back into their cultural system in order to secure the legitimacy of its central axioms. To confirm the existence of biblical sites by one's own presence and the truth of photography was to corroborate the essential religious truths enshrined, the travellers believed, in the values of their own societies of Western Europe and Anglo-America. The journey also served to establish the difference, in fact the superiority of the travellers' culture from those encountered in the *contact zone*. At the same time it underlined the travellers' status within their own social context as ones who could afford to travel. The travel photograph displayed and viewed at home contributed to this ritual of status reinforcement.

Photography had further attractions for the religious traveller. The extreme iconophobia of sixteenth- and seventeenth-century puritanism responsible for a truly systematic destruction of England's pre-Reformation religious imagery was no longer shared by the nineteenth-century middle class. In fact visual images were being used widely by religious organisations to educate the public against various perceived social evils such as alcoholism and indolence. However, residual suspicions remained. For that reason, the uncoloured sobriety and accepted visual honesty of photography, and its associations with science, made it an especially appealing kind of image-making for Britons and North Americans living in cultures still strongly marked by puritanism. A case could be made for regarding the medium as a puritan technology. A high proportion of its inventors and developers were from the nonconformist traditions, so often strongly represented in science, technology and utility. Sir John Herschel had himself been a biblical scholar.

The pious may, as Hegel said, be content with poor-quality images, yet even the most mediocre nineteenth-century photograph had something that traditional visual forms lacked – the facility for reproducing presences, an essential effect for religious experience. This even gave photographs the edge over the exaggerated intensities of Orientalist paintings. By the reproduction of the visual world of the Holy Land – the ruins, the landscapes – biblical events could be shifted in the mind from the mythical to the historical, from the imaginary to the actual. As Nissan N. Perez puts it, 'The nineteenth century travellers were able to both recreate a fact and experience a symbol' (Perez 1988: 62). The inventorising procedures of materialist science could be employed to rescue and reaffirm the spiritual – positivism at the service of metaphysics. More than mere records, many of these photographs were like relics, traces of the sacred. They were objects somehow touched directly by the divinity: the light of the Holy Land, the shadow cast by the trees on the Mount of Olives, the 'very stones on which He walked'.[2] In the photograph the sacred becomes concrete, or rather it becomes manifested in things, in places, as it had when Christ entered the material and temporal world in human form. Within the religious imagination two orders of time play on each other inside the single spaces of these photographs: the time of the everyday, the single lifetime (*chronos*); and mythical time, the time of God (*kairos*). These sacred documentaries, photographic fragments of the world through which Christ once passed, could be gathered like parts of a mosaic into the pre-existing unity of scripture within the mind of the believer – facts embedded in a substratum of faith.

As the believer could match any image of the Holy Land with numerous

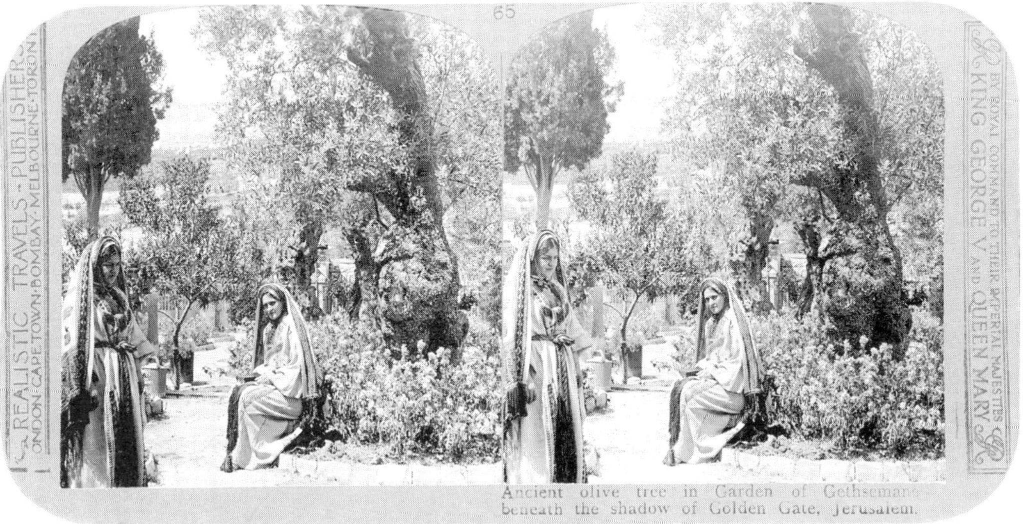

Fig. 9 Realistic Travels Publishers, 'Garden of Gethsemane' (stereoscope), n.d.

biblical passages, the photography of the region was never anything less than a sign mixing image and text. In fact many Victorian photographic albums accompanied the prints with biblical quotations. In this, their function as a means of selecting and intensifying the experience of significant places and buildings is comparable to that of today's tour-guide to the religious sites of the Middle East, whose rhetoric must focus the imaginations of the tourist on the sacred place and bracket out the surrounding offices or fast-food restaurants – the banalities of the profane contemporary world.

In García Márquez's *One Hundred Years of Solitude* José Arcadio Buendía attempts to prove the existence of God by the scientific method of photography:

> Through a complicated process of superimposed exposures taken in different parts of the house, he was sure that sooner or later he would get a Daguerreotype of God, if he existed, or put an end once and for all to the supposition of his existence. (García Márquez 1987: 51)

The Victorians may not have believed they were literally photographing God in the Holy Land. But their images were taken as proofs that the sites of God's dramatic appearances in the world existed. Photographs of the region were empty stages for the religious imagination to fill or opportunities for the travellers to introduce themselves into the biblical scenery as a display of faith. In both instances the photographs were forms of what Nissan Perez has described as the 'spiritual appropriation' of the region (Perez 1988: 100). Barthes speaks of the photograph as a '*tableau vivant*' or 'primitive theatre' (Barthes 1982: 32). And Félix Bonfils, among others, evoked the biblical events by hiring locals to re-enact them for the camera at the original site. The fictional reprise puts its truth beyond question; it is as solid as the ground on which the bemused actors, often Bedouin, were seated (figure 9, see Thoman 1979: 43–5).

This use of visualisation for religious contemplation was not new. In his lecture 'Visibility' Italo Calvino reflects on certain spiritual excercises using the visual imagination employed by Ignatius of Loyola, the founder of the Jesuits. For the more effective contemplation of Christ, Loyola urged the devotee to visualise a physical place, the *mise-en-scène*, as Calvino puts it, wherein Christ may have appeared (Calvino 1992: 84). Edward Said has spoken of Christianity as 'a religion of imagination and recollection' (Said 1991: 178). And, in a study of the sources of Romantic thought, M. H. Abrams describes how the Christian imagination internalises the apocalypse, 'by transferring the theatre of events from the outer earth and heaven to the spirit of the single believer' (Abrams 1971: 47). Consequently the individual soul advances towards its personal apocalypse, imitating the passion and resurrection of Christ. Those Victorian travellers pictured at the holy sites continued this practice. Rather than 'transferring the theatre of events' back to the outer earth they were claiming those places as the settings for their own personal spiritual drama. They are pictured in the home of spirit, 'Out There'. They will be viewed in the personal home, 'in here'. They stand in spaces where absence is most pronounced, where Christ was, but no longer is; but where the possibility of his presence was to be experienced most powerfully. The absence is filled by their presence which signifies the faith that might re-create the lost presence. They embody what they believe. Photography offers visual testaments of their act, and in its ability to indicate presence and signify absence, it mirrors perfectly their theology.

British India

Among Great Britain's colonial possessions India was special. To begin with, its economic importance was pivotal in the British colonial economy. But the political, even psychological involvement of the British with the aggregation of ancient and frequently highly complex cultures that made up colonial India had an intensity rarely seen elsewhere in the Empire. This is explained by the fact that as a unified entity India was not only the product of British material interests but also the creation of the British cultural imagination.

British India was composed through a process requiring a variety of mythologies and representations to which both photography and travel contributed. Under Lord Curzon, Viceroy at the end of the Victorian epoch, the process culminated in the Durbar of 1902 in Delhi when the *idea* of India was given a material or, perhaps, theatrical form. The Durbar was an enormous spectacle or assemblage of Indianess, much of it anachronistic or half-invented by the British. The historian Bernard Cohn describes it as 'a living museum'. 'Rulers', he writes,

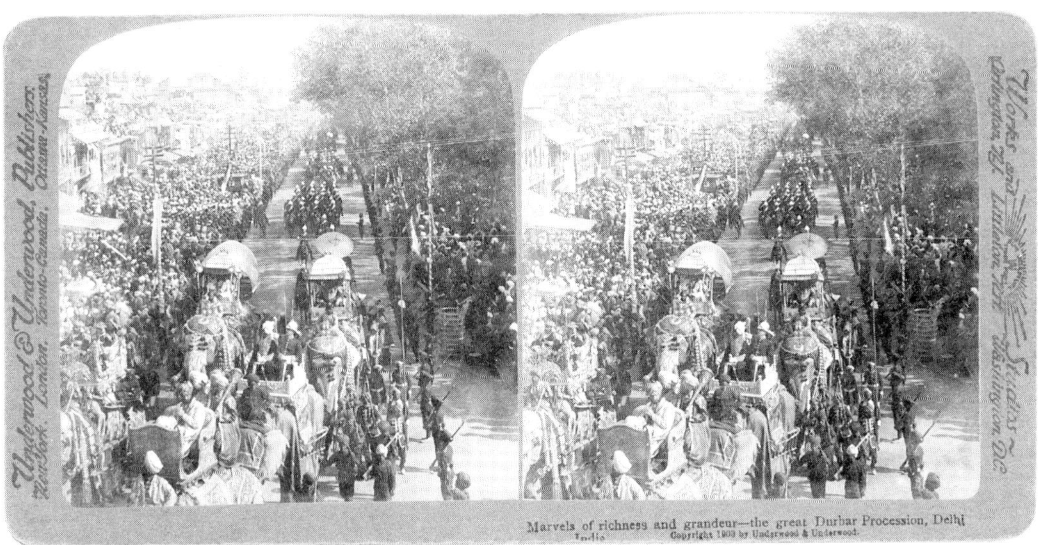

Fig. 10 Underwood and Underwood Ltd., 'The Great Durbar Procession, Delhi' (stereoscope), 1903.

'and ex-rulers [were] arranged like exhibits structured according to the British view of the Raj' (Cohn in Hobsbawm and Ranger 1984: 193).

The Durbar took the form of a great parade of brightly costumed soldiers and erstwhile regional potentates from all the Raj territories paying homage to the Viceroy and through him to the absent British monarch. The ceremony displayed the diversity of India and in the colonial mind dramatised the belief that only through the totalising force of British rule could national unity be realised (figure 10).

Photography's first function in colonial India was as an apparatus of control. Most of the early European photographers were British army officers, or individuals working for the East India Company or the British colonial administration itself.[3] With the unsentimental, perhaps unreflecting, candour of many imperialists certain of the righteousness of British domination, the photographer Samuel Bourne was quite clear about the camera's role in India:

> From the earliest days of the Calotype, the curious tripod with its mysterious chamber and mouth of brass, taught the natives of this country that their conquerors were the inventors of other instruments besides the formidable guns of their artillery, which though as suspicious perhaps in appearance, attain their object with less noise and smell. (Bourne 1863a: 268)

Such photographers were fulfilling the colonial authorities' desire for what Janet Dewan has called a 'comprehensive photography', a means of mastering space (Dewan 1992). Photography formed part of the practico-symbolic management of the vast subcontinent which demanded the classifying, recording, census-taking, mapping, displaying and licensing of everything, so rendering it knowable, imaginable and controllable by means of European systems and on British terms. Photography was directly linked with the establishment of road, rail and telegraphic networks and, above all, with the great trigonometric survey of India from the southern tip to the Himalayas begun in 1802 and continued for a triangulising half-century afterwards. David Harvey writes:

> The world's places were de-territorialized, emptied of their preceding significations, and the re-territorialized according to the convenience of colonial and imperial administration. (Harvey 1989: 264)

Travel in India for pleasure or edification reached significant levels only after the Mutiny of 1857. However, it was never separable from the colonial process. Indeed travelling had always formed an essential part of the business of ruling. Colonial officers frequently criss-crossed enormous territories in their endless administrative peregrinations. There is an account of Raj life at the highest level, written in the mid-1880s by the Marchioness of Dufferin and Ava, wife of the Viceroy himself, in which she appears to have done little else than travel. The Marchioness was progressed by a multiplicity of conveyances across the archipelago of colonial stations and cantonments, and the palaces of subordinate Indian royalty. (She also took her own photographs en route, though they do not appear in the published account of her time in India. See Dufferin and Ava 1889.)

The function of such travelling was in part managerial and in part social – it established ties among Raj officials. But in great part its purposes were symbolic. The journeyings of the rulers and administrators represented British power as ubiquitous – its face appeared across all the territories under its rule. It also showed the Raj as all-seeing. To be visited by the Viceroy was to be inspected by the colonial power's most senior incarnation on Indian soil. Later, the itineraries of tourism – itself a form of inspection – would re-enact these ceremonies of power by holding to the routes the Raj had established. Tourism in general often follows the itineraries and simulates the comforts of the rich and privileged of earlier generations and remains haunted by their values. In India the tour of the Prince of Wales in the 1870s laid down the routes of the countless visitors who have followed.

The most influential travel guide of the Raj, its 'Baedeker', was *Murray's Handbook to India*. It was an aid to travel for pleasure and interest, but one organised by the same template that structured the colony's administrative and military knowledge. The second volume of James (Jan) Morris's study of the British Empire contains an exposition of a British town map of Agra published in *Murray's*. Morris shows how the map displays the colonial system's spatial and social logic. The map is the diagram of a territory, a social formation and a mentality.

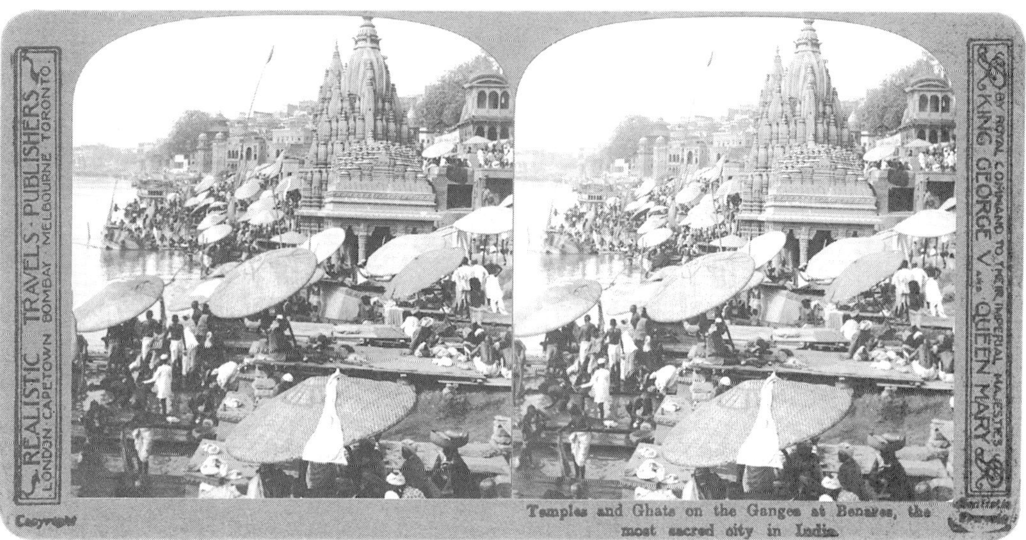

Fig. 11 Realistic Travels Publishers, 'Temples on the Ganges at Benares' (stereoscope), n.d.

> The maps delineated in three or four colours the detachment of the British from their subjects. There in the centre of *'Agra and its Environs'* is the red splodge of the Indian city, shapeless, solid, raggedy at the edges, relieved only by suggestions of stinking backstreets. Hygienically to the south of it, separated by a patch of green and linked to it by Hastings Road as by a causeway, is the neat enclave of the cantonment, with its churches, its government gardens, its high bungalows ... just the look of it on the map suggests the absolute self-sufficiency of the cantonment. It was a world apart. (Morris 1979b: 131)

Such maps informed the (European, male) traveller not merely where he was but where he belonged, and therefore *who* he was. A journey would confirm the map and thereby confirm the politics of the map. Organised and serviced in this manner, the traveller was moving as much away from India as towards it.

Mobilising the qualities of photography's visual pleasure – which equally distanced and intensified the viewer's relation to the object – travel photography was a symptomatic element in the culture of post-1857 British Raj with its closer identification with the *idea* of India and greater spatial and cultural distance from the actual subjects of its rule. In its own way, photography was a form of mapping. It helped establish the range of locations and experiences deemed important to British visitors or viewers and made them visually manifest. Photography's visual structure mediated the visitor's relationship to the sites in ways that ensured they would be consumed aesthetically and interpreted ideologically. In short, travel photographs functioned to educate viewers and would-be visitors how to see India and produced for them an India to see.

A number of places where the colonists had been besieged and massacred during what the British would call the 1857 Mutiny became unmissable sites of British pilgrimage and tourism and soon featured among some of the most commonly photographed. Cawnpore and Lucknow above all became the most hallowed locations of sacred ground in colonial mythology.

In the siege of Cawnpore all but a few of the thirteen hundred European officials, soldiers and their families died from deprivation or disease in the siege or were killed by the rebels. Women and children often died in particularly horrifying ways. The 'violation' of European women by the mutineers was assumed by the British, though ultimately unproven on any scale (see Robinson 1996: chapter 7). However, the anguish of cultural difference and, most acutely, masculine identity was visited as usual on the female body, itself the contradictory site of both otherness and identification.

The final massacre of women took place in a house that had been built in an earlier period by a British officer for his Indian mistress. In the house of the sexually available native woman, her female Others, the Memsahibs, were slaughtered by Indian men. To the Imperial British male the symbolism would have been unbearable. European women embodied sexual purity and racial integrity. For a colonising masculinity based in the power to protect its women from the polluting native, the victim of the mutiny was as much the stability of masculine identity as the specific women and children who perished. The actions of the Indians bore the hallmarks of ethnic rage and sexual humiliation. For the same reason the British revenge that was brought down on them later was of comparable savagery. The sieges and massacres entered 'the mythology of the Empire' as 'sacramental episodes' and in the post-mutiny Raj its sites generated sights, which in turn produced photographs (Morris 1979b: 232–6).

The major consequence of the Mutiny was the deepening of British political-military control – India became part of the British crown – and of Britons' identification with India, many speaking of themselves as being part of India, something more than colonising foreigners. European deaths in the mutiny came to be seen as the sacrifice by which the British had earned the possession of India more than ever before.

Not only does nationhood need martyrs, it also requires locations and memorials dedicated to them. Such death spaces mark the ritual hotspots of national energy. They are foundational spaces at which the national destiny is forged and reforged with every ceremony, every visit. The Mutiny sites took on the same kinds of meanings the more India came to be regarded by the British as more intimately their own. To visit them and to travel from one to site another gave the idea of British India and its somewhat mythical history a geographical reality of which travel photography was both proof and celebration.

Shock photographs of siege defenders' bleached bones were known to the

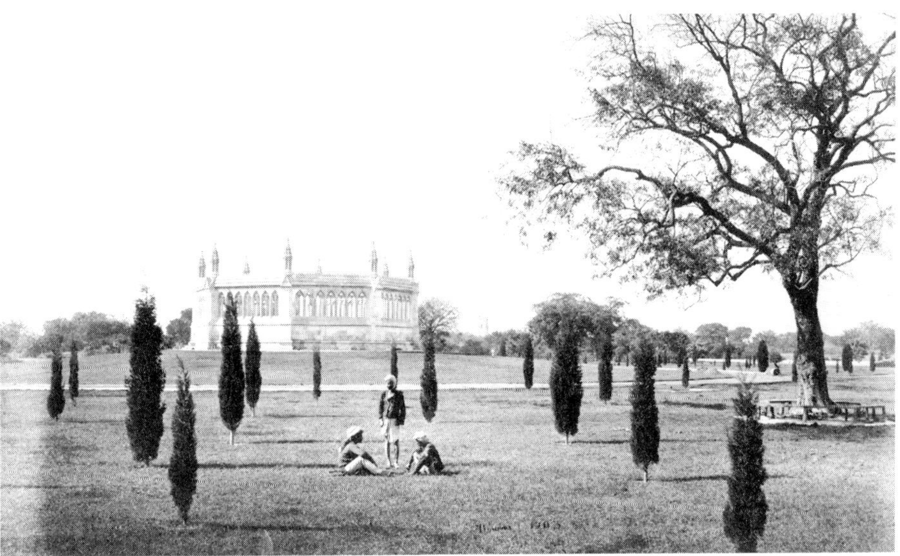

Fig. 12 Samuel Bourne, 'The Memorial Well and Gardens, Cawnpore' (albumen print), *c.* 1864–70.

Victorians, but what later visitors and viewers of the photographs would see was tranquillity restored and British representations imposed utterly on the space and the meanings of the event. In the photograph by Samuel Bourne (figure 12), Victorian space is viewed *from* Victorian space, that of the viewer. The neo-Gothic monument and that emblem of Victorian civic safety, the urban park, cover the horrors they memorialise. The visitor or the viewer recollects the traumatising events but sees here the British colonial order beyond them. Nothing disrupts the space, everything belongs. The Indian men in the foreground submit to being contained by the quiet triumphalism of the place. The British viewer, carrying an unease that would stay with them until 1947, may have wondered what was in their minds.

A companion photograph by Bourne shows the angel statue within the monument. Officially it signified the Angel of Resurrection. Additionally it most likely evoked, for the viewer at home, the figure of the Angel of the Hearth, the female spirit of Home. It was Home with all its meanings that had been violated in this place, a place which the viewer was invited to see as his or her own. It is an image of both fear and reassurance.

There was a density in British attitudes towards India and much that was contradictory. India was a call to duty, a chance to make a career or to embrace obscurity. It energised some, enervated others. Some were overwhelmed by it, lost in it; others were horrified. Many remained determinedly ignorant of the country even as they administered it. Some fostered a constant disdain for its people and cultures. Some, as I've suggested, regarded India as quite simply a continuation of England. There were a few who more or less converted to its values and some who became notable scholars of Indian history and culture. There were others for whom India was a bazaar of novelties, a display of exotic attractions. Many had some or all of these responses continuously. Directly or indirectly all would have been marked by the trauma of 1857; but almost all assumed the necessity for European rule.

A further examination of some of Samuel Bourne's work can show how travel and travel photography reflected certain of these attitudes and in some instances attempted to resolve or repress their contradictions and sedate their fearfulness.

Bourne was a commercially successful travel photographer in India. A non-conformist who gradually adopted many of the less sympathetic attitudes of the Raj ruling class, he spent most of the 1860s on the subcontinent. To him India was business, the whole continent visual raw material waiting to be refined into photographic commodities. He described India as 'the land of rising British enterprise' (*JPS* 1864b: 70). His company, Bourne & Shepherd Ltd, was founded in the 1860s and based in Calcutta, with a studio in Simla, agencies in various parts of India and outlets in London and Paris. It included a mail order service. Bourne's work was widely exhibited in public exhibitions in Europe and India and featured in the Paris Universal Exposition of 1867. The business continued in other hands after Bourne left India in 1869 (see Sampson 1992; Ollman 1983).

In its global reach Bourne's enterprise shadowed the colonial system in more ways than one. His photographs both visualised and mapped the lineaments of the colonial relationship. To travel his India actually or solely by means of his photographs was to reproduce ritually that relationship. His customers were offered not simply neutral images of India, but, in a choice of subjects and styles determined by English visual taste and imperial preoccupations, he produced representations containing British *attitudes* towards India. His photographs located India and the viewer, in most cases British, in a relationship that was as ideological as it was spatial, as ideational as it was visual. This was equally true of his studies of Indian nature such as the Himalayas as it was of those of Indian society and culture, the 'types' and temples imagery. Tourism in general offers the world for consumption. Bourne's business was selling the consumption of colonialism, and selling it primarily to those who had produced it. From this period onwards it would prove difficult to separate the two processes.

Bourne's operation met and shaped demand. His undoubted photographic skill, his traveller's stamina and the modern distribution system of Bourne & Shepherd Ltd made this possible. But none of this would have been effective if he hadn't either shared the attitudes of his customers or cut his ideological cloth to theirs. This affected both the content of the images and also the manner in which they were made available. For example he marketed Indian 'Views', 'Types', 'Ruins' and 'Landscapes' in particular to travellers who wished to make up their own albums documenting their own itineraries. Not only could they make their own selection, they could also purchase prints of the same building or site photographed from different points of view and thereby impose their own *découpage* on the world Bourne and his associates had photographed. The service favoured the viewer or consumer of the representation above its object.

Bourne recorded his responses to India in a number of reports prepared for the Photographic Society at different points throughout his Indian career. In their mélange of wonder, repulsion and the recourse to imperial certainties, they are typical of the responses of many British residents and visitors of the time. They also translate into his photographic work and haunt the India it invents.

In one moment Bourne is elated by India. He speaks of the brilliance of the Indian light, of a 'coming alive feeling', of the 'crispness of imagery' (*JPS* 1863a: 269). In another moment, it is fascination that overtakes him. He writes of Benares as 'truly magnificent and imposing'. He wonders at its 'temples and mosques with their gilded domes glittering in the sun' (269). Later this is replaced by bewilderment as he becomes 'lost and confused in the intricate labyrinth' of India (269). This in turn modulates abruptly into horror when Bourne appears to cross some threshold in cultural space and gets too close. He is sickened by a public cremation, 'the roasting skull and feet' (269), and some kind of existential panic ensues. His apprehension of India's strangeness lurches from the fascination with the Other as exotic to the horror of the Other as abject and unclean. What had been so beautiful in Benares were elements composed into a view, something seen far off, from a position of contemplation. But they don't bear closer involvement. Bourne's admiration is violently displaced as he takes refuge in a cultural contempt that will recur in later responses to the villages on his travels and in his dealings with porters: 'On every hand you are reminded of the religious zeal of these deluded people. Their gods – hideous, shapeless monsters – are daubed on every wall, and adorn hundreds of filthy so-called temples' (269).

Bourne was a self-elected member of a colonial culture devoted to the maintenance of ethnic distance from the societies it dominated, which of course were themselves deeply structured by caste difference and the classification of the pure and the unclean. Bourne's own language expresses a fear of contamination. Better to keep one's distance and avoid being touched. Better to return to the safety of the 'view'. And what better than to view the immaterial beauty of the Taj Mahal? Before it Bourne's horror transmutes again to wonder.

Already a tourist attraction, the value of the Taj Mahal is judged according to the intensity of the affect it can produce in the tourist. Bourne recalls his amazement at the 'dazzling brilliance of the palace' and speaks of his 'enraptured gaze'. 'One stands', he writes, 'in mute astonishment' as though in 'a dream', and he wonders if some 'fairy ... has transported me' (1863a: 269–70).

Bourne is incapacitated. His rhetorical fairy seems to have ferried him towards the unreflecting perceptions of infancy. This is a language of speechlessness; of the pre-rational. The traveller is lifted out of time. Like the sacred images of pilgrimage the Taj Mahal becomes Archeiropoietic, a product not of human work but lowered down from heaven by divine hands (see

Freedberg 1989: 100–3). It floats outside of history airborne on the rhetoric of Bourne's reverie and abstracted from social reality in the way it is represented. Bourne is cleansed of the dirt and difficulty of the all-too-real India in the bodyless state of pure vision, in the somewhat self-induced rhapsody of the tourist before the attraction. The relationship to India is transformed from one of colonial power to one of aesthetics and touristic pleasure; from an ideological relationship to one of sensation freed from moral response. India becomes a source of reverie, a picture, with the viewer safely dreaming before it. And for Bourne, gathering himself back to professional consciousness, 'the camera is the only instrument that can give to those who have not seen it any idea of its proportions and beauty' (1863a: 270).

Journeys made to be read or viewed or otherwise consumed after their completion are journeys home, journeys made to be reviewed at home. 'The roads we follow', writes Paul Carter, 'are travellers' constructions, ways to find home' (Carter 1987: 259). Bourne's Photographic-India is a set of selected, intensified locations and events along a narrative road destined for the safety and resolution of home. Home was an actual social space, a place of viewing, reading, recollecting, which might be equally the middle-class fireside in Great Britain or the exclusive space of the British cantonment in India. But home is also in the visual form and structure of the photography, itself part of a culture's way of seeing, part of Pierre Bourdieu's *Habitus*. It resides in the objects selected, in the visual mode in which they are presented. If the Indian experience confirmed the European's sense of superiority, it was also clearly one filled with the anxieties of the kind related by Bourne, or fictionalised in Kipling. Bourne's work refined out what was disturbing in India. However distant his subjects, they remain viewed from and through 'Home', a point of origin and state of mind which has its visual equivalence in what Bourne calls the 'pictorial'.

In 1869, reviewing his time in India, Bourne writes: 'I make no pretensions to *scientific* travels – my object was purely pictorial' (*JPS* 1869b: 570). His understanding of the term had been indicated in an earlier report to the Photographic Society of 1863 lamenting lake-deficient Simla's insufficient appeal for the lover of the picturesque. 'It has', he writes, 'no single objects of architectural interest, no rustic bridges, and no ivy-clad ruins, trees and mountains' (*JPS* 1863b: 345).

Bourne's most obvious motivation here is to find architectural forms and landscapes that will please the sub-Romantic taste of his clients. The former he found in ruined temples and palaces of the Hindu past.

The British carried out archaeological surveys in the 1860s. Curzon would commission more at the turn of the century. There is a view that he privately accepted the inevitability of Indian independence and wished to preserve and develop scholarship and conservation of the Indian past as preparation for it (see Morris 1979c: 114). Another view takes such projects as further examples of the transformation of India into a museum (Cohn in Hobsbawm and Ranger 1984).

Bourne's studies of ancient Indian architecture presented the subcontinent as

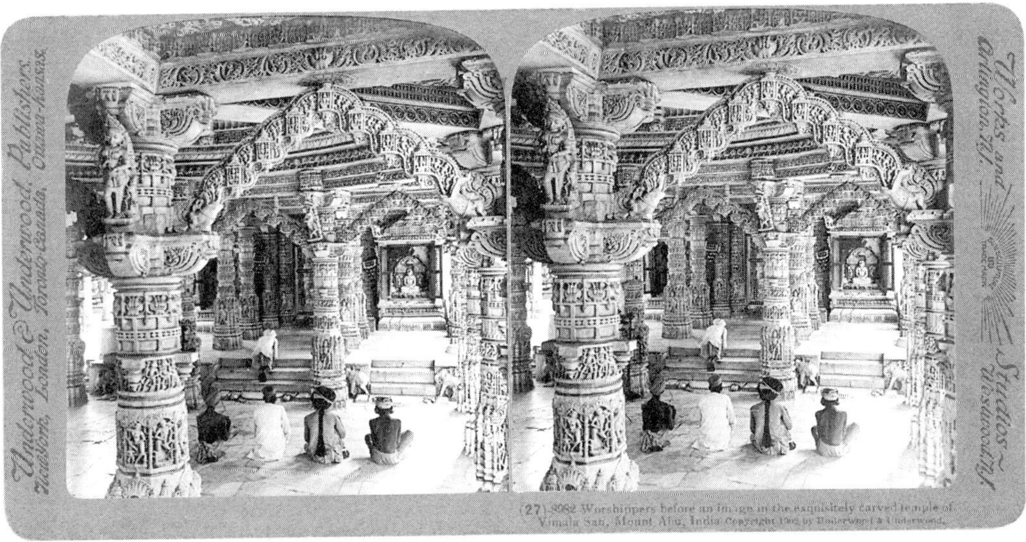

Fig. 13 Underwood and Underwood Ltd, 'Vimla Sah, Mount Abu, India' (stereoscope), *c*. 1902.

a living antique. In this they match Cohn's view of the function of British conservation projects. As Bourne himself said, his purpose was not scientific. The images of architectural ruins offered instead the pleasures of the picturesque's melancholy tendency. The ruins were emblems of time and nature's inevitable triumph over civilisation. But the pleasure would have contained a certain flattery for the British visitor or viewer. The interest in these ruins, their incorporation into the tourist itinerary, while acknowledging India's past accomplishments, also sequestered India in the past. They came to signify the end of something, as if saying that for old India history had indeed finished and that the future lay with the British, those who looked back from that future like time-travellers from a more advanced place gazing at these traces of an ultimately failed past. Photography and the restoration programmes were feats of resurrection and salvation, imitations of the divine power that many British believed to be sponsoring their presence in India.

Bourne was also able to discover Indian views whose tidy grandeur fulfilled the requirements of the other form of the picturesque, landscape – ones that recalled the preferred landscapes of England.

Bourne's imagery made the viewer, the client, necessary by transforming space into place, a process achieved by containing spaces within enclosures or boundaries (Carter 1987: 148). In the lake view (figure 14) contingent spaces and objects are *placed* by the ordering, excluding frame and by the internal orchestrations of elements into a necessary arrangement – sky, water and land disposed into balanced proportions; near and distant trees, hills and their watery reflections echoing each other. The viewer is placed on superior ground from which, across the park-like foreground, the vista opens out, a point of view

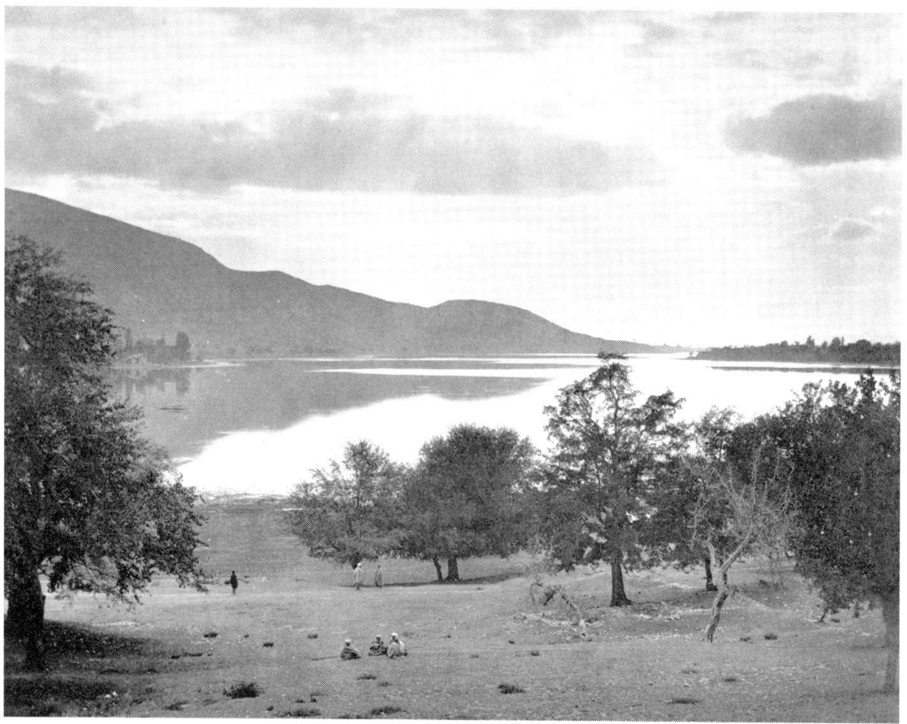

Fig. 14 Samuel Bourne, 'Sunset on Mount Bul Lake, Kashmir' (albumen print), *c.* 1864–70.

which contains that of the Indian figures who, as in the gardens of Cawnpore, are rendered spatially inferior (pun intended). And yet the viewpoint is not so elevated as to suggest the viewer does not belong. It is an overseeing. The world arranges itself for the viewer. It flatters colonist and traveller alike by means of this familiar pictorial language of landscaping and ownership. There is safety here too. The image is filled with the tokens and qualities of settlement. A building or town promotes itself out into the water. There is a series of containments or encirclements. The hills encircle without overwhelming, the lake is contained by the land. The lake is natural, restless energy stilled through containment. It is held by the land which is humanised space where figures move at ease. The lake is encircled by the human gaze as is the whole scene. The look is inward. The contemplation of rather than the struggle with nature prevails here. The dissonance between nature and culture, between world and self has been overcome. The order of the place is determined by the viewpoint; and the one who occupies it creates the place, is necessary to its existence.

This photography also secretes an ideological charm – described in Salman Rushdie's novel *The Moor's Last Sigh* as a 'mirage of Englishness' (Rushdie 1995: 95). The intensification of Britain's identification with India resonates through such imagery. Within the celebration of 'English' qualities in the Indian landscape lies the celebration of the English presence in India. As

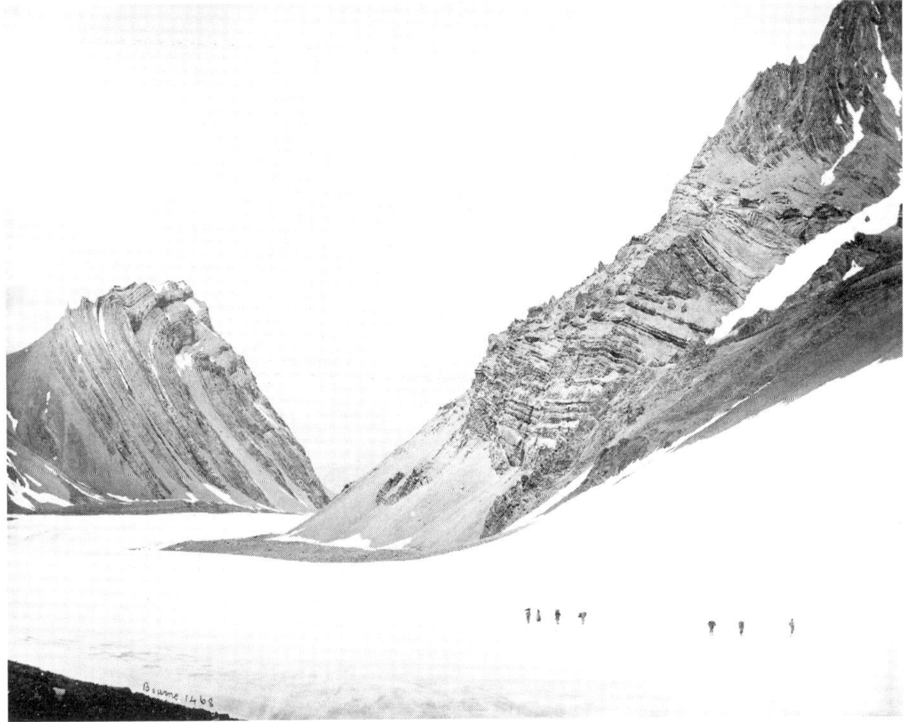

Fig. 15 Samuel Bourne, 'Manirung Pass in Spiti, 18,600 feet' (albumen print), *c.* 1864–70.

European tastes are harmonised with (certain fractions of) the Indian landscape, so the colonial presence is harmonised with India in general. European standards of natural beauty dominate, the hegemony of their cultural and political standards is further naturalised (see Mary Louise Pratt on the 'rhetoric of presence': Pratt 1992: 205).

The images reassure. The restful, benevolent qualities associated with this type of landscape symbolise a desire for a displacement of the turbulence and actual or implicit violence of colonial rule. They also permit the English to look as if they belong. By means of them the viewer can equally recall home and feel *at* home in India – for home, the qualities of English landscape, can be seen in India. The faraway is rendered near-at-home and either could be India or England. Much depends on how the land lies.

Bourne's pictorialism also embraced the sublime. This he found in the Himalayas, from which he descended, a photographic Moses, cradling his magnificent 40×20 inch glass plates speaking as if he'd looked into the face of God. It was probably the highest photography carried out at the time and the effort to get it was formidable. It is recounted in further reports to the Photographic Society. The steep rocky roads, the problems of organising porterage, of making pictures in remote, cold conditions; of transporting the glass plates down narrow trails provide Bourne with the elements of a narrative of practical difficulties and colonialist exasperation that concludes less in the euphoric grandeur of the high passes – although they moved Bourne to religious as well as photographic enthusiasm – than in the serenity and stillness of the photographs: products and objects of pure contemplation.

But they were not the fruits of exploration, however much they resemble the work which came out of later mountaineering or polar exploration projects. Bourne made no measurements, nor did he plant the Union flag on any peak. It was not knowledge that he sought but visibility: the conscious pleasure of seeing for its own sake with no obvious purpose. It offered the viewer the same freedom from utility or necessity that 'unnecessary' travel supplied (figure 15).

Visually, Bourne formed his response to the mountains in terms of an imagery that reproduced their 'wild sublimity' and organised them into objects framed for contemplation. In the Himalayas Bourne effectively relinquishes social India. Along the roads into the foothills he produced a few portraits of villages and villagers. But in the high, antiseptic emptiness history is displaced by geology, weather and space, which are in turn transformed, as they are so often in the religious minds of the nineteenth century, into metaphysics. The only human presence might be a few ant-sized porters a mile or two before the lens and of course, Bourne's own point of view. Where the Taj Mahal had astonished with its brilliance and beauty, here it is the enormity and endlessness of the Himalayas that overcomes him. As before, the experience generates a surge that trip-switches the reasoning mind to the off position:

> Peak rose above peak, summit above summit, range above range, innumerable and boundless, until the mind refused to follow the eye in its attempt to comprehend the whole in one grand conception. (Bourne 1864b: 69)

The power of visual experience – the boundless space, the work of gigantic telluric forces – leads Bourne's uncomprehending human consciousness to the acceptance of God's unmatchable creative power and greater understanding by the 'uplifting of the heart to him who formed such stupendous works' (Bourne 1864b: 69).

Photography's art of conveying visual power beyond ideas will, Bourne believes, lead the viewer's mind to the same conclusion reached by his own. He writes 'it must be set down to the credit of photography that it teaches the mind to see the beauty and powers of such as these' (1864b: 69).

And yet it is in one of his accounts of Himalayan travel that Bourne spoke of India as 'the land of rising British enterprise' (1864b: 70). His experiences there and the work he produced remain as much the projection of a British mentality and as deeply embedded in the historical realities and requirements of colonial India as any other. Remember that Bourne included the photographic camera among the conqueror's inventions. The mountains function for him as an 'axiological desert', to appropriate Bakhtin's term for nature, on to whose vacant features ostensibly free of social meaning the core axioms of a culture are projected. The iconography of distant horizons and deep space already carried strong connotations of the sublime, of the going beyond. It visualised Victorian energies and ideas concerned with progressive movement. Space is given purpose. Look at the figures on the glacier in figure 15. They are travelling for ever into a distance – towards a future. For the Victorian viewer space was something to be filled, a lack to be replaced by the fullness of possession. An imagery which in the eighteenth century had invited the viewer to contemplation had become for the Victorian a call to action.

Bourne's photographs reproduce this lack – the emptiness into which we must travel – and thus stimulate desire which, as a form of symbolic and aesthetic possession, the photograph satisfies. The viewer is pleasured further by the knowledge that the power of their own society is implicit within these photographs: the power of Victorian technology, the camera; and the power to be where one chooses. If Bourne can be said to have been looking through the eye of the Raj, these photographs are saying that British endeavour and organisation have risen to the highest order in India; that British representational technology and British religious belief supersede all others. Bourne's apparent humility before the elevations of 'the Almighty Architect of the Universe' has another more presumptious intent: the assertion that the divine is the only force higher than the power of the British Raj (Bourne 1870a and b: 39).

Notes

1 For some reflections on the association made by Europeans between degeneration and the Orient see Perez (1988): 105–7.

2 In Islam there is a belief that when a person is touched by divine grace or the spirit of revelation, visible traces in the form of light remain at the location of the event. Such a place often becomes the destination of pilgrimage where believers hope to glimpse the abiding luminosity of divine presence. The force that transmits it is known as *Baraka*.

3 See Captain Linnaus Tripe, Madras-based 1858–9; Captain Melville Clark, *Journey to Simla, Ladac and Cashmere*, 1862; Captain T. G. Glovers, Ganges 1864; Major Robert Gill, *Indian Temples*, 1864; and see Mackenzie 1987.

3
Worlds in a house: the consumption of travel photography in the Victorian middle-class home

> Private space is marked by an exterior material boundary and an interior surplus of signification. (Susan Stewart, *On Longing*)

> The Stereoscope is now an institution of every home – a veritable 'Household World'. (*La Lumière* 1851)

> Home is where the heart is
> Home is so remote.
> (Lena Lovitch)

In the nineteenth century only a minority of those who consumed travel photographs covered any distance themselves. But what did images of distant places mean to those viewers who remained behind, and what needs did they serve? This chapter attempts to answer these questions less by discussing photography than through an examination of the most important place in which photography was viewed and from which the worlds beyond it were imagined. This was the middle-class home. The portrayal of this place that follows will of necessity be general, even abstract. It is unlikely that many Victorian homes will have resembled it in every detail and many counter-examples can be found to contest it. Without doubt, I have exaggerated the degree of separation between the public and private realms where it concerned women. The cultural historian Lynda Nead, for one, would contest not only the degree of separation but even the decisive role of any separate domestic sphere in determining Victorian female identities. One of Nead's studies attempts to reveal a significant presence of 'respectable' women in public spaces and claims that the movement and activities of women through them was often more negotiable than effectively prohibited and for such reasons female identity more fluent than has been commonly assumed (Nead in Porter 1997: 167–85). However, my intention is to uncover something of the home's underlying cultural logic – its *grammar* rather than its *speech* – so as to elucidate its role as a lived mechanism for processing cultural meanings which originate from the outside. The relationship between the home and exterior social spaces will be examined; but the chapter's central interest will lie with the home's reception of the colonised world through the consumption of photographs.

The Victorian middle-class home was at once a location, a set of social and spatial practices, a state of mind, a cultural subsystem. It was also an active and determined component in a wider system, that is a world within the world of globalising capitalism. Eric Hobsbawm describes the establishing of a global capitalist order with its attendant systems of communication and transportation and, over time, structures of political control, as 'probably the single most important development of the period'. The period of its completion, from the 1840s to the end of the century, had, he maintains, an importance equal to that of the late fifteenth century, the time of the voyages of Columbus. By the end of the nineteenth century it was possible for the first time to speak accurately of 'world history' (Hobsbawm 1977: 48–52). For its first two generations, this new world order was dominated by England. The evolution of the Victorian middle class, wherever located, was part of the wider evolution of this world order.

Born also of this time, photography, and travel photography in particular, formed part of the cultural armoury and of capitalism's expansion. In his study of the British colonisation of Egypt, Timothy Mitchell notes how the communications media including photography aided colonialism in its penetration of Egypt, among many other places, with both its power and its truth:

> They gave global political power not just its detailed practicality but its facticity. From the tourist spectacles of bombardment and the displays of weaponry to the telegraphed news report and the postcard home, global colonialism came into being not only as a local method of order, seeking to work with individual minds and bodies, but as a process that was continuously reporting, picturing and representing itself. (Mitchell 1991: 130)

The process of colonisation involved the linking together of colony and metropolitan centre at every step. It was developed in such a way as to enter equally the private realms and subjectivities of Europeans in the colonial spaces and those at home.

In a move mirroring its domination of the external world, capitalism began to colonise and re-order the interior domain of existence – private life. It invented new structures of home, family and sexuality, and constructed a 'bourgeois domestic space' which generated new selfhoods.

This new private life was a set of actual spaces founded on certain kinds of separation of private and public existence and formed from the interior social and architectural arrangements of the Victorian middle-class house. It was a psychological space, an evolving topography of new subjectivities and emotional regimes. It was also an economic space, a breeding ground for consumer fantasy and a site of consumption and consumer display.

Rooted in both the external realm of positive events and in the interior domain of idealisation and fantasy – in both science and romance – photography became as essential to capitalism's re-ordering of the interior world

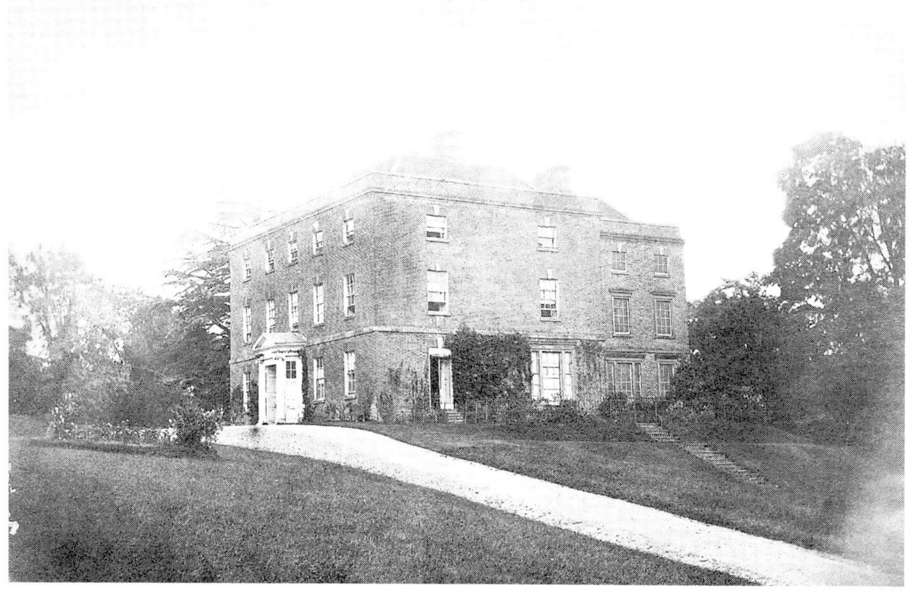

Fig. 16a From a Victorian family album, n.d.

as it was central to its domination of the exterior one. Like a two-way mirror it would both function as a conduit between them and a means of keeping them separate.

The exterior and interior worlds were distinct, even opposed, but interdependent. The individual was increasingly pulled in both directions – held between mobility and stasis, by 'abroad' and 'home', by the force of an actual or imaginary relationship with a developing imperialist world system on the one hand and by the affective pull of personal existence, always both powerfully material and deeply imaginary, on the other. The home was producing human subjects for empire; the house was filling with its products. The wealth of empire made the 'cluttered opulence' of the Victorian house possible. Like all houses that call themselves homes, it was a punctuation mark at the ending of all roads; the still point at which a journey could be recollected, anticipated – or imagined (Carter 1992: 9–27). The Victorian home was the destination and point of departure, at the beginning and end of the roads of a globalising capitalism.

Throughout this period photographic images became established as the dominant visual mode in which journeys and distant places were recollected, anticipated or simply imagined. The home filled with visual representations and more and more the world became experienced as image. The industry of mass-produced graphic and photographic representations that grew up from the 1830s onwards formed part of the cultural mechanism which located the individual in relation to different dimensions of social existence. The middle-class photographic portrait, to take a prime example, mediated between the private and public. In standardising its subjects' mode of dress, posture and expression before the class-eye of the studio camera the portrait was both a

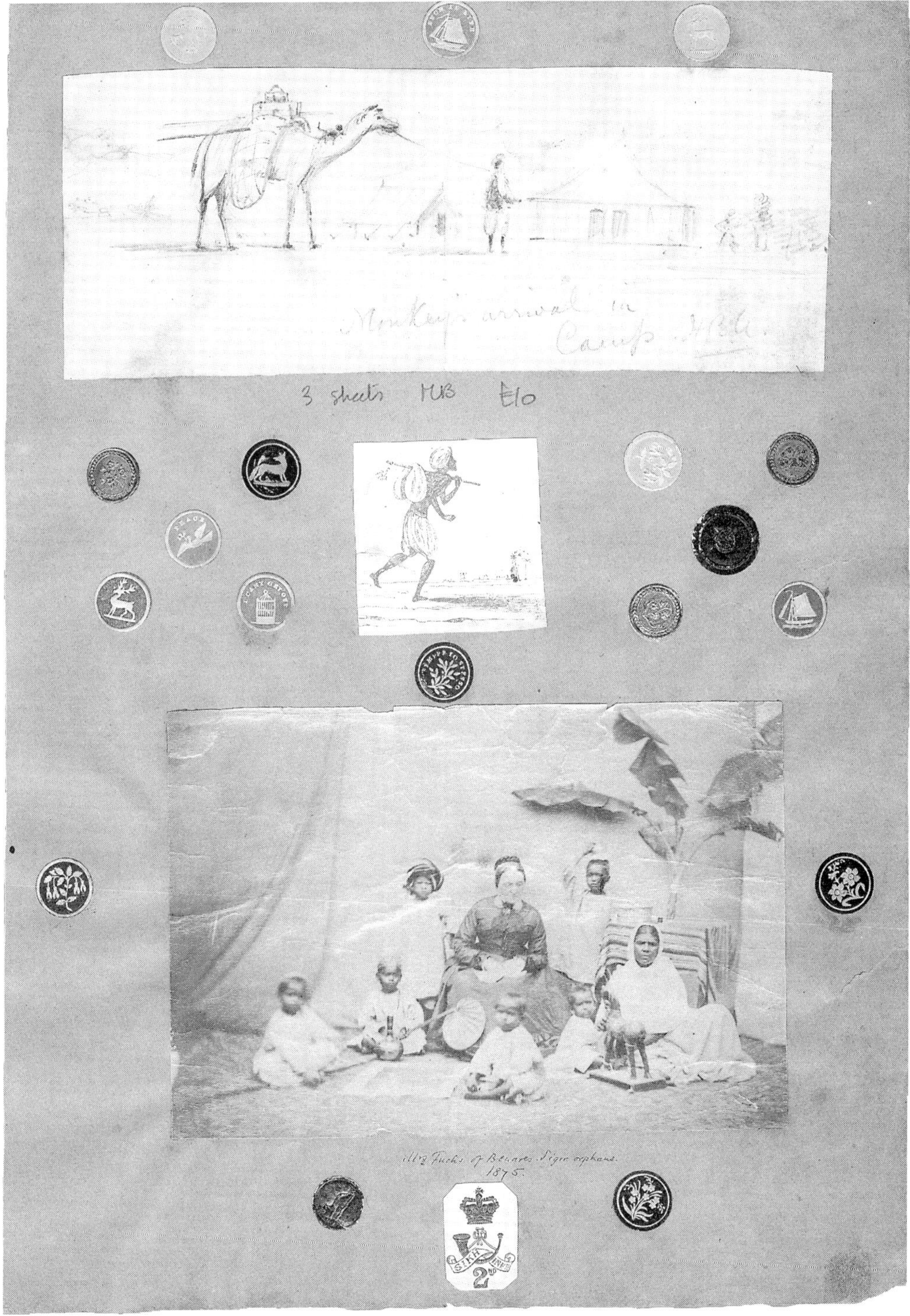

Fig. 16b From a Victorian family album, n.d. On opposing page to 16a in original album.

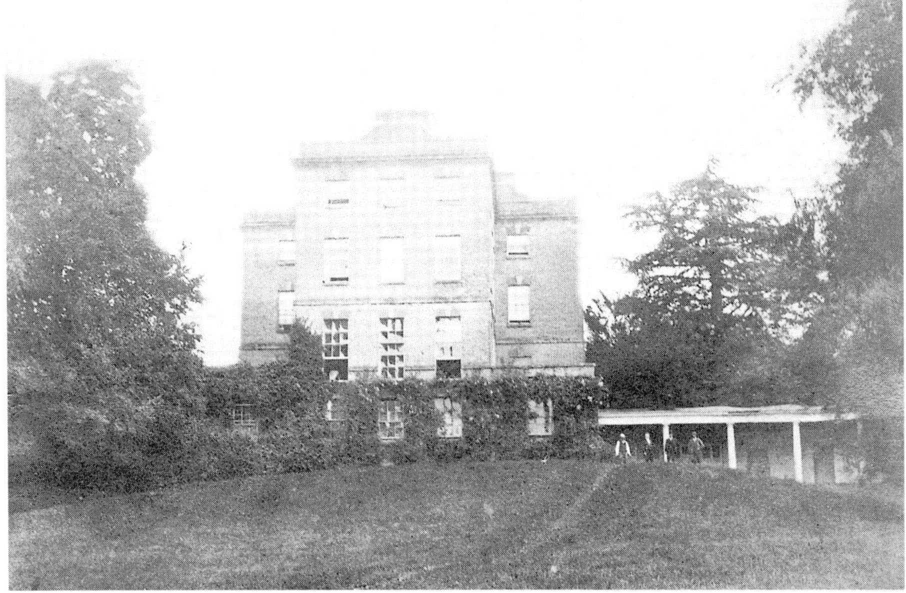

Fig. 16c From a Victorian family album, n.d.

private image of self and at the same time a publicity still for a whole social group, an 'outward sign of inward grace'. It mirrored individuals back to themselves and out into the system of middle-class appearances. In John Tagg's lapidary phrasing, it was 'a sign whose purpose is both the description of an individual and an inscription of a social identity' (Tagg 1988: 37).

The travel photograph mediated between the private or local and the global. Where technology was shrinking space through speed, the photograph was reducing the world the better for it to pass through the promiscuous iris of the West. For the consumer of images in the metropolitan centres photographs of distant possessions and colonised peoples confirmed their sense of being at the compelling heart of the new world order and relocated their own identities within it. Travel photography provided middle-class viewers with the means of identifying themselves in and with the global system in which, as members of a colonising state, their lives and fortunes were already invested.

Photographs were also commodities, sign-commodities, prototypes of the informational and aesthetic goods which dominate our era. In them market and politics coincided. It is said that the goal of marketing is to persuade consumers that the world of goods and experiences on offer is no more than the precipitation of their own desires. If this is true, then in the placid confusion of actuality and fantasy that is the engagement in the photographic image, the European middle-class viewers of all kinds of early travel photographs may have imagined that the world as held in those images was now arranging itself for them. In fact many travel and expedition photographs of the Victorian period were portraits of the travellers themselves – the viewer's agent-surrogate – in which the sights and monuments they posed before seem recruited as indicators of the knowledge, taste and social power of the subject. Certainly, both travel and portrait photography were transporting the self-image of the middle class across all space under its mastery and across time by inscribing it into the history they were themselves making. Their portraits remain with us – the repetitiously dead, renewing ownership of their epoch every time we view them.

As a commodity form and bearer of class values the photograph established for the viewer a relationship to travel which was at once commercial and ideological. As discussed in an earlier chapter, the fact that the photograph shifted optically aided perception from direct observation to the consumption of representations admitted fantasy and daydream into the viewing process. It made possible one of photography's most popular uses: as a form of imaginary travel.

Photography recorded journeys made by the viewer. It supplied other viewers with the spectacle of journeys they'd never undertaken. In these alternate functions photography was reflecting the mixed meanings that the word 'travel' carried in the Victorian world which were themselves reflections of that world's own contradictory nature.

Victorian society promulgated revolutionary social and technological processes but feared the disorder it expected in their wake. Consequently it imposed on itself a regime of conformity and prudence. On one hand it could promote both social and global mobility as its central myth (Gay 1985: 65). On the other it could represent itself as a hierarchical social order fixed by tradition and by moral and even biological laws. It was a culture torn between the retentive values of work, savings and self-restraint and the sensuous prospects and fantasies of spending and consuming which wealth made increasingly possible. In the realm of travel Victorian society could generate both the most fearless and remorseless adventurers and the most timid stop-at-home daydreamers. Each was equally representative of their world.

Many of these oppositions are condensed in two singularly modern conditions which became common in the Victorian period and were immediately catered for by the new culture of travel and its imagery. They were boredom and the yearning for novelty.

Boredom was a word almost unknown in English speech until the eighteenth century (Spacks 1995). It became ubiquitous as the routines of mass society became widespread. While boredom was normally seen as a listless and uncreative state of mind, in some instances it could be regarded as a form of psychic opposition to modern life's repetition and conformity or as a defiance of the bourgeois enthusiasm for work and productivity. Boredom could also be seen as a creative expression of dissatisfaction which might drive the individual towards change, as in Baudelaire's 1859 poem *Le Voyage* (see Petro in Petro 1995).

The pursuit of novelty was in part the solution to the problem of boredom; in part it was the product of the commodification of the idea of progress. Moral and social evolution were replaced by the illusory transformations accompanying consumption. This created an existence passed in a state of both permanent curiosity and managed dissatisfaction. Boredom and novelty each became a function of the other.

Reflecting such developments, opposing positions began to form in the individual subject. Middle-class citizens had every reason to feel they inhabited blessed identities. The exterior world belonged to them, and their private life was sanctified by the reigning value system. However, the market required the production of consumer need, which in turn required convincing individuals their lives were deficient and in need of fulfilment. It demanded a subjectivity which was a continuous dreaming of being other than itself – a yearning for some authentic, free or happy existence somewhere in a distance more imaginary than real. But it was a subjectivity that had somehow to remain convinced of its own perfection.

Travel photographs helped establish both of these positions. As representations of conquered regions they confirmed the viewer's sense of his or her own power. Their realism and, especially for nineteenth-century viewers, their visual brilliance, their luxuriance, corresponded to the viewer's wealth derived in all probability from the same regions as depicted in the photography.

And yet, as images of the 'extra-ordinary' world beyond the drawing room, as the products of others' adventures, they were equally capable of confronting viewers with intensities lacking in their own lives and leaving them feeling diminished. Additionally, the sense of spatial distance and cultural remoteness that travel photography conveyed and the incidental image of disorder or violent death all threatened to insinuate into the home themes which might unbalance its mythical stability. However, the Victorian home was a cultural device, a mechanism whose function was the maintenance of order achieved through the expunction or neutralisation of whatever threatened to negate it. For example like other practices in Victorian culture it was able to transform a disruptive desire to wander into an affirmation of settlement, into an entertainment, and to translate prospects of the strange and fearful into sources of reassurance. In this context, travel photography was the solution and the problem. What follows is an attempt to clarify this.

In 1855 Ernest Lacan, who from time to time corresponded with the Photographic Society in England, looked out from his study across the roofs of Paris at a patch of blue sky in the distance and wrote:

> You dream that there are under this same sky ... pleasant lands where the eye loses itself in distant perspectives, where the pupil dilates, where thoughts are transformed and purified, where the soul can plunge into reverie as you look at the luminous atmosphere. You dream that you are there instead of here, you dream of dark forests, dappled plains, picturesque valleys posed like rests along your route, majestic mountains and frothing seas, the Alps, the Mediterranean, Italy, Spain, the Orient. Wait, open that album! (*Le Moniteur universal* 1855; quoted in Teynard 1992: introduction)

This passage was composed during the Paris Universal Exposition and displays the signs of a visual taste in the process of being re-shaped by and for the photograph. Many of the qualities of the scenes are photographic. It's no surprise he demands his Album – it's photography he's missing.

A market in books and images catering for the sedentary reader or viewer interested in the world beyond their own existed as early as the 1600s (Hale 1994: 181). From the seventeenth and eighteenth centuries this new kind of reader and viewer, the imaginary traveller, had become more common. He or she was the traveller who never left home but was regularly transported by means of fictions, recollections and visual images; the traveller who journeyed in the imagination. Two of the earliest novels of all, *Don Quixote* (1605) and *Robinson Crusoe* (1719), were both in their ways travel stories.

In the same period the accounts of numerous 'Grand Tours' were familiar to aristocratic readerships. This was a genre devoted more to the effects of travelling on the taste and psychology of the traveller than to descriptive accuracy. By the late eighteenth and early nineteenth century the widely read chronicles of trips made by explorers and topographers such as Cook and Von Humboldt were laying claim to more objective or scientific intentions.

In the nineteenth century the explosion of cheap publishing and mass-produced imagery made the imaginary traveller a commonplace. David Livingstone was able to sell thirty thousand copies of the expensive six-volume account of his African adventure in the 1850s (National Portrait Gallery 1996; Hobsbawm 1975: 330; Richards 1991: 123). Livingstone's journey would now be described as a media event. It was plainly an entertainment. Readers were able to lose themselves in what was a search-narrative with Africa acting as the wilderness backdrop to an adventure in Western meaning and identity in which Europeans or Euro-Americans got lost; and then found themselves – famous.

By the end of the century it was possible to reproduce photographs in travel books. Many recounted trips to colonial possessions such as Canada and Australia. Some combined the aim of giving readers and viewers the pleasures of second-hand experience with that of encouraging emigration. This was especially true for Canada, concerned at a time of increasing American power to fill the great spaces of the western provinces. One can see this in the Countess of Aberdeen's book *Through Canada with a Kodak* published in Edinburgh in 1893 whose print run went into 'tens of thousands' (Harper 1994: xv). It included eighty-four photographs, half of them Kodak snaps by the author, half by professionals. The snaps are notational, like diary entries: a moment on the train journey, a train wreck, a quick view of a settlement, some portraits. The professional photographs are for the most part picturesque landscapes.

The modulation between two kinds of imagery had a purpose. On the one hand the immediate, quotidian style of the snap presenting encounters with particular moments and ordinary individuals showed Canada as a land filled with busy migrants from the Old Country, folk like the reader of the book, perhaps, whose vision is unfussy and primarily pragmatic. On the other hand, the 'timeless' grandeur of the picturesque, revealed a continent of spectacular even sublime natural beauty which promised liberation, even transcendence. Such visual seduction might have converted an imaginary traveller into a settler.[1]

However, while even non-utilitarian travel increased in this period, most voyagers never left their seats. 'All my modes of conveyance have been pictorial', confides Mr Booley, the superannuated banking clerk who cruises the world by means of the Panoramas in Dickens's 1850 feature *Some Account of an Extraordinary Traveller* (Dickens in Slater 1996: 202–12). For every Sir Richard Burton, or Flora Tristan, there were ten thousand Mr Booleys or Emma Bovarys, precursors of the Pooters, Blooms, Mittys, Lisas (in Ophuls's film *Letter from an Unknown Woman*) and Billy Liars of later generations. For many the stories and images of travel functioned to postpone or replace actual travel. Experience postponed and enjoyed as contemplation rather than action had become a privilege of wealth, a conspicuous consumption of non-consumption, an attitude famously personified in Huysmans's 1884 character Des Esseintes, who held travel to be a 'waste of time, since he believed the imagination could provide a more than adequate substitute for the vulgar reality of actual experience' (Huysmans, *Against Nature* (1959); 1984 repr.: 35; see also Moretti in Nelson and Grossberg 1988: 339–46).

But for those whose financial options or stocks of courage were more limited, travel stories and images could provide compensation for their immobility. Indeed, this may have been their social function, especially among the lower middle classes. Photographic travel imagery was commonly promoted as a means of enjoying the world beyond the doorstep free of dirt or mortal risk. In 1852 Louis de Cormenin, to whom Maxime du Camp dedicated his Middle East Album, wrote:

> It will be the glory of this society so fecund in discoveries of every kind, and also its reward to have reduced space and time in relation to man. By a happy coincidence, photography was discovered at the very same time as the railways. We need no longer embark on the ships of Cook or Laperouse in order to go on perilous voyages: heliography, entrusted to a few intrepid practitioners, will make the world tour on our behalf, without ever having to leave our armchairs. (quoted in Lemagny and Rouillé 1987: 54)

A generation later the American photographer James Ricalton was promoting the same advantages. His guide for the vicarious and immaculate traveller, *India through the Stereoscope*, came complete with stereographs and a viewer. It was published as part of the series *Underwood Stereoscopic Tours* and went through several editions before the end of the century, each featuring a new selection of images. In his introduction, Ricalton not only offered the buyer an experience of travel free of heat and disease to 'a wonderland you can reach directly from your fireside' but also promoted the superiority of the simulation over the actual: 'Besides there is often a witchery and a charm in Stereoscopic images not found in the real presence of places and things' (Sharma 1987: 54–5).

This feature of bourgeois culture was notably identified by Roland Barthes in his *Mythologies* piece 'The Nautilus and the Drunken Boat'. 'Imagination about travel', he writes, 'corresponds in Verne, to an exploration of closure.' Barthes accounts for Jules Verne's wide popularity in his success in reflecting the desire to 'enclose oneself and settle' like a child in a hut or a little tent. Verne's *Mysterious Island* features, he says

> The man-child [who] re-invents the world, fills it, closes it, shuts himself up in it, and crowns this encyclopaedic effort with the bourgeois posture of appropriation: slippers, pipe and fireside, while the storm, that is, the infinite, rages outside in vain. (Barthes 1972: 65)

Rather than indices of adventurousness, Verne's fictional vessels – the ships, submarines and rockets – embodied for the reader an inclination to be enclosed and, as Barthes writes, 'of having at hand the greatest possible number of objects, and having at one's disposal an absolutely infinite space' (Barthes 1972: 66). 'A ship', he adds, 'is a habitat before being a means of transport' (Barthes 1972: 66).

For the stay-at-home Victorian, deep in reveries of travel furnished by the photographic album or the stereoscope, the habitat, the house, too, will have become a means of imaginary transport. Through the porthole of the photograph, the world of infinite objects lay safely disposed in an outside at once introduced and deferred by representation. He or she was subject to an interior regime driven by an ulterior motive.

Yet, for those who did embark, travelling might still be undertaken in a variety of enclosures, in vehicles such as the coach, the steamer, the railway car, each extensions of the house, mobile homes from which the world could be observed by the lonely and untouchable consciousness in detached and leisurely mastery through the frame of the window.

Of course, travel was already framed, already associated with pictorial experience before 1839. The world had been sliding past in the magic lanterns and in the pre-photographic stereoscope for some time. Photography transformed this popular magic into a popular science, a medium no less magical for being realistic. In panoramas and dioramas foreign parts and imperial moments had been staple subjects from the beginning. However, these spectacular visual entertainments were consumed in public. Photography, on the other hand, quickly became associated with the domestic, much of it accumulated and consumed in the privacy of the home. And this introduced specific complexities into the manner of enjoying and interpreting its imagery.

Space, as Heidegger has shown, is *for* something. Space structures relations between actors within and beyond it; it establishes relative value and meanings between different spaces; gives those participating at the interior of their own space a relationship to a horizon which defines the interior as well the outside and the beyond. The interiors and horizons delineating the Victorian middle-class home constituted part of the mechanism through which its inhabitants looked out at the world. It was a mechanism that helped form what Stuart Hall has called their 'imaginative geography' by which a structure of being is intensified, 'by dramatising the difference between what is close and what is far away' (Hall in Rutherford 1990: 230–2). As we shall see, the ordering of space is always an ordering of meaning.

It is more or less redundant to say that the Victorian middle-class domestic space was gendered. Alongside reproduction, the structuring of gender relations was its most important purpose. It determined interior relations and relations with its defined exteriors.

The nineteenth century is justly renowned for its development of civic spaces and amenities. Yet these positive spaces had their opposites in the zones of negativity which existed as categories in the Victorian cultural imagination and in the actual manifestations of the social inequalities attendant upon Victorian economics. An over-preoccupation with the negative spaces was crucial to the mythology of the middle-class home.

The outside social world became classified as a masculine domain from which the unchaparoned middle-class married woman was expected to be excluded. Although the source of wealth, the outside was commonly represented as a place of strangeness and instability where self-interested individuals 'gave themselves up to', lost themselves in, the struggle for money and influence. With its mysteriously autonomous industrial processes and its commodities forever shifting in value, identity and function, it connoted a frightening loss of control. Full of the dangers of class hatred, crime, sexual predation and disease, it was considered a place of risk.

The distant spaces of the colonised regions beyond were more ambiguous. They were stages on which European men could make themselves economically and morally through playing the imperial part. But they concealed hazards to both the physical self and to the norms of European identity. Again, with few exceptions, this did not apply to European women, who were often largely absent prior at least to permanent European settlement. (See Lawrence 1994: 21, on colonial stories written about those women who travelled to the colonies; written for 'Housebound Females'.)

Against the degraded social realm on the outside the domestic interior stood as place of refuge and moral certainty. Under the caring hand of the presiding female – the eponymous and necessarily asexual '*Angel of the Hearth*' of Coventry Patmore's popular poem – the economic warrior could be restored to his true moral and emotional self; re-humanised in the bosom of his family. Within this orthodoxy the middle-class male self was made in the public domain, and realised in the private (Sennett 1986: chapters 2 and 8).

As refuge for economic man the home was required to dispel the harsh utilitarian facts of the exterior market place by the idealisations of family life and its pastimes. The home not only established a condition of security it also secreted a distracting unreality. Writing of mid-nineteenth-century Paris, Walter Benjamin says:

> The private citizen who in the office took reality into account, required of the interior that it should support him in his illusions. This necessity was all the more pressing since he had no intention of adding social preoccupations to his business ones. In the creation of his private environment he suppressed them both, from this sprang the phantasmagorias of the interior. This represented the universe for the private citizen. In it he assembled the distant in space and time. His drawing room was a box in the world-theatre. (Benjamin 1973: 167–8)

Jean Baudrillard echoes Benjamin's observations when he describes the home as 'a narcissistic territory ... wherein the subjectivity can fulfil itself without let or hindrance' (Baudrillard in Elsner and Cardinal 1994: 10).

The home was where the man 'collected himself' or perhaps 'recollected himself'. The association between home and collecting is important. More and more the home exerted a powerful centripetal force, pulling things and people towards its core. The home was itself a collection. It stood as a fullness, a clean, still place of stable authenticity against the outside. Within the home things came together: a family, a moral order, a set of treasured objects and memories which helped define the integrity of the home and of the self. The home became a second world in which the orders of the first were rearranged by the collective solipsism of the middle class. The fondness for wax fruits and stuffed animals was a symptom of a desire to control time and decay through replication and simulation. The cabinets of fossils and the butterfly collections represented nature re-ordered as a museum with its indispensable frock-coated curator – the owner. The cabinets of curiosities were each a miniature cosmos. Being arbitrary assemblies of heterogeneous and frequently bizarre objects, they celebrated the collector as the only source of unity and coherence. The *primum mobile* of a personalised universe, the collector's subjectivity transformed contingency into necessity. The universe of the collection could even be an alternative to that of utility, the sovereign principle of the outside world. In Benjamin's words, 'the collector dreamed that he was in a world which was not only far-off in distance and time, but which was also a better one ... in which things were free from the bondage of being useful' (Benjamin 1973: 168–9). And collecting may even have confined the strayness of lust. One social historian has suggested that the collector's investment of time and desire was driven by 'a need, common in men over the age of forty, to control or check the libido' (Corbin in Ariès and Duby 1990: 545).

Collecting mirrored in miniature the colonial processes of surveying, classifying and gathering up. It was a game of ownership and control. In her biography of Darwin Janet Browne notes that for men of his class natural history, collecting and hunting were simply 'different expressions of a single urge for possession' (Browne 1995: 220). Timothy Mitchell highlights the desire of imperialism to transform the world under its control into a shop display, an exhibition, a collection (Mitchell 1991: 18). And Stephen Kern wonders whether the suppression of space brought about by the collection-like clutter of nineteenth-century interiors was a symptom of the coloniser's fear of the colonised other's space. In these rooms crowded with objects, he argues, distance was suppressed and the uncharted, incomprehensible emptinesses of the colonial zones were symbolically filled and rendered familiar (Kern 1983: 156).

Photography also represented a symbolic suppression of distance and acquisition of space. It too was a form of collecting. It gathered up the world as an infinite series of image-objects, fossilised presences, places, all stilled, preserved, miniaturised and thus classifiable. It rendered the world comprehensible and manageable under the evening lamplight.

On the other hand, in atomising reality and by confirming the non-presence of the objects, photography could, in Susan Sontag's words, 'confer on each moment a mystery', granting the means of indulging in pleasurable reverie (Sontag 1978: 73). Not only did these hybrid characteristics of photography enable the photographic album to match the strangeness of the cabinets of curiosities and also confirm the unifying power of the collector and his subjectivity, they meant that photography was the perfect medium for the project of simultaneously acquiring the world of objects and of dreaming reality. Possession and control and the ideal of stable order and identity were the goals being sought by these activities. This included the control not only of the lives of women but also their 'meaning' in the cultural order. How the woman became represented in the domestic space had important implications for the meaning of representations in general and for the ways in which the outside world was viewed from the house.

The function of women in the domestic space was central but contradictory. In addition to generating the famous comforts and repressions of the Victorian home, the evolving arrangements of private existence did increase both the responsibilities and the influence of the woman in relation to home management, child rearing and, in certain households, the frequency of reproduction (Smith in Hartman and Banner 1974). Given the increasingly central position of the domestic in the evolving economy and culture of consumerism and in cultural reproduction in general, some have seen in these developments the beginnings of a feminisation of culture.

However, the Victorian woman's task remained essentially unchanged: to nurture and sustain a social order dominated by men or at least by the masculine principle. In this she became a crucial agent in the transmission of culture and therefore the mistress of fictions and images. The mother or daughter or an unmarried female relative resident in the house, for example, was most commonly the guardian of the photographic album in which the private history and moral narrative of the family paralleled the wider story of their class and nation (see, for example, Warner 1992: 28–32). For the home had become a place where stories and pictures abounded, a place of safety from where the world could be told and imagined through these products of the Victorian culture industry.

The position of the female carried profound symbolic values. At the core of the Victorian family resided a refined hypocrisy. The home may have been idealised in the male psyche yet many men evidently preferred their homosocial life on the outside. More significantly, the home was at once defined as the heart of existence and yet regarded as junior to the reality-making realm of male projects. Women were associated with a secondary social reality and reflecting this they were associated with appearances rather than truth.

This complex calls to mind Luce Irigaray's critique of Plato's famous 'shadows in the cave' analogy elaborated in *The Republic*. In the language used by Plato to describe the cave, Irigaray detects the ghostly presence of the maternal body, in particular the womb. This sensible, worldly, corporeal and mortal vessel is demoted by Plato and placed below and after the realm from which truth or reality is taken to derive – that of the intelligible, disembodied, self-originating Idea – the realm of the Father. 'Engendering the real is the Father's task, engendering the fictive is the task of the Mother – that "receptacle" for turning out more or less good copies of reality' (Irigaray 1985: 300; see also Whitford 1991: chapter 5).

Again the feminine is associated with secondary appearances; the masculine with primary, intellectual reality. In Irigaray's Plato the repression of woman's presence in the creation of meaning is a denial of sexual difference – a denial driven by fear of the primal scene and the castration complex. It is a disavowal of the body and its mortality and thereby of the probability that truth, rather than being singular and universal, is located in specific times, places and persons – in particular bodies.

The features of Plato's metaphysics are recognisable in those of the Victorian domestic culture and its use of representations. The home was itself a cave of shadows; the bright shadows of stories, pictures and magic lantern slides through which a world systematically defined as outside and opposed to it was pictured. It was also a culture which generally attempted to impose a repressive order on sexuality, especially that of women, while sanctifying the idea of the 'female'. These activities were not unrelated.

In dividing the family off from other social groupings, middle-class private life had increased the husband's power within the house and yet had encouraged a greater affirmation of affection between spouses. At the heart of private life these developments built a tensile structure of relations between men and women in which the potential for a democracy of the feelings remained in conflict with the fact of the enhanced power of the individual male head of household. By the nineteenth century the re-emphasised distinctions between the public and private worlds added to these established contradictions an overestimation of family existence which deepened the intensities within the house. The man needed the home to put himself back together, but the woman was caught in a *double bind*. The companiate marriage sanctioned the expression of feeling and raised emotional expectations but as a cultural system the family could not admit the open expression of female sexual desire (Stone 1982: chapter 8). The threat posed to the cultural order by the woman's autonomous desire, her difference, was buried by idealisations and repressive definitions of femininity. Her physicality was swaddled by euphemism or silence. In this way masculine identity was provided with a womanhood which appeared to have its foundation in masculine needs and desires. The echo of Irigaray's Plato is clear. The repression of difference with its effect of installing the masculine singular as the origin and master of both knowledge and identity is present both in the Platonic metaphysical tradition and in Victorian sexual culture. The reassuring unities that male culture sought at home rested on the denial of that *primary* otherness, sexual difference. If the home's function was the restoration of a reassuring unity, its ultimate promise was the resurrection of unity with the Mother in whom all difference, all separation is overcome. For Gillian Rose therein still lies the source of male nostalgia for the domestic space, the place of return. For woman, she argues, the home is historically a site of exploitation; for man it is a place which stands for 'none other than the inaccessible plenitude of the mother' (Rose 1993: 60).

As we have seen, one of the cultural functions of 'Woman', assigned a position as a representation in the signifying order and a space as a social individual in the domestic order, was to restore or sustain a sense of integration and effectivity in masculine identity. It was to be achieved predominantly by means of the imaginary removal or repression of the destabilising threat of difference that patriarchal culture imagined her to quite literally embody. Allied with the dominant social and economic power of the middle class, this ordering of identity and meaning around sexual difference helped form the cultural optic through which photographic representations of the outside world and its peoples were viewed and understood.

In the previous chapter it was discussed how the strangeness and dangers of the colonised regions were overcome by photographic modes which re-imagined their objects as exotic, ethnographic, abject, archaeological or Europeanised. It was not by chance that this imagery was collected, viewed and interpreted in a space from which the foundational otherness of female sexual difference had, in theory, already been removed. This space, the home, was as much a part of the institution of photography as the studio or the camera. In the process of receiving photographic images into the home the two modes of repression and denial – the domestic and the colonial – were brought together. They spiralled inseparably around each other like the two helices in the structure of DNA one transmitting the principle of the integrated male subject, the other that of social dominance. In a very particular manner, the outside world was being domesticated.

The translation of the outside world, the colony, into the home's significations was not achieved by specific uses or readings of photography alone. The translation was made possible additionally because of a certain isomorphism between it and the ideological aims of globalising capitalism. This is seen most sharply in the conceptions of visual truth associated with the photographic image. Its realism had its origins in the acquisitive individualism embodied in the monocular perspective of sixteenth-century Italy, in Renaissance visual surveying of land-capital and in the celebration of personality in oil painting and eventually photography from the sixteenth century onwards.

Photography's illusionism was an equal partner with its realism in the business of representing capitalism. This was most pronounced in the stereoscope, a form strongly associated with the domestic consumption of the medium.

As we have seen, viewing a stereoscopic photograph is closer to visual immersion. In a modest way it anticipates virtual reality systems. The presence of three-dimensional objects is accomplished so powerfully that a hyper-presence is given to the world of independent events. The viewer feels himself or herself to be 'out there', moving deep into the multiplanar space. At the same time, objects and figures are transformed into the frozen instants of performances staged for the viewer alone, taking place 'in here', in the private theatre of the viewer's head.

When photography's effects were recruited as conveyors of Victorian middle-class mentalities the primary task was to conceal any sense of the viewer's implication in either the production or the reading of the image. It was 'disappeared' in the blindness of the 'purely' visual. The way the world was and the way the viewer saw were one. Similarly, any independent mentality beyond the home in the pro-photographic event originating, say, in a colonised culture with diverse traditions in the ordering and understanding of representations, was erased as thoroughly as were the ordering power and agency of the photographer and the viewer.

Like Plato's bloodless intellection the representation of truth in a visual realism without authorship has been linked to the visual culture of patriarchy. Three-dimensional visual realism, with its disembodied mastery and proprietorial gaze, has been regarded as its most classical form (Rose 1993: 39; Gregory 1994: 160 and passim; William Cowper's 'monarch of all I survey' poem on Alexander Selkirk). Photography, a medium designed from visual realism's template, held a further claim on truth. The guarantor of its truth lay elsewhere, in its referent situated in the world of masculine projects. Viewed at home, the photograph of distant imperial sites may have brought on Romantic reverie – the domestic, feminised mode – but all such daydreams rested securely on the rock-hard fact of the colonial process that governed it – the realm of the masculine. 'In Plato', writes Irigaray, 'the mother-matter gives birth to images, the father-God only to the Real' (Irigaray 1985: 112). This notion, too, was mythical. As Sara Mills notes in her study of women's travel literature, 'Representations of women have been central to the process of constructing a male national identity in the colonial period, but that paradoxically has been based on the excision of women's involvement in colonialism' (Mills 1991: 58). In needing to disavow, even forbid female productive activity in the exterior colonial world, patriarchal culture was confirming the possibility of its existence.

The fetish or fantasy-effect of the photograph was also enlisted to these ends. Out of what Christian Metz has called 'the immobility and silence' of the photograph an effect of pleasure and mastery is brought about (Metz in Squiers 1990: 39). By snatching the image from the disturbing flow of independent time and the logic of what might be an incommensurable social reality to that of the photographer or viewer, such as that of Indian society, the photograph comes to act as a fetish. Its apparently definitive completeness denies not only its own fragmentary nature but also the heterogeneity of the world from which it has been taken. It is still; the immobile content submits and can be viewed and re-viewed at will, giving viewers the pleasurable sense of a world disposing itself for their contemplation.

It can be argued that what is seen and how it is understood depends in part on where it is seen from, on the structure and social organisation of the position and space of looking. If this is so, then the travel photograph's contract to reduce the multivocal to the univocal was ultimately fulfilled in the gendered and class-structured space of the house (Wigley in Colomina 1992: 347). There the destabilising potential in the oppositions of fantasy and realism, fetishism and science, self and other, male and female, interior and exterior, home and abroad, ruler and subaltern, civilisation and savagery were pacified in such a way as to ensure the preservation and safety of masculine order and European power and their cultural categories against whatever was conceived of as alterity and chaos.

Note

1 In the nineteenth century it was common to use visual documentation and spectacle to encourage emigration to the colonies. An earlier example of the latter was S. C. Bree's *Colonial Panorama* of New Zealand displayed in a Leicester Square gallery in the late 1840s. The Panorama was sensational enough for *The Times* to believe 'it would do more to promote emigration than a thousand speeches and resolutions' (quoted in Slater 1996: 202) – which was its makers' intention.

Part III

Tourisms

4
Paradox amusements: tourism and the modern image

> Between them, the camera and tourism are two of the uniquely modern ways of defining reality. (Donald Horne, *The Great Museum*)

> The themes that haunt the contemporary era (advertising, image, leisure, freedom, travel). (Marc Augé, *Non-places*)

As contemporary societies would be unimaginable without the photograph, they would be unrecognisable without tourism. While attempting to examine as specifically as possible the defining presence of photography in relation to tourism and as one of its active elements, the discussions which follow will reflect also the ultimate inseparability of the medium from tourism's general culture and economy and from the varieties of modern culture of which they are constitutive.

I begin, if not with a tourist photograph, then with a photograph of tourism. In one of Martin Parr's sardonic transcriptions of world tourism, two parties of tourists, one Japanese, the other probably European or North American, are shown gathered on the Acropolis above Athens (plate 1). Much of what is central to the condition of mass tourism is presented in this photograph; both in its arrangement of actors in the scene and in the obvious subject matter.

Here tourism is visualised as a collective event, a social ritual and as international. There is a certain cultural consensus, for the tourists have all congregated in the same place, at a tourist sight, presumably for the same reasons. At the heart of the sight stands the 'attraction', to use Dean MacCannell's term, the Parthenon. It has been awarded this status by a cultural system which appears to unite these otherwise distinct peoples. The temple seems to generate a force field organising the tourists into orderly architectural formations that echo its own. Before the attraction things come together, are harmoniously constituted. The tourists are incorporated into the system of tourism. They physically mimic its forms.

And yet such integrities are countered by the isolation of each group from the other. The principles of harmony, of unity and universal human reason given form in the Parthenon are here unsettled by the thought that these groups might

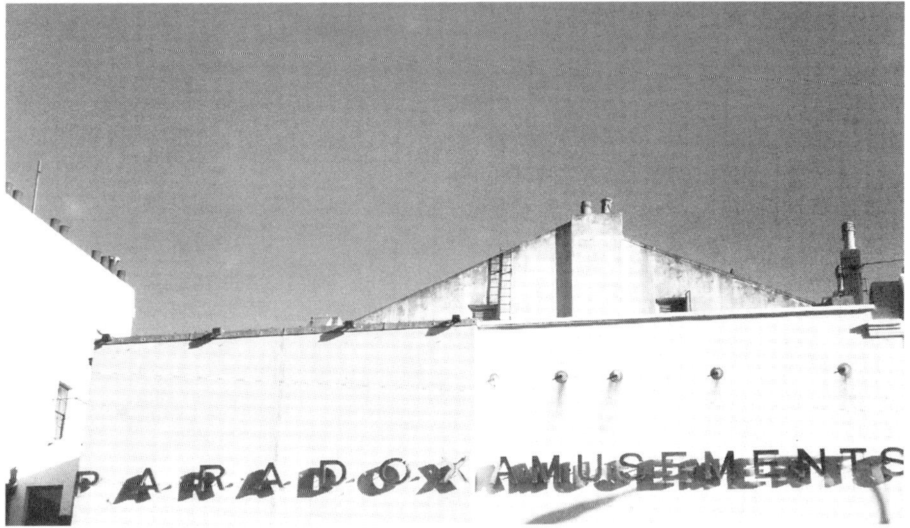

Fig. 17 'Paradox Amusements Arcade, Brighton', 1994.

be united only in a shared *mis*understanding; that, against expectations, tourism serves to confirm the *dis*unity of humankind. The groups look in different directions. The Westerners, abstracted in tourism's word, have their backs to the camera as they attend to the discourse of the tour-guide. The Japanese, given up to tourism's optic, face forward, arrange themselves for the group photograph under the monument. Perhaps by means of this global and yet so Western setting they wish to demonstrate their desire to conform to the practices of the world system to which their wealth admits them, and at the same time display their difference within it. They too are being seen seeing; their presence on the world stage is also being confirmed, legitimated, by the all seeing global subject, the imaginary eye of world culture through which tourism peers. Perhaps they look towards an absent Japan, their families, their future selves in a domestic posterity recalling the moment back home.

Tourist spaces are public and global but also private settings. By their visual association with the Parthenon and its cultural status, the tourists absorb its cultural energy. They link themselves to a world of public culture, of global identity. At the same time the photographic framing extracts the building from its own history and context and transforms it into a backdrop for the drama of the tourists' personal histories. The moment is absolutely public and entirely intimate. And Parr, in a small act of treachery in which we now collude, usurps the perspective into which they have surrendered themselves to photography. He photographs their being photographed and disturbs this fragile privacy.

Parr's book photographs tourism as the making of photographs, or as a series of interchangeable domains made or occupied by photographs. Ten of the sixty-nine images in *Small World* (Parr 1995) feature the act of photography. Many others foreground the repeating litter of promotional images drifting across the world's tourist sites. A T-shirt for Bali is worn outside Barcelona's Sagrada Familia; a Disneyland icon appears at a miniaturised Sacré Coeur in Japan; a Hawaiian shirt is displayed in a Florentine piazza; a tourist carries away from the basilica at Santiago de Compostella the image of its façade printed on her carrier bag, a trace peeled from the original like the features of Christ on Veronica's shroud (plate 2).

Things are transforming into images of themselves. Nothing is quite where it's supposed to be. Everybody's proclaiming having been somewhere else. Everything signifies everywhere else – or perhaps everything is at home in the nomadic world-without-centre of the image-commodity. Like the consumer in Baudrillard's system of object-signs, the tourist never quite arrives, never completely connects. Each sight is interrupted by the signifiers of other sights. Each sight signifies all other sights in the system of sights, most still lacking our visit and thus generating our desire for them (see Baudrillard in Poster 1988a: 45). Serial production under capitalism makes any distinctive form abstract and interchangeable. In this process these sights have become 'deterritorialised', translated into the economy of exchangeable images and tourist experiences (Deleuze and Guattari 1978: 205–58; see also Crary 1990: 10–11).

Tourists and their sights exist in order to be photographed; indeed are photographed in order to attain their existence. In the realm of tourism, 'the world [has become] the reproduction of its reproductions' (Anders 1980: 113). The excitement at finally seeing a long-familiar attraction, such as the Eiffel Tower, comes from being like the pilgrim arriving at the origin of an image, the source of representation, the still point beyond it, in the presence of the (Holy) Referent (Father). If this image has an origin, then there is truth in the world in general. Meaning does after all purchase on the real just as the tower presses down on the world with all the reassuring force of its industrial mass; before, that is, the cameras are raised, the postcards are gathered, and its materiality begins to leak away and, borne up by the signs, images and spectacles of touristic Paris, the tower floats off into the weightlessness of its own significations. After all the Eiffel Tower's rigid density was put up to penetrate high into space and facilitate a new experience of looking, a modality more comfortably associated with floating, with light and the clear fluids of the eye, with space and unbounded consciousness. As tourists, we seek authenticity, an object, a truth somehow precedent to all representation – and then take photographs, lapsing back into the realm of image.

This modulation between the hope for the encounter with singular authenticity and the actual immersion in a plurality of representations is a constant in tourism. In the accidental Classicism into which they have assembled themselves, in which they come to resemble and thereby identify themselves with the object of their visit, Parr's Japanese on the Acropolis seem to express a desire to come to rest in something beyond tourism's unstable representations. As we shall see in a later chapter such mimetic gestures recur throughout Parr's book. Like all tourists, his tourists are caught up in, and revel in, a global entertainment of ever-shifting bodies and iconolatry – and yet appear to yearn for stasis and fixity, for meaning, for certainty. In this the tourist system iterates the old Romantic promise of authenticity, of the rediscovery of the unity between subject and object, of an intimacy between the object and its representation. Its historical roots lie partly in that promise.

In the same moment we know it is unlikely to be fulfilled. Against the Romanticism of its clients, Parr pictures tourism as a process which endlessly defers its object. As he or she moves or is moved on to the next semiotic intensity, the tourist enters the flat excitement concluding in neither disappointment nor satisfaction which typifies the postmodern. If nothing lies outside of tourism's system of representations then the true object of tourism must be tourism itself.

In an article on anthropology and tourism Dennison Nash, deriving his oppositions from MacCannell (1976) and Boorstin (1963), asks whether tourism should be regarded as 'a quest for "authentic" or "pseudo" experiences' (Nash 1981: 465). One is inclined to answer: 'Both!' Their co-presence forms the central paradox of tourism, one efficiently contained in Dean MacCannell's summation of tourism as 'staged authenticity' (MacCannell 1976). In the context of this discussion, MacCannell's conceit refocuses our attention onto the staged reality of the photograph and the confused realities of modern and postmodern culture.

> Oh Tourist.
> Is this how this country is going to answer you
> and your demands for a different world,
> and a better life, and complete comprehension
> of both and last, and immediately ...
> (Elizabeth Bishop, *Arrival at Santos*)

It is difficult to isolate tourism as a single activity. Even speaking of mostly mainstream tourism Valene L. Smith identifies as many as five different kinds, distinguished by different objects (Smith 1989: 4–6). Eric Cohen finds four types of tourist motivation, each seeking different goals and satisfactions (Cohen 1974: 527–55). Trinh T. Minh-ha suspects that with the rise of global mass tourism the age of 'real' travellers is over. 'The role', she writes, 'of the traveller as the privileged seer and knowledgeable observer has ... become quasi-impossible' (Minh-ha in Robertson et al. 1994: 22). All travellers, if they are not exiles or migrants, are now tourists.

However, if all non-essential, voluntary travelling must now be considered some species of tourism it does not follow that all tourism is the same thing. There are notable differences between Smith's and Cohen's categories; and there are further distinctions. Even when they share the same motivations and objects as other tourists, social groups can be required to relate to tourism in ways that continue to set them apart. Tourism is no less marked by the anxieties and complexities of divisions such as class, race, gender and sexuality than any other social activity.

What is common to all varieties of what we call tourism is their notable conformity to both the structures and qualities of modernity. So many of tourism's affects and meanings are produced by way of images and much of its energy is discharged from out of the friction between unity and fragmentation. Both are essential attributes of the modern. Given this, tourism needs to be seen as more than a 'cultural appropriation of modernity', as Don Slater has it, but as modernity itself in action (Slater in Jenks 1995: 233).

Dean MacCannell sees the tourist as a singularly representative figure of the modern age, 'one of the best models available', he claims, 'for modern-man-in-general'. The vicissitudes of modernity are a central presence in his still indispensable study, *The Tourist* (MacCannell 1976: 1).

For MacCannell tourism is both symptom of and cure for modernity's discontents. On the one hand, it displays modernity's restlessness; its self-centredness and feeling of personal incompleteness; its commodification of desire and aspiration and its sly transformation of the hope for change into the taste for mass-produced and repetitious novelty.

On the other hand, tourism provides encounters with the authentic experience and integrated selfhood deemed absent in the disassociation and insufficiency of modern life, and imagined to be located always elsewhere and in other times 'in purer simpler lifestyles' (MacCannell 1976: 3). More often than not these lifestyles will be found in regions all but destroyed, ruined or devalued by the process of modernisation itself; their remnants and traces turned into objects for the nostalgic modern visitor to gaze upon – to photograph.

This is an idea that Baudrillard appears to have drawn upon when he describes postmodernity as 'the simultaneity of the destruction of earlier values and their reconstruction. It is renovation without ruin' (Baudrillard 1990: 171). Baudrillard encounters the phenomenon described by MacCannell evolved to the point where the original, the authentic, the past can no longer be seen as anything but the fabrications of the present. They are idealisations, unreachable beyond the present because they have no existence outside of it.

MacCannell specifies tourism's functional connection with modern needs by means of one of its most typical manifestations, *sightseeing*. Through the systematic visiting of the established sights, acquiring souvenirs, postcards, making videos and, of course, taking photographs, sightseeing is, he writes:

> a kind of collective striving for a transcendence of the modern totality, a way of attempting to overcome the discontinuity of modernity, of incorporating its fragments into a unified experience. (MacCannell 1976: 13)

Here we have a triangulation of cultural meaning in the quest for unity or authenticity; visual experience in its specific touristic mode; and the optical ordering of looking and the production of visual metaphors and allegories equivalent to the cultural meaning in the form of touristic photography, both promotional and personal. Together, they invent the terrain of tourism in the activity of picturing it.

Another salience of modern culture is its reflexivity. Modern societies are accompanied by sets of meta-systems through which they experience themselves, reflect on themselves, re-stage themselves as spectacle, or become detached from themselves. Each establishes a relationship *to* social reality; it is, as it were, stood-off from and revisited even as it is inhabited. We have become the permanent reviewers of our own experience. In his study of tourism's cultural system, John Urry writes:

> In some ways the 'social organisation of the *experience* of modernity', beginning of course with Thomas Cook's, is as important a feature of modern western societies as is the socialised production of manufactured goods. (Urry 1995: 164)

Both separate and ensembled photography and tourism are mechanisms of this reflexivity. Preceded and followed by photographic representations, the tourist visit to a social history museum, a beer factory, a living village of tribal people, or merely watching and photographing the waiters at work, or even other tourists being tourists, are all examples of this function – watching the social, turning it into images. The experience is as likely to be mythical as sociological. Whether discursive, narrational or representational, meta-systems permit us to transform something experienced or endured into something contemplated, something looked on, something consumed. They enable us to possess something which possesses us and, perhaps, to engage in the uncritical pleasure of venerating rather than challenging what exists (MacCannell 1976: 3).

The collective distancing of modern individuals from their own cultural processes, itself a phenomenon of their culture, is a pattern which evolves at speed through the nineteenth century. As the privacy of the individual entered public arenas, as the city filled with unspeaking strangers, as appearances such as dress became more ambiguous and yet more essential for scrutinising the other's social identity, as the retail revolution and shop displays emphasised the pleasure and necessity of visual experience, a mode of silent looking began to dominate earlier modes of public engagement (see Sennett 1986).

Don Slater links these shifts to technology. 'Technology', he writes, 'becomes culture by virtue of its ability to produce spectacular cultural forms' (Slater in Jenks 1995: 231). In this way modernity demonstrates its power to transform fact into magic, to fill the indifferent material and historical world with human subjectivity. The world becomes an entertainment; we its spectators. Heidegger, more brusquely, insists that technology (and this would include the camera) functions to arrange the world so as to avoid experiencing it (Heidegger 1977: 3–35).

The link between photography and tourism features also in discussions concerning the question of postmodernity. Zygmunt Bauman, for example, places travel and tourism at the heart of the modern world's preoccupation with the process of identity. Where modernity, he argues, was taken up with the making and maintenance of a stable identity, the concern of the postmodern world is to resist fixed identity, to seek out play and replay, to multiply the options for the self.

At this point Bauman ushers in the role of lens media. He associates successive modes of identity with historically successive media appropriate to their nature. Thus, modernity is linked to the permanent, 'irreversible' and accumulating family photographic album, with its inventory of 'identity-yielding events'; whereas postmodern identity is seen as characteristically embodied in the videotape – 'erasable', 're-usable', 'calculated not to hold on to anything for ever' (Bauman in Hall and Du Gay 1996: 18).

For Bauman 'the most fitting metaphor' for modernity's task of establishing identity is the 'pilgrim' who seeks the special elsewhere, the sacred place to connect to, a place where meaning and selfhood can finally be re-established (Bauman in Hall and Du Gay 1996: 24).

The emblem of postmodern identity, on the other hand, is the figure of the 'tourist':

> A conscious and systematic seeker of experience, of the experience of difference and novelty ... The tourists want to immerse themselves in a strange and bizarre element ... on condition, though, that it will not stick to the skin and thus can be shaken off whenever they wish. (Bauman in Hall and Du Gay 1996: 29)

Bauman's rather too neat periodisation of modernity/'pilgrim', postmodernity/'tourist', seems to ignore the fact that throughout the whole modern period the tourist has been as much amused as made anxious by the doubtful authenticity of tourist sights. Mark Twain's *Innocents Abroad* (1869) comes easily to mind. So too does the cheap, cheerful and tacky style of the old-fashioned British working-class resorts which were always enjoyed for just those qualities. Reality lay elsewhere then, in the adult worlds of production and child rearing. The holiday world was unreal, daft, a mildly carnivalesque assortment of the consciously infantile and the near-pornographic, the bad-for-you food, the transient conviviality and the confetti of images. There the photograph – jokey, fun-with-strangers or family group – was as much about acknowledging the passing nature of the show as attempting to hold on to it.

This is not to deny that there's been a shift in the condition and sensibilities that obtain in contemporary culture in the direction of those qualities Bauman nominates as postmodern. Their repercussions for tourism and photography are significant. But, rather than being the replacement of the modern by the postmodern, it seems to me that the shift represents a dramatic magnification of tensions between tendencies that have co-existed in modern culture since at least the advent of consumerism and mass-produced imagery.

The neatness of Bauman's account is purchased at the expense of more accuracy when he characterises photography's effects and meanings as static and immutable. This he does in order to fix the medium in the pre-postmodern. But it's a designation challenged by the nature of the viewer's reception of photographic imagery. While videotape's wiping and rerecording facilities clearly shape or coincide with the postmodern sensibility, the moving image nevertheless *imposes* on viewers a fixed succession of image-events dragging them along with it and significantly determining involvement and interpretation – 'without remission, a continuum of images' (Barthes 1995: 54).

In comparison with videotape, while the codes of culture and the traces of actual phenomenon form its perceptual and semiotic substance, the photograph simultaneously offers its meaning unanchored, contingent, open to multiple if not infinite interpretations and reflections. It lacks mobility but possesses another kind of dynamism in what Régis Durand terms its 'implosive character' (Durand in Petro 1995). That is to say, it achieves its affects by provoking rather than organising the workings of the viewer's unconscious. The photograph causes the viewer to, as it were, dream into it, causing it to become subjectivised by the viewer's desires, memories and associations.

Photography's double facility for mobilising and being mobilised by fantasy on the one hand and for an immanent visual realism on the other features importantly in its role as promoter of tourism. This will be examined in some detail in the next chapter. For now, we can see how this double facility has helped to shape tourism's general cultural system through the making of one its most important elements – the tourist fiction.

Using the term 'fiction' in something close to Frank Kermode's usage to mean representations which, as opposed to myth, accept their own fictionality, which require the assent of their public rather than its belief, which are experiments on reality and expressive of modern, post-symbolic cultures, mass tourism, at least, is happily based in fictions (Kermode 1968: 35–64). The enjoyment of a mass tourist sight such as Blackpool Tower, Benidorm's Aqualandia, any Disneyland, is not critically dependent on it having any meaning outside the tourist system. Tourists use the photographic images of tourism, including their own photographs, as both proofs, records and mementos of tourist actualities while accepting these same actualities as set-up performances, idealisations or romanticisations – fictions. Photography uses actuality – a view, a national type – to produce fictions for tourism; tourism uses these fictions to produce its own actualities which lie beyond truth and representation. They are akin to Kermode's 'necessary fictions', fictions that permit actual events to take place. The fiction of zero, for example, permits us to begin counting. They might also be likened to Pierce's 'performative metaphor', a sign which makes something happen.

As with the enjoyment of all types of fiction, much of the pleasure of tourism lies in its text – in the symbolic forms that construct its worlds which are at once actual and virtual. Tourists read the images, play with the signs, disdain them or are seduced by them, and add a few of their own to the system. All over the world, as Jonathan Culler writes, tourists are 'engaged in reading cities, landscapes, and cultures as sign systems' (Culler 1989: 155). Playful sign-surfing and casual textual analysis now form one of the apparent freedoms of our reflexive cultures. Like the right to reverie of the nineteenth century's post-Romantic culture, it represents the apparent triumph of individual subjectivity, that is, freedom. Here, perhaps, we can locate the clearly 'postmodern' character of the tourist's activity.

But tourism is not entirely the preserve of consumer-*flâneurs*, chilled ironists content to drift in the wakes of Situationists or Baudrillard's fan club. And the 'pleasure of the tourist text' is not without a certain desperation. Once again, as with the viewer of the photograph, the desire for the authentic eternally returns, unrenounceable. Some will be seeking in tourism the reassurance of a world re-ordered by the cliché, hoping to pass through the fluidity of fiction to the solidity of myth. Culler writes:

> The tourists are fanning out in search of
> Frenchness, typical Italian behaviour,
> exemplary Oriental scenes, typical American
> thruways, traditional English pubs. (Culler 1989: 155)

When Dean MacCannell wrote of sightseeing as an attempt to 'overcome discontinuity', he added that 'of course, it is doomed to eventual failure: even as it tries to construct totalities, it celebrates differentiation' (MacCannell 1976: 13). To be a contemporary tourist, then, is to live a dual consciousness; to be in effect both 'pilgrim' *and* 'tourist'. The contemporary tourist is not indifferent to the quest for authenticity but must engage in it agonistically, knowing that the images and significations of that authenticity, promotional or self-created, photographic or video, are precisely what place it almost without doubt, out of reach. Tourism plays out year after year, consciously or otherwise, part of the central condition of being modern, the awareness that, in Umberto Eco's words: 'there is no classification of the universe that is not arbitrary or conjectural' (Eco 1997: 208) while remaining loyal to the vision of finding the redemptive felicity of authentic, unmediated experience.

5
Travel products: promoting the tourist vision

> Wow, that's so postcard! (Western visitor on first seeing the Victoria Falls, 1995)

> After you have paid, everything is free. (Philipus, London hairdresser, enthusing about his package tour to Acapulco)

> Is it lack of imagination that makes us come to imagined places, not just stay at home? (Elizabeth Bishop, *Questions of Travel)*

Tourism specialises in visual goods and services, variously described as 'virtual', 'non-material', 'symbolic' or 'postmodern': views, spectacles, environments, simulations, 'experiences', sensations, home movies, videos and photographic images. Brochures, posters, postcards and other promotions stock the traveller's visual combinatorium, picturing the world of tourism and its objects, establishing how they are to be seen, their desirability, the weight of their cultural meaning. Additionally they secure the peculiarly visual, or rather, visualised nature of tourist attractions and experiences. All tourists, whether or not they take photographs, consume places and experiences which are photographic, as they have been made or have evolved to be seen, above all to be photographed (plate 3). A resort's photogenic qualities can determine its fortune. If it lacks them it can be re-invented or re-shaped so as to acquire them: a beach imported, some palms realigned, a Moorish gateway constructed, some viewpoints created. Such places are often photographs materialised in three-dimensional form. Consequently, much tourist photography is quotation – a reprising of the contents of the brochures, or the reproduction of a view that as likely as not came into existence as a consequence of photography. Tourist photography is more a process of confirmation than of discovery; a practice which takes place within the system of tourism, a system so self-enclosed it bears comparison to Marc Augé's description of a 'symbolic universe':

> they constitute a means of recognition rather than knowledge, for those who have inherited them: closed universes: where everything is a sign: collections of codes to which only some hold the key but whose existence everyone accepts: totalities which are partially fictional but effective. (Augé 1995: 33)

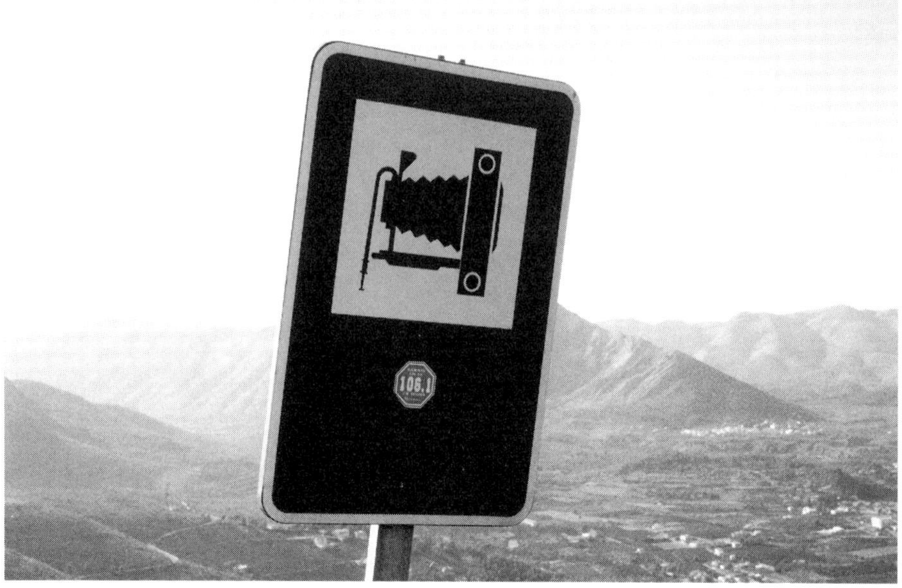

Fig. 18 'Photo Point Sign, near Tárbena, Spain', 1996.

What follows is a discussion of how and in what forms the photograph, or the *photographic*, has come to be so central to the production, promotion and expression of the tourist experience and to what Baudrillard would call the production of the tourist needs.

From its beginnings tourism has been identified with the intensification or overestimation of the power of visual experience and visual images to pleasure and transport. As indicated earlier, by the end of the eighteenth century visual experience and travelling for instruction and entertainment had become closely, indeed systematically, associated. Primary uses of the word *tourist* in fact denoted the traveller who sought pleasure in viewing '*picturesque*' landscapes, and tourism's earliest practices were concerned with the organising and standardisation of such a traveller's activities.

Thomas West, for example, was the author of an influential early guide (1778) to the English Lake District in which the region was re-imagined as an aesthetic and devotional object. The Lakes became a kind of text and therefore required critics and interpreters, roles which tourism was eager to take on. West has been described as 'the inventor of the way of looking at landscape from certain pre-ordained viewpoints or stations so that the experience of tourism, instead of a jumble of impressions, should be a series of properly composed and memorable tableaux' (Victoria & Albert Museum 1984: 14).

Some generations before the advent of modern tourism with its commercial and professional infrastructures and mass visitations, landscape painters, drawing instructors, guides, guidebook writers, lake poets, hoteliers and coach owners were inventing that assemblage of rhetorical and practical services that are now so familiar. The world was being arranged to facilitate the smooth and profitable 'throughput' of groups of visitors whose itineraries were governed by criteria determining which *sights* were noteworthy and how they were to be viewed. Aesthetic experience was being enthusiastically valorised and tightly routinised and, following a pattern which had appeared in the Renaissance, it was becoming a particular activity within the general consumption of goods.

Much impetus was added to the visual dimension of these developments by new optical mechanisms. The camera lucida and the Varley Graphic Telescope, to take two examples, centred objects and fixed them 'in the field of vision' (Gifford 1990: 20). They intensified the viewers' apprehension of what was before them, but also imposed an order, a discipline on the way the viewer looked. The camera lucida in particular optically concentrated the viewer's immediate visual experience of the present scene, and at the same time displaced the scene into a representation in the form of an image projected on to a surface which the viewer could trace out as a drawing.

By standardising visual experience, by suppressing the impact of other senses less easy to organise, the sense of smell for example, and by providing picture-making devices, the way was being prepared for the full commodification of travelling, looking and the experience of space. Attempts in the nineteenth century to patent viewpoints used by photographers and the Kodak Picture Spots at contemporary North American tourist attractions spring from these developments.

Pre-photography visitors to the English Lakes, or wherever, learned to look not so much at natural forms as at nature aspiring to the condition of visual art. They were being taught to look for *images*, and, indeed, to make them – both the camera lucida and the Varley Graphic Telescope were drawing aids. Anticipating Baudrillard's concept of the Simulacrum, the model preceded the mountain. The most meaningful encounter would apprehend nature as the materialisation of a primordial aesthetic idea, a representation. By the time contemporary mass tourism emerges in the 1950s – affluence, cars, jets and cameras – tourist activity was entirely inseparable from the framing and fixing of visual experience. This is highlighted by Andy Grundberg in a discussion of Lee Friedlander's study of tourists observing and snapping at Mount Rushmore (figure 19).

As Grundberg notes, Friedlander's terse depiction shows both the sight and the tourists themselves being brought into existence through the effects of looking, reflecting, framing and imaging. These, he adds, are all linked to the general project of culturally appropriating the natural world. 'Natural site has become acculturated sight' (Grundberg 1990: 15).

As the image makes clear, the 'sight' or the 'site' is a 'seeing' without a subject, for it pre-exists the arrival and activity of any individual tourist-photographer, who, once located there, is framed as much as framing. The sight is not so much an object to be viewed as an already structured condition of seeing, a situation which *places* the sightseer even as he or she freely chooses to look or shoot.

Fig. 19 Lee Friedlander, 'Mount Rushmore, South Dakota' (gelatin-silver print), 1969.

The effects of photography's presence in the tourist system merely completed a process under way before photography's birth. As tourists, even at the moment of photographing, even if touring cameraless, we are not so much looking as looking at images, or looking *for* images. Tourism provides us less with experience than with events to see, or rather, events to look at. The privileging of the visual grants us separation from our own experience, as if we are on holiday from things – tourism's little transcendence. We look on or look in through the distancing arrangements of the camera or through eyes educated to see with the same ontological remoteness. The world of the tourist is 'over there', in the past-present, in the exotic-ordinary. It is framed off, the object of imaging or description, in some spectacular distance, or set back as performance (Greenwood in Smith 1989).

John Urry argues that a particular form of organised visual experience in fact constitutes tourism's distinctive product. This he calls 'the tourist gaze'. He writes:

> The minimal characteristic of touristic activity is the fact that we look at, or gaze upon, particular objects such as piers, towers, old buildings, artistic objects, food, countryside and so on. (Urry 1995: 131)

The 'tourist gaze', 'endlessly reproduced and recaptured', is the end result, he argues, of a combination of discipline and pleasure aligned with the ascendancy of the visual. Not only does the 'tourist gaze' marshal the visual experience of the tourist, it transforms ordinary visual experience, normally pragmatic and habitual, into a self-pleasing end-in-itself whose perceptual sensuality is carried over into other forms of the tourist experience. It provides enjoyment for the tourist and bestows order and shape on to what Urry describes as 'a rather complex and inchoate process' (Urry 1995: 21).[1] The tourist knows what to do and what to expect, and is equipped with some competence with which to evaluate the experience. In its difference from everyday looking, the 'tourist gaze' strengthens the essential demarcation of the time, space and perceptions of the holiday from those of the working year, which gives touristic experience its identity. It integrates the production of taste and consumer expectations with a service that caters to them. The 'tourist gaze' is constructed, experienced and maintained by visual images which remain typically photographic.

The systems and practices by which modern tourism invents and establishes its locations and charges them with the power to draw visitors are more systematically brought to light in Dean MacCannell's analyses of two processes, which we have already encountered, 'the system of attractions' and 'sight sacralisation'.

MacCannell's 'system of attractions' combines a semiological understanding of tourist sights with an account of how subjectivity is bound into commodities and their consumption. He pictures the attraction, in fact tourist activity in general, as a social practice established to an inordinate degree, in discourses and representations. Watson and Kopachevsky describe tourism as 'sign-driven' and 'media-driven' (1990: 643–60).

A tourist attraction consists of a set of relations between three elements the sight, the marker and the tourist. Like the ghostly image forming in the developing tray, the attraction emerges out of their in-between – out of the matrix formed from the force of their relations (MacCannell 1976: 41). The marker is a pragmatic sign, simply a means of representing a sight to a tourist. It can take many forms both on and off the sight's location: as guidebooks, plaques, travel writing; advertisements on billboards or television, in magazines; as posters and postcards; and as photographs, which can feature in all.

But the marker is dedicated to a more complex process which, drawing on the language of pilgrimage, MacCannell calls 'sight sacralisation' (1976: 44–6). Through a series of phases a sight is invented, given full cultural existence by being charged with meaning and power, becomes able to bestow grace on its visitors, if only of a secular kind. In one of these stages the sight is 'mechanically reproduced'. Effigies, prints and photographs of the sight and its associated objects are distributed through the culture increasing its fame and therefore its value. It is this phase, he writes, that 'is most responsible for setting the tourist in motion on his journey to find the true object and pictures of the object' (MacCannell 1976: 45).

When the sight's connotations are fully absorbed into the cultural and language of a society it becomes capable of generating significant cultural energy as the virtuous object, as a location in the spatial dramaturgy of a national or cultural identity, a relay in an international system of cultural values. The sight has becomes a transmitter of meanings and sentiments and at the same time a magnet drawing to itself those who wish to experience them embodied in material form.

The sight is tourism's essential object and location, and not only is the essential mode of consuming it visual, it is itself the result, the invention, of predominantly visual representations. The image originates the sight which originates the image of the sight. And yet, tasked with providing authenticity, tourism accords originary status to the sight, establishes it as the cause rather than the consequence of its representations and thereby makes it the source of their truth.

Nevertheless, the sight is more 'presence' than thing or even place, as its existence is always extended in space by its Markers. Indeed, the process studied by both MacCannell and Urry is essentially the manufacture and consumption of 'presence'.

But it is not only its cultural existence that a sight owes to photographic representations. Its identity as a commodity is similarly achieved. Tourism's curious second world was not solely camera-engendered. Almost from its beginnings, tourism's visual culture has been a fellow-traveller of and participant in the evolution of the culture of consumption.

In Michel Tournier's fable *The Legend of Painting*, a caliph holds a competition to establish the better of the two paintings commissioned to cover opposing walls in his palace. The first painting, by an artist who'd never left home before, is unveiled to show the beautiful picture of a Chinese garden. A week later the second, widely travelled, painter pulls back the curtain to uncover a vast mirror in which the first painting is brilliantly reflected. He hadn't lifted a brush but was immediately declared the winner as not only did his secondary image contain the beauty of the first, but its garden was also alive, populated by those viewing it (Tournier 1992).

In tourism the distance between the promotion and the promotion's object has been all but abolished. With photography and photographic seeing as prime commodity forms in tourism, the photographic image that promotes it is in many instances the very item consumed – the advertisement has become its own commodity. Given the uncertainty of the use value of such goods, they must be promoted as not merely serving the needs of the consumer, whatever they might be, but as being the precipitations of the consumer's very being, as if it is consumers who conjure commodities into life. Like the viewers of the second artist's mirror, whose reflections are contained in the copy and yet whose presence originates it, distinguishes it from the first, the tourist is allowed to walk in tourism's secondary garden as if he or she had brought it into being by simply looking at it.

The advertiser's ideal tourists see what they expect to see and expect to see what the advertiser has intended. Tourists are positioned as both consumers and producers. Some promotional images reflect this by portraying the tourist location as a world structured by the tourist's pleasure. A typical example would show empty beaches where the waterline or a run of trees or a pier pass diagonally into and across the image. The diagonal introduces into the image the tourist's excited anticipation, a hedonistic rush, the line of the viewer's desire entering into, being entered by, the tourist scene and its pleasures.

Another familiar trope features empty seats before a vista which is not merely incomplete or wasted without the tourist, but cannot even be produced until one has taken up their position before it.

Take this image promoting Florida (plate 4), which anticipates the still-to-arrive spectator or a film director with the power to shape the events that will unroll before the empty 'director's chair'. As a female companion or assistant has already been provided, the mainstream consumer is encouraged to read thc absent tourist as male and to see the female as a figure whose holiday will remain incomplete without his arrival.

Tourism's ability to sell a world already suffused with thc tourist's own desires comes from its drawing on the appeal of popular cinema, a world already deeply lodged in most tourists' psyches. Hollywood, in particular, has provided tourism with continuous infusions of glamour and influenced much of its visual style: for example, the use of imitation technicolour with its movie connotations in the promotions of the 1950s and early 1960s, or the use of exact widescreen ratio in the design of billboard or double page magazine advertisements.

The association between vacation in warm places and the lives of movie stars was more common before mass tourism headed south. However, there are plenty of contemporary promotions whose images are effectively publicity stills for non-existent movies in need of leading players for the roles of happiness.

The necessity of the tourist is reinforced by the connotations which promotions can give to photography itself. The editors of guidebooks will often select work from photographers which are at the same time professional and striking enough to impress the viewer and yet appear uncomplex and simple enough to persuade would-be tourists that they could have taken them and indeed will. Photographically speaking, the guidebook, and therefore the world it evokes, appears to be speaking the language of the tourist. Another approach is to use photographs styled as tourist photography. For example a brochure promoting the Indian state of Karnataka presents each attraction as an already mounted colour transparency (figure 20).

Here the world has already translated itself into the language of the tourist. Rather it is already spoken for. To photograph these South Indian sights will be a form of quotation, the production of duplicates. Put another way, the repetition of the same gesture – photographing the photographed – forms part of the ritual behaviour of tourism, a choreography of mostly foreknown movements and encounters. The tourist is one who joins a dance that's been under way for generations. When one photographs a tourist attraction one is confirming the general system of tourism and one's place within it where

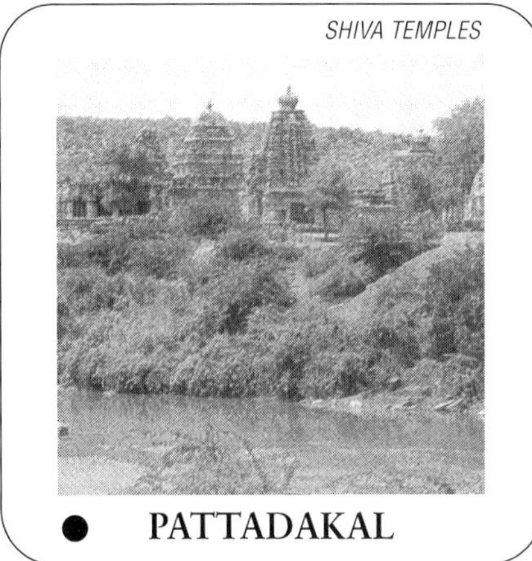

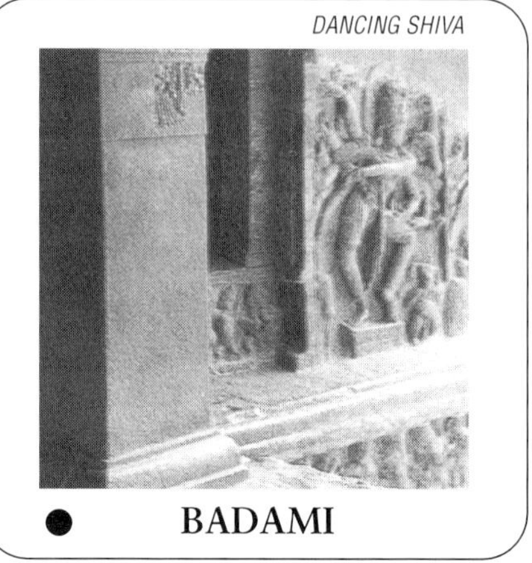

Fig. 20 Promotion for Karnataka, India, 1994.

everything is already done and seen, and where it is still to be done and seen; where everything is foreseeable and yet remains unexpected.

Tourism goes further than transforming the world into an infinity of photographic appearances. It is capable of representing a place or a whole culture as if its origins and most essential identity lie in photography.

A notable example of this is the *Kodak Hula Show* in Hawaii in which the culture has been absorbed by the institution of photography in both its rhetorical and corporate manifestations (plate 5).

Hawaii has been processed, developed, one might say, re-presented and relaunched in the colours, in the livery of photography itself, of the Eastman Kodak Company. Hawaii has thus becomes Kodak-Hawaii, a state and an identity photographed from within. Photography doesn't represent Hawaii so much as Hawaii represents photography. The country exists to sell the photography which in turn sells the country.

A comparable example can be found in publicity material for Papua New Guinea which interpellates different types of tourist client by means of the connotations conveyed that attach to the distinctive photographic styles picturing the locals: Colour-Exotic-Primitive for the more mainstream tourist; Ethno-Doc-Monochrome for the independent traveller – a culture tourist clutching, one supposes, if not a Leica then at least a serious Nikon (figures 21 and 22).

The country-as-photograph becomes a sign signifying less itself than the varieties of foreign touristic taste and self-image. As in the world according to Benetton where, through icons of the tragic and tumultuous planet, the world and its events are reduced to the status of a collective sign signifying the dull but reassuring safety and order of casual wear, here, even the appeal to primitivism in the portraits of Papuan warriors is overridden. They become signs less of themselves than of the identities of tourism manifested in the making of images.

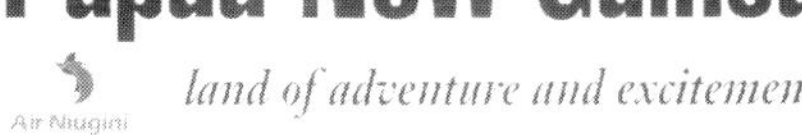

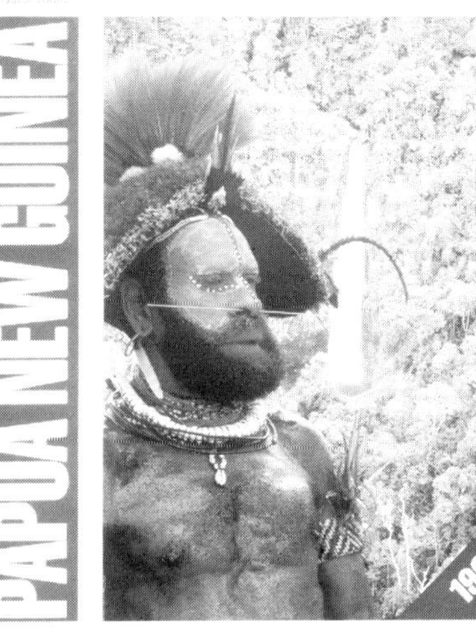

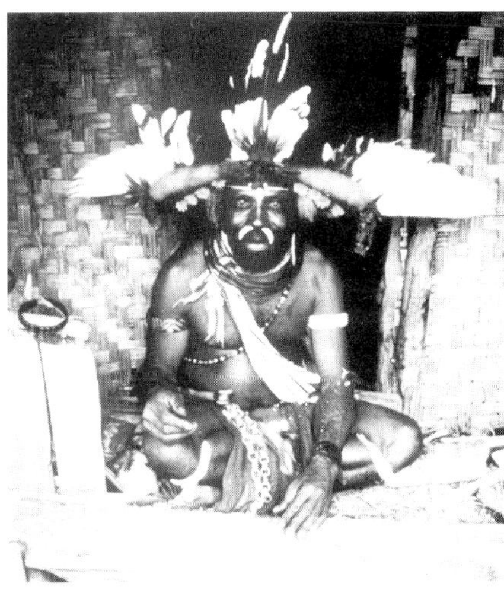

Fig. 21/22 Promotion for Papua New Guinea, 1994. Original in colour.

Tourism and its imagery can be seen as commodified Romanticism. It has another important cultural antecedent, religious pilgrimage, which, like Romanticism, was linked to a faith in the potency of visual images and to a deep interest in the ritual aims of travelling. Much in tourism's imagery can be linked to it.

Pilgrimage and its related festivals took place in sacred time when ordinary, cosmically insignificant time was abandoned for a set period. Many pilgrimage shrines contained an image, relic or statue believed to have been touched by the sacred or able to radiate its force. Such images drew the traveller to the shrine. Churches were built to house them, and became filled with their sacred atmospheres. Around such centres and along the pilgrim routes rose up small industries dedicated to the service or exploitation of the devout. These included the production of religious images and pilgrim badges associated with particular shrines.

By proximating themselves to the numinous power of relics and religious sites pilgrims not only physically shifted themselves out of the space and time of the everyday or profane world, they connected themselves more powerfully with the sacred, with the source of things, with a truth and a unity located elsewhere. Almost invariably the connection was made by means of a sacred image. To look upon such an image was to observe the sacred manifesting itself in the world with an immediacy seldom encountered in ordinary existence. Faith would be reconfirmed, illness and misfortune might be overturned and a 'communitas' built among the travellers (Turner 1978).

Common to all of this was the desire for the restoration of lost wholeness. The pattern in so many rituals of travel which commence in dispersal and conclude in a re-coming together – in a collection – is certainly common to both pilgrimage and tourism. We have seen MacCannell's argument that sightseeing and the collecting of postcards, souvenirs and photographs offer the modern tourist a means of imposing an order on things. Although moving in a different cosmos to that of the fractured modernity of MacCannell's tourist, medieval pilgrims also saw themselves as fragments in a fallen, broken world. But the disunity of their world had been brought about by humankind's sinful separation from God. The collecting of relics in one place, the collecting together of believers at the sacred location where the material world had once been reconnected to its source in the divine by martyrdom, miracle or apparition, and the pilgrim's powerful identification with the sacred through its traces or intimate representations – literally in the case of an anatomical relic – were all components of a ritual drama of *re*-collection. It represented the coming together of believers, of signs and their objects; the gathering in of the sundered parts yearning for a unity they had never known but could not forget.

Photographs function as elements in tourism's secular cultural system guaranteeing a supply of experiences which are simplified and, in most forms of tourism, unthreatening. Yet, like sacred icons, they also tender the possibility of the transcendence of everyday existence. As we have seen, they are active in the establishing of tourist sights as places surpassing the ordinary. Watson and Kopachevsky see in the tourist attraction the qualities of Durkheim's religious symbolism through which believers 'assign sacredness to ordinary objects and/or experience'. Additionally, they note that Urry's tourist gaze also involves 'the transmutation of many ordinary objects, places and experiences into sacred ones' (Watson and Kopachevsky 1990: 648).

Photography itself shadows certain moves of the sacred: the replication of worlds, for example, or the redemption of things from oblivion, or the transubstantiation of objects into signs. Whatever is photographed is changed as, of course, are our perceptions of it. Simply through the actions of selection and framing, the object is lifted beyond its surroundings. Our visual engagement with it is enhanced. It becomes a favoured object of enquiry, of enjoyment and desire, elected as significant – numinous, even.

The size, colour and ubiquity of tourism's promotional and souvenir imageries simply deepen the force of these effects. Like much of advertising in general, their 'salvational-aspirational' rhetoric reveals its sources in religion. But their visualisations of the paradigms and ideal-types of touristic pleasure offer practical transcendences. Their prospects, tableaux and little allegories translate the intangible noumena of tourism's mythologies – freedom, wonder, surprise, novelty, authenticity, conviviality, boundless physical pleasure, beauty, consumption without production, the liberation from time and so on – into the empirical phenomena of depictable, tangible objects, places, events and flesh. The photograph gives us reasons, evidence, with which to dream. It transports us in fantasy but to places that appear to exist. As already noted, Greenwood has argued that tourism transforms the world into a performance. Photographs provide visual guides to the right settings, moves and gestures of the performance. Like religion, tourism and photography transform the world into a dramatic text but a text illumined, suffused with enhanced perceptions, with the desire for happiness. The most effective tourist promotions often have an intensity of colour, pattern or allure which are the visual equivalents of the transforming potency of the promised tourist experience. The emotional registers of its utopian brightness and extreme colour saturation make up the score of a popular sublime. A memorable example of this is the work of John Hinde and the studio he established in Ireland in the 1950s (plate 6).

These photographs are less the representations of what tourists have seen; more like tokens of the world as the marvel they would have wanted to encounter. Hinde, with his Quaker and Christian Scientist background, derived his visual style from religious impulses (Lee in Hinde Ltd 1993: 16–19). They contain something reminiscent of religious Enthusiasm and its visual form, Excess – the enlargement or magnification of perceived forms as witness to a joy in things bathed in the light of God's grace (plate 7).

Of course, in these little technicolour stained-glass windows, the light of the divine is assisted by the corporate hand of the holiday business colouring up and casting glittering over its sometimes rather commonplace offerings.

While tourism's iconographies present the holiday as micro-paradise, Western tourism still operates out of predominantly post-religious cultures. Like the pilgrim, the tourist may be seeking a connection. Yet, as argued previously, unlike pilgrims, most tourists understand that they also move through fiction; that tourism's icons and values are contingencies peculiar to their own culture and epoch – symbolic devices which invent their own world. They understand that, if nothing else, they can at least hope to surrender themselves to tourism's spectacles, to bathe in the light of the images that have enticed them into tourism's spaces. The modern consumer has long been taught to separate actual possession from the spectacle and fantasy of possession; has learned that the pleasure of consumption lies as much or more, and often exclusively, in the looking and in the wishes and imaginings it calls up.

Tourism's roots in nineteenth-century retail culture break surface here. Display and looking were central to new kinds of urban experience ushered in by the vast trade fairs and expositions and by the shopping arcades and *grands magasins* or department stores appearing from the 1840s onwards. The most famous were the Great Exhibition in London in 1851, Paris's *Exposition Universelle* four years later and the *Bon Marché* department store which opened in the same city in 1869.

The new stores, in particular, were designed to permit as much light as possible to fall on the carefully patterned arrangements of merchandise. The affluence of illumination transformed necessity, utility and the gross materiality of things into a glittering theatre of goods, a temple to the spirituality of the commodity. The new skills of window dressing weaved mythical associations around the goods (Miller 1981: chapter V).

The public were free to wander the stores and arcades without buying. They could simply look, dazzled, it was hoped, by the utopian abundance filling every space: the radiance of the chandeliers, the lustre of glass and diamonds, the colours and textures of the clothing and textiles. They might picture to themselves the other worlds whose existences were whispered in the displays. *Son et Lumière* and other musical entertainments were sometimes held in the *Bon Marché* after business hours, strengthening the association between the commodity, visual spectacle and the freedom of the daydream (see also Richards 1991: chapter 1; and Buck-Morss 1989: chapter 8).

For the window shopper – the sightseer – looking and daydreaming were ends in themselves. Everything in the store seemed to exist to guarantee their pleasure. It conferred on looking the illusion of mastery, of autochthony. Like the tourist subject emerging in the same period, the looker became possessor of everything seen because everything seen was born from their look.

This process, begun as a visual sensation, was brought to fulfilment as economic consumption only in the purchase of the item. But this became almost secondary, simply the necessary gesture that closed the ritual and sustained the fiction that utility rules the transaction. The true consumption had already taken place in the eye and in the imagination.

Clearly, much of this is at work in modern tourism which, inheriting the combined effects of colonialism and consumerism, looks on the world as a department-store-without-walls, a great display, laid out, available for visual purchase.

For example, a common visual trope in tourist promotions is the refining of landscapes, natural forms, objects and so on into abstract or near abstract patterns and serial forms: the lines of a vineyard photographed from above; the regimented patterns of line and colour made by fields of variously coloured tulips, or fruit on an open-air market stall (plate 8). The images do not seek to inform but to please the eye. All aim to reduce the world to an object designed for looking at, or to the enticing order of a shop display. The chaos of forms, fragments and unpredictable events is refined away to reveal a world whose essence is shown to lie in some underlying order, some unchanging structure.

While this visual refinement of things helps fulfil tourism's ordering-reassuring function it also offers a world experienced differently, more vividly; a world where the rules of hedonism and the aesthetic dominate. On holiday one must see unusual things, or at least see familiar things unusually. It is a popularised form of 'making strange', that playing with traditional forms and habitual perceptions employed by the Cubists and Russian and other Formalist critics and artists in order to revitalise and make conscious our experience of the world. But, unlike the aesthetic or political applications of this practice, there is no subversion at work here. In the same moment that mainstream tourism takes its clients out of the ordinary, it returns them unaltered. These images might be visual intensities but they are not convulsive ones. Tourism is more Busby Berkeley than Brecht. It takes the world as it is, and renders it apparently even more perfect, certainly more entertaining – extraordinary but not truly wild. It is finally, a celebration of things as they are, a beautiful pacification.

Another source of this language of patterns lies in a certain kind of modernising eye whose recent ancestry lies in the photographically illustrated magazines of the 1920s, above all those in Germany. These publications were creating or feeding the demand for visual novelties and spectacle. Besides offering glimpses of the normally inaccessible lives of the rich and powerful, or of strange and distant cultures, some featured photographs of mostly inaccessible unreachable perceptions: images shot from balloons and aircraft, photographs of remote galaxies or highly magnified plant and crystalline structures. Though posing as popular education, appearing in magazines positioned as weekend reading, these images functioned as holidays for the eyes, more ocular travel for the homebound.

The work of German photographers Karl Blossfeldt and Albert Renger-Patzsch was central. Their imagery 'discovered' in natural objects the machined precision and the serial forms of factory products – nature as industrial design. In industrial goods, on the other hand, they revealed the patterned morphologies of a perfected Nature.

Such photography helped grasp the world by a mode of seeing expressive of advanced industrial capitalism moving into its product-fetishising consumerist stage. Variations of it have always been common in the pages of the *National Geographic* and many other illustrated periodicals since. It informs the eye of contemporary tourism pleased by those patterned forms and landscapes not only because they are reassuring signs of order, or that they lay the world out for us to see, but also because they reveal the characteristics of a world remade by mass production; a place in which the modern tourist can truly feel securely at home.

Note

1 This echoes Susan Sontag's description of tourist photography as an 'anxiety-reducing' activity. It gives, she says, purpose to a sometimes aimless activity. 'Unsure of other responses, they take a picture' (Sontag 1978: 10).

6
Sabulous: the beach, the camera and social display

> Under no circumstances is it anything ever anywhere near a beach.
> (Walker Evans on photography in Sayre 1997)

Tourism produces objects for tourists. It also makes tourists for objects. Tourists may accede to their identity as objects of tourism but equally they aspire to be the subjects of their own performances and self-descriptions. For example, when writing their holiday postcard messages, tourists inscribe their own features on to the reverse face of tourism's most common and conventionalised visual form. Some release their sarcasm on to the card's clichés and advertise the tourist's role-distance. But most pen messages that are often as conventionalised as the images they accompany. It is as if, given that the postcard is a kind of ritualistic public discourse open to the scrutiny of all those through whose hands it passes, many feel obliged to adopt the customary tones and formalities of postcard greetings, however trite.

And yet the postcard is also a private letter – certainly a personalised one. Whatever the style of their message, by means of it tourists can add something of their own narrative, their subjectivity, to the plot that tourism has devised for them, if only the names and addresses of families and friends.

More than anywhere else, though, it is on the beach that the tourist plays between the two positions of tourist-as-object and tourist-as-subject. Almost from the beginnings of tourism the beach has been its *locus classicus*. As such it is, like Friedlander's Mount Rushmore, a place and a *situation* of seeing and of being seen; a social space where social being puts itself or at least its appearances on display.[1] For this reason, almost since its inception as a specialised 'location of culture', the holiday beach has been scrutinised and celebrated by the painter, ranged over by the photographer. Clearly they have understood that what took place there offered them an irresistible access to manifest social meanings and diverting performances. Even today, the camera retains its link to the sea and the sand.

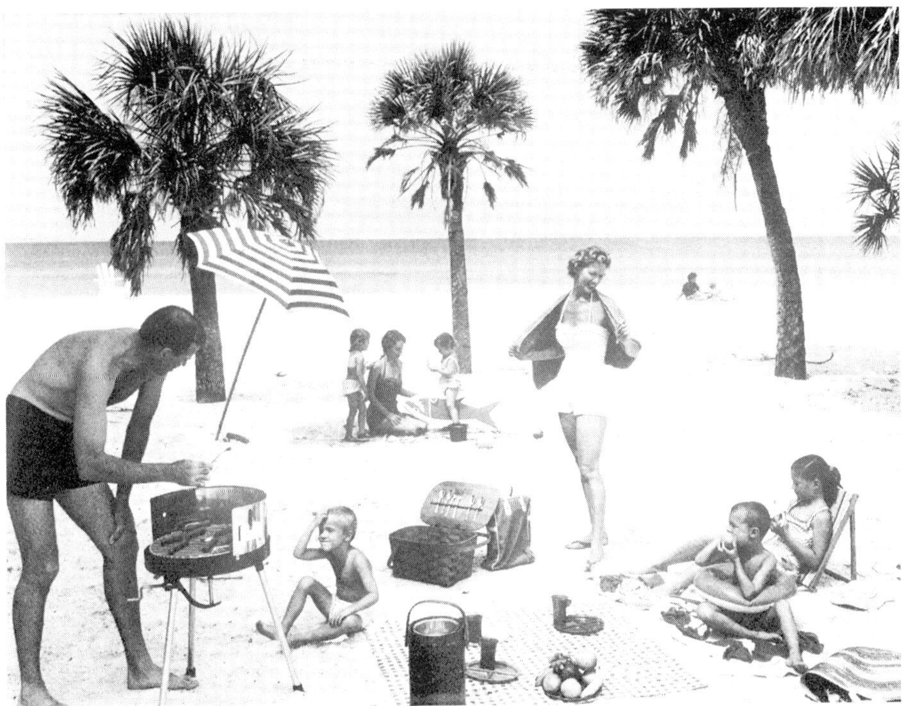

Fig. 23 Jo Steinmetz Studio, 'Longboat Key, Florida', 1958. From *The Champion Pig*.

As a site of cultural meanings the holiday beach tends to be associated with the liminal (Shields 1991; Lencek and Bosker 1998). It stands littorally, literally at both the social and geographical edge. It is fluid, part in nature and part out, spaced-out, a slip of land where society leaves its slip showing, where things slip out to be seen, and for these reasons an appropriate context for the out-of-the-ordinary activities of holidaying and tourism. Transformed from a place of work to one of play – from the onerous to the ludicrous – the beach is where necessity may be disavowed.

Of course the separation on the beach between work and play is never complete. Tourism is work for many, traditionally underpaid; and even on some well-established holiday beaches there remains an uneasy co-presence of visitors and those who live and work off them. Horace Nicholls pictured this in the 1900s in his study of Nice washerwomen at work on the beach with the fantasy architecture of the Casino and its Orientalist domes and towers rising beyond them (Royal Photographic Society Collection).

It is evident that in the early years the camera was just one of the numerous odd, cruel and carnivalesque novelties available at the beach. Ramsgate, on the Kent coast, was described in the late 1850s as 'a paradise of photographers' (alongside) 'nigger melodists and donkey drivers ... the provider of shocks from a galvanic battery and the tame cat who allows canaries to hop about under her nose' (quoted in Linkman 1990: 54).

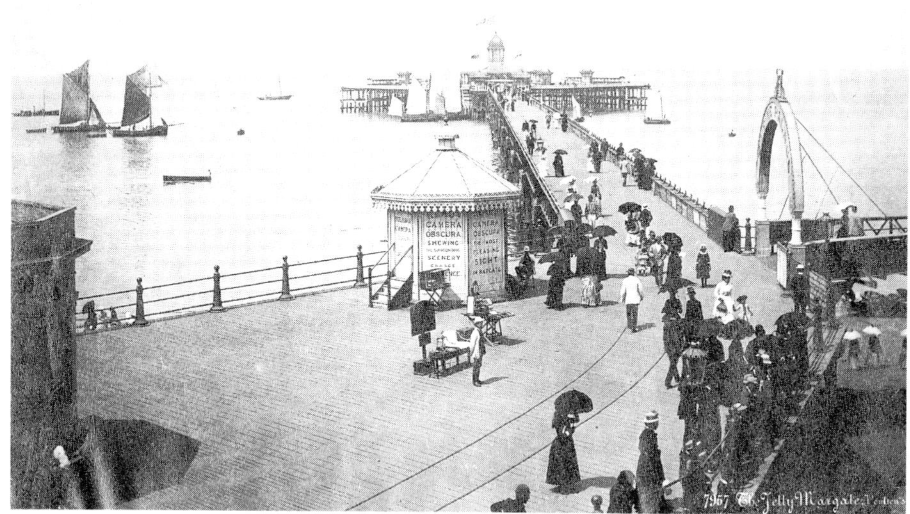

Fig. 24a 'Margate Pier with Camera Obscura', n.d.

But clearly the beach is also a stage, a studio, indeed an *arena*, sabulous or otherwise, at the heart of the culture. It is a common, public space and in the United Kingdom relatively few are privately owned.

Against a neutral backdrop of sand, water and sky social performances take place, people make an appearance, display themselves in front of each other and before the collective eye of the camera. As a place to see and to be seen the holiday beach holds the most essential and attracting object of modern tourism – the social itself.

In the nineteenth century the paintings of W. P. Frith depicted the presentation of social identity at a number of public gatherings: the crowds at a London railway station, at Derby Day on the Epsom Downs, and on Ramsgate beach. But the character, status and class of his Victorians were not self-determined. They were founded in biology. Their physiognomies represented the outward expressions of an immanent physiological and even moral necessity. The face and the skull could be read for immutable qualities of character and consequently of social worth. Beneath the turbulence of the nineteenth-century crowds Victorian ideology saw a fierce and irresistible order. The function of the paintings was to demonstrate its existence and by so doing to confirm the order of the Victorian social system as righteous and natural.

Where Frith makes objects of his painted subjects, the camera on the beach, in the hands of the professional or of the holidaymakers themselves, has tended to produce more democratic statements. The beach performances of holidaymakers are never free of the shaping force of social reality. And they are in great part a set of types and situations scripted by the tourist system itself. As Bourdieu says, even the apparent 'casualness' of the poses adopted for the holiday snap are structured and staged, 'because here as well as elsewhere the "natural" is a cultural ideal which must create itself before it can be captured' (Bourdieu 1990: 81).

However the beach performance can be a type of delinquency, a refusal to accept the facts of social existence. It might be inspired less by what determines the individual – the realities of, say, class and income – and more by what the performer would like to be or feels they should be if the social world was governed by desire or the principal of equality. 'In Greek and Roman texts', writes Foucault, 'the injunction of having to know yourself was always associated with the other principle of having to take care of yourself' (Foucault in Martin et al. 1988: 19). It's this latter principle that predominates on the beach. But it is not necessarily delusion. There is much that is fictitious in the way people present themselves on holiday but, as with carnival, while the holiday alters the order of things only for a time, the subversive principle which holds that things could be other than they are is made visible. So, the tension that is set up between the ideal and the actual self is less a mark of self-deception than of the awareness of a deficiency to be overcome in social reality itself. Commenting on Walter Benjamin's critique of mass culture, Susan Buck-Morss writes: 'it takes mass culture seriously not merely as the source of the phantasmagoria of false consciousness, but as the source of the collective energy to overcome it' (Buck-Morss in Levin, 1993: 316–17).

It was on the beach that in the late nineteenth century Paul Martin made some of the first photographic portrayals of working and lower-middle class people in pursuit of their own pleasure, celebrating themselves – somewhat dissident behaviour in a hierarchical society where the frostier puritan values retained influence. Although probably as a consequence of Martin's candid-camera approach and, ironically, because of his lack of any reforming interest in his subjects, for once their lives seem to lift themselves free of the weight of necessity and utility by the self-creating activity of enjoying, that is, re-creating, themselves.

In these photographs their identities are not reduced to that of social objects lacking interiority or made to stand as abject or heroic signifiers of whole classes or conditions by the usual documentary or carte-de-visite types and generalities such as the 'street types', the 'London poor' or the 'toiling masses'.

Although frequently part of a crowd Martin's faces and bodies are memorably particular. In spite of being recorded in public spaces, his subjects often appear seceded into some private realm – unreachable, autonomous: lovers absorbed in each other, an audience transported by a Punch and Judy show into a collective privacy. For a time, they belong to nobody but themselves. They exist in free time, always a precious goal of organised labour. To that extent at least his beach photographs are political.

Challenging the apprehension of the crowd as an anonymous, engulfing

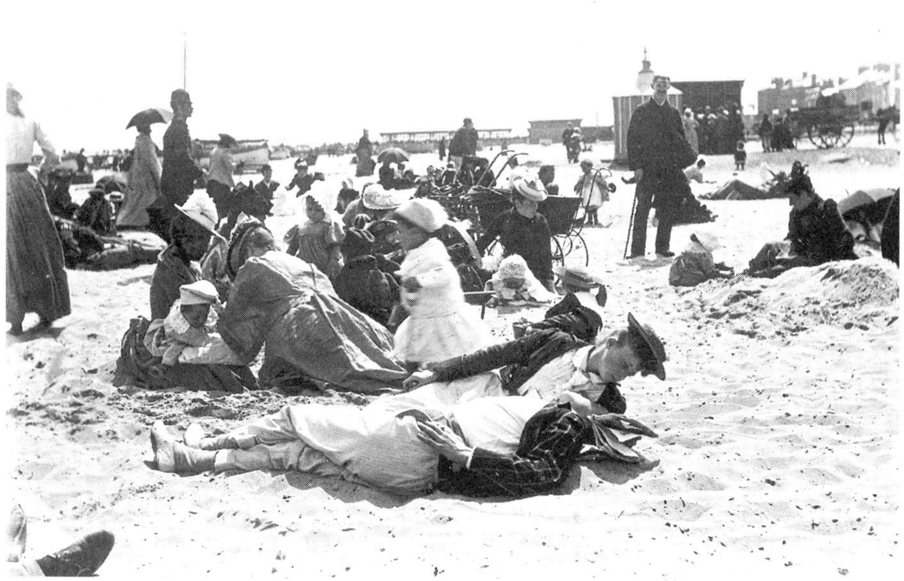

Fig. 24b Paul Martin, 'Beach Scene at Great Yarmouth', *c.* 1894.

otherness, Martin's photographs show the masses on the beach instead as a voluntary association or a temporary community – as self-enjoyment achieved within the social group. The holidaying crowd becomes a kind of plenitude, a place of belonging where *communitas* does not overwhelm selfhood, in which difference is magically overcome without the expense of identity.

This notion is fully developed in the 1930s and 1940s, by which time it had been filled out by a progressive populism voicing itself through the rhetoric of the 'romance of the masses'. It is present in Bill Brandt's *Brighton Belle* of 1936 in which a young woman on Brighton beach offers the camera a humorous parody of Britannia, turning the stern portentous meanings of the battle figure into the popular jollity of seaside cheekiness.

It's there too in Weegee's mass portrait of the democratic crowd cheering itself through the camera at Coney Island in 1940 or 1941 which seems nothing less than a record of the oneness of humanity or, at least, of America. Coney Island had long been regarded as a place where normally unacquainted social groups could rub bared shoulders in the levelling zone of pleasure and play. The temporary community seems to have been achievable only in a place which is in a sense outside society and half shrouded in dream – the Other place, the fairground – but from which one returns with the gifts of memory and photography, the proofs that Utopia had been glimpsed if not quite grasped.

However, this Coney Island throng is overwhelmingly white; an amicable

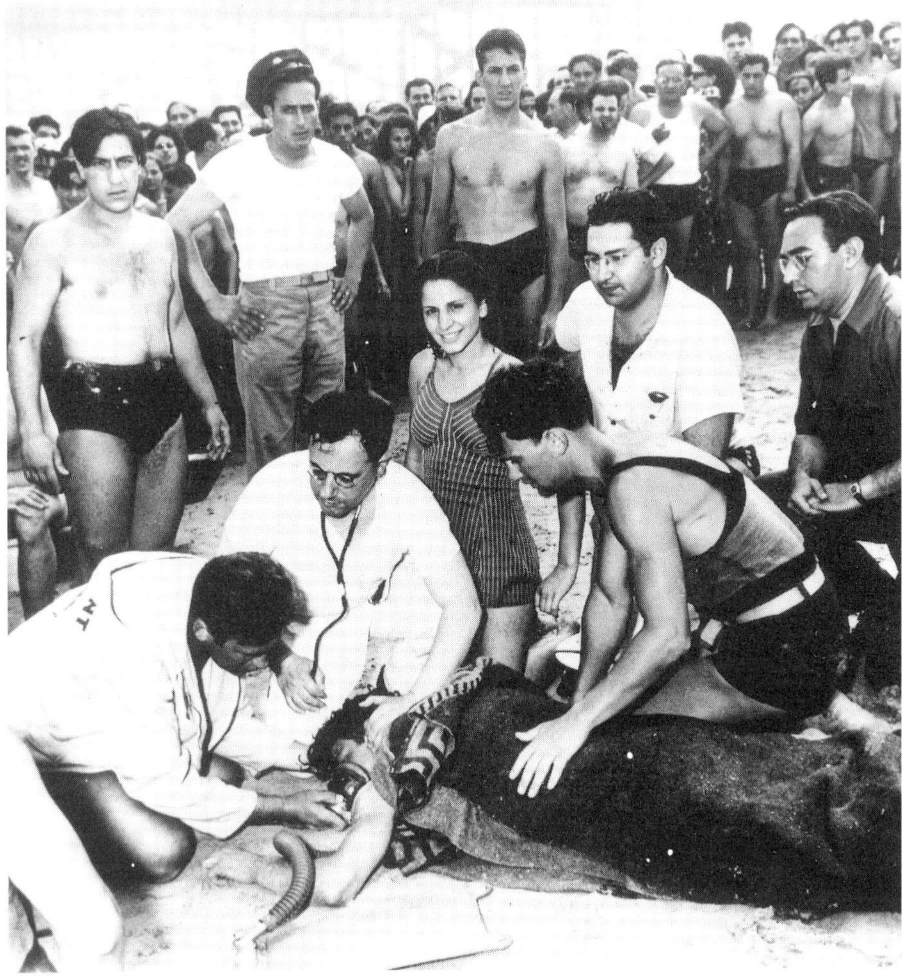

Fig. 25 Weegee (Arthur Fellig), 'Coney Island Drowning Incident', 1940/2. © International Center of Photography, New York, bequest of Wilma Wilcox

assembly for sure, but one that crowds out attention from the great exclusions of America which remained beyond the borders of the image. In this light the photograph is really just a family snap and not the human family.

But Weegee is normally associated with less idealised versions of the human than this. The denizens of his other worlds, from the jolly dipsos and shame-free transvestites, to those baleful nocturnal killers caught out in the flash, attest to his hard-boiled acceptance of the multitude of selves and their harsh motivations operating beyond the morality and sentiment of official pieties.

In another of his Coney Island epiphanies Weegee challenges the assumption of the moral and psychological integrity of the individual – that necessary complement to the notion of a universal human unity (figure 25).

No doubt selfless attempts are being made to revive the swimmer collapsed on the sand. But within the mass of concerned faces there is the young woman, whose costume and proximity to him suggests she is a close companion or relative, who looks up and out from the edge of tragedy and beams attractively at the camera.

In a way her action is scandalous. It appears to confuse duty to self and duty to others in a manner that defies propriety. Of course, this could be taken as displacement, the symptom of trauma. The very inappropriateness of her smile may have been the mask of her anguish. Read in this manner the image shows a singularity of intense feeling whose expression transforms under stress into its opposite.

Read differently, the image rains scepticism on notions which see human sympathy and response as unparadoxical or purely altruistic. This is, after all, the beach and people here are getting something out of the situation, including the viewer. Within the image a voyeurism drawn to accidents and the misfortunes of others is unmasked. The image's structure of reception provokes the voyeurism of the viewer who can enjoy the unexpected 'availability' of the woman; especially if the viewer entertains the fantasy that it is the consequence of 'his' own autonomous look which coincides with the aim of the male photographer but is not constructed by it.

Certainly the woman's divided response attests to the power of a masculine viewpoint and how women were and, arguably, continue to be formed to respond to it by being, in John Berger's words, 'almost continually accompanied by her own image of herself' (Berger 1972: 46). Weegee's woman on the beach is cut between a being self-enclosed within its own precise situation and one propelled into the general, into a position prepared by the culture for the feminine – a being-for-others as a function of the look of the camera.

As with everything else on the beach the value and effectiveness of self-display is not equitably distributed, is not experienced by all as pleasing or emancipatory. Even the most socially cohesive beach in at least the capitalist cultures is alive with competitive status markers or positional goods such as dress, body accessories and, of course, cameras. And the beach is also a beauty contest with judges and losers and those deemed unqualified to enter. The licence given to all men to ogle any woman on the beach is experienced by women in contradictory ways. Some claim to find fun and flattery in it, to accept it as one of the necessary and manipulatable moves in the ritual of sex. Others submit to it ruefully. Others, again, regard it as a visibility in which the woman's sense of self disappears in the blindness of the public voyeurs who are incapable of seeing beyond the body of their own fantasies. On the beach the desire to coincide with one's own self-display is haunted by the sense that the process always leads to estrangement in the eyes of others.

In Weegee's image the woman's look transports her from the realm of human compassion and aid, from the realm of conscience and social duty encircling the man on the ground, to the equally human and co-existing realm of self-love and amoral desire, here an affect of photography with its links to the cultural systems of glamour and fame.

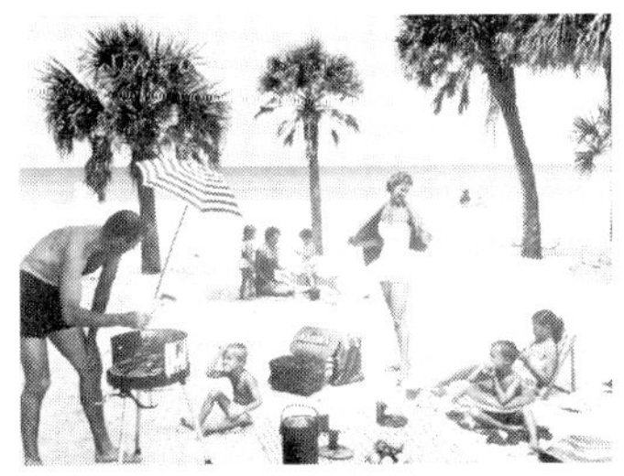

Fig. 26 Jo Steinmetz Studio, 'Longboat Key, Florida', 1958. From *The Champion Pig*.

However, the antinomies in Weegee's picture might be merely apparent. They call to mind Freud's contention that opposites share beginnings. In the unconscious, where love and self-love are indistinguishable, the woman's behaviour is beyond or perhaps before contradiction for, Freud maintained, compassion shares its origins with narcissism (Freud 1953–, vol. 13:88, cited in Rorty 1989: 31).

Such oppositions serve to remind us once more that the ritual space of the beach is itself built from embracing oppositions; a place of interior private fantasy where public roles and meanings are reconfirmed. Its ostensible individualism – the self-display, the self-satisfaction – coincides with the voluntary gathering of often huge numbers of people in constricted territory. It's a place of unclothing in which material and social differences off the beach might be replaced on it by the *communitas* of the body. Alternatively it is the battle on which the visual war of appearances are fought out by the flaunting of the unequally distributed capital of physical beauty – though a distribution not necessarily reflecting economic wealth.

No differences are allowed to unsettle this mythical beach (figure 26, larger-scale reproduction figure 23 on page 93). The creation of a commercial studio, it was taken and perhaps even taken seriously in 1958, Eisenhower time, a period in the United States falsely chronicled as stable and even serene, whereas the dominant order was beset by Cold War unease and demanded frequent reassurance from its culture. It was certain of one thing though, its (white) affluence. This tableau contains both. It confirms the permanence of traditional gender roles and family structure and celebrates leisure as the fruit of productivity.

The beach acts as pure extra-social space, a nature that endorses the truth of the performances taking place upon it so naturally; and a pleasure zone where the hardworking nuclear family with its picnic and barbecue gear goes to receive its reward for being what it is. In the background the flat, uncontroversial sea plays its familiar part as symbol of eternity, of unchanging order.

The participants may be outside history on the beach but they know what they must do. The man is primitive man – the hero who brings fire, the hunter who provides meat and feeds his family. He relays his best piece to the eldest boy, the next in line for his position.

The woman is reproductive rather than productive. Closer to nature than her mate, she has just emerged from water. She mediates adulthood and infancy,

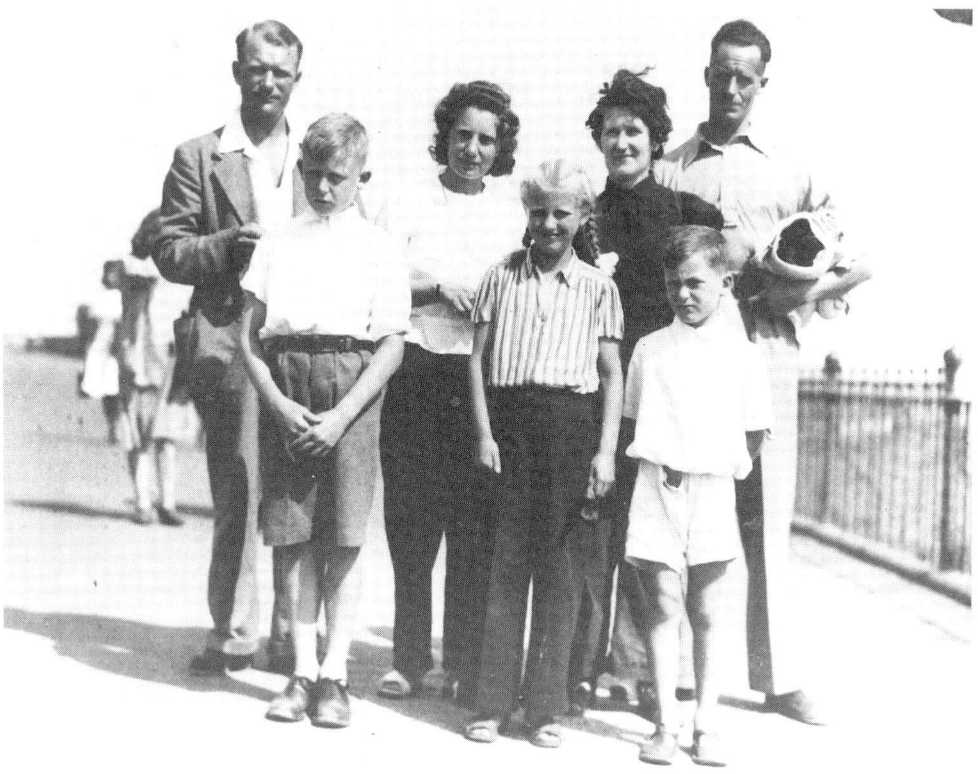

Fig. 27 Family holiday snap, Margate, 1946.

sharing the space of the younger children. She is decorous; she does him credit. Her body displays what he has. She awaits the gifts of the man's production.

This photograph was taken by a helpful stranger with one of the subjects' 1933 Brownie Box camera in Margate (figure 27). It was exposed in the summer of 1946 and shows two comfortably-off British working-class families on their first vacation following the Second World War.

As a personal icon its functions would have been the usual ones of celebrating and memorialising a special moment in the families' lives. Photography's effect of suspending an event out of the flow of time corresponds appropriately to the suspended, 'sacred' time of the vacation, the holy day. This image is a 'trophy' snatched by these people from the hand of time, a witness to a time they consume as they choose, rather than the time that consumes them – the time of work, history and death. In this form at least their act has survived. Such images are always holiday gifts for ordinary time to come, for posterity. When given over to these functions, Bourdieu describes the photograph as 'the object of collective and quasi-ceremonial contemplation', and the medium as 'festive technology', a 'technology for the reiteration of the party' (Bourdieu 1990: 26–7).

However, although it is an image made by and for the private uses of the holidaymakers themselves, the group still surrenders to portraiture's public formalities and to the collective family ideology it serves. The male, female, child hierarchy is naturalised by the physical hierarchy of relative body size emphasised or invented by the men standing at the back, overseeing the women and the children. Family unity and stability is indicated by the close grouping, by the preordained poses, the convergence of looks towards the camera 'so that the whole picture points to its own absent centre' (Bourdieu 1990: 81). As in all such portraits the subjects enter into a form of cultural exchange. The language in which they might normally behave, move, gesture, is given up for the collective code of portraiture. An idiolect is all but silenced in return for a presence in the general culture of representation.

Yet specific lives leave their unique prints. There are uncertainties: some smile, others do not. The two families, neighbours, never got on all that well. The unity of the photograph may have required some compromises, even a small defeat: the women twin their smiles, although one thought the other a little 'common', and the other thought her 'a bit stuck up'. The slumped shoulders and facial expression of one of the boys suggest a sulky resistance to being part of the ritual. The girl appears to be trying her best to please in unpropitious circumstances. The younger boy fails to smile. His father, the man who went to war, retains his 'military bearing' – his sharp trouser creases; the one who didn't wears a baggy jacket, amiably rolls a smoke.

Bourdieu describes this kind of visual arrangement as 'frontality', an imitation by the popular classes of the traditional bourgeois photograph expressing their desire for social respect. 'Honour demands that one pose for the photograph', he writes, 'as one would stand before a man whom one respects and from whom one expects respect, face on, one's forehead held high and one's head straight' (Bourdieu 1990: 82).

In 1946 the people in this group felt they were due a deeper kind of respect. They were still buoyed up by having voted in a socialist government with a huge majority. The adults, veterans of the Depression, had secure employment. Above all they had survived a dreadful but, they'd concluded, necessary war and the images and memories of other beaches still haunted them: the sacrificial sites where the dead of the democratic armies had floated in the surf, or were drowned in the sand. 'The last beach I paddled on was at Salerno', recalls Lenny in Graham Swift's novel *Last Orders* (1996), thinking of the allied landings in Italy, 'I ain't so keen on beaches'.

For several years Margate beach had been negative space – out-of-bounds, wreathed in barbed wire, mined and guarded. What had been a festive edge-space had been transformed into a perilous border sealed against Fascism, the enemy of all edges and difference.

Now, in their shy and solemn manner, these two families begin to venture again on to their own beaches, to repossess them as ordinary victors, modest survivors. They are defending nobody, taking no orders – simply being there, doing nothing other than celebrating themselves and people like them, restoring the temporary community – and, in doing all these things they re-purify the beach, the once infected border.

The Cuban writer Edmundo Desnoes notes that 'frontality' is common in Latin American photography because Latin Americans live in the 'Plaza', happily accepting and returning the gaze of their fellows. Unlike North Americans in their separate, privatised lives, they continue to inhabit a public culture, still have truly public space (Desnoes 1987: 7). By the 1940s in the United States, affluence, the suburbs and the motor car were putting distance between more and more people and the old proletarian intimacies. In Britain, as early as the 1930s the more collective culture of the British working class was also beginning to disperse towards the nuclear fragments more typical of our own time. Perhaps the frontality of this photograph betokens something additional to respect – and something fragile. This was probably the last generation of British people that could walk on the beach as though it was Desnoes's 'Plaza' – to see and be seen celebrating a collective belonging constituted by enjoyment and social morality in equal parts. The sand was still a public place more than a market place. They may have received their photographic cues and legitimation in the layouts of *Picture Post*, but the meanings that once lived within the moment of this portrait rose out of a class and national moment once both real and widespread. Against this, Martin Parr's photographs of a shabby New Brighton in the 1980s and 1990s, where underpaid people huddle in the margins of a littered ugliness, seem to mark some kind of degradation of popular hopes and pleasures in which significant themes of Britain's recent social history can be read (see Parr, *Home and Abroad*, 1993).

The integrities of the old working-class cultures are vanishing, taking with them their suffocating limitations as well as their democratic warmth. Longer holidays and the leaking of recreational culture into the working year have reduced the near ecstatic difference from the everyday once represented by a week on Margate sands. But the holiday beach and the beach photograph continue to stage the rituals of leisure and transient association, and on a few occasions they have offered a central visibility for new kinds of social performance.

In at least two instances since the 1950s the beach has been the space in which 'youth' performed itself into social existence, got itself seen, filmed, photographed, then theorised and mythologised and recycled: the Mods' seaside ructions of 1964 and the more recent Rave culture on the Balearics in the 1980s and since. On the beach young people could realise their need to relocate themselves symbolically, to gather on the 'outside' and create their counter-families and communities. The beach was an appropriate setting for the expression of adolescence's fervour and transience, its need to get away and to be noticed, an effective resonating space for intoning youth's refrain of marginalisation, for the living out of the liminal, pilgrim's journey that being young is.

But no modern cultural movement feels complete without the legitimation of publicity. The Mods and the Ravers required the visibility as well as the displacement of the beach. They became nourished by an imagery that both confirmed and compromised their revolts and withdrawals.

The beach's significance as a *central* social stage has declined with the certainty of knowing what a central social experience is and for whom: that is, with the passing of the centre. Social spaces and their meanings are multiplying, fragmenting – like the social eye, like the social itself – and like the varieties of vacation.

In the 1990s the Dutch photographer Rineke Dijkstra portrayed a series of young people standing on beaches in various countries. They were exhibited at London's Photographers' Gallery early in 1998. The style is uniform. Photographed frontally in full figure, they stand isolated in their swimming costumes with their backs to the sea. Some are in pairs but also extracted from others on the beach. They stare uncertainly into the lens. The desaturated colour and the bright almost shadowless light reduces emotion. The shallow depth of field blurs beachline and sealine leaving the background without depth, like a wall or flat backdrop – a visual block. Having no other distractions in the image the viewer's scrutiny of the subjects is fully concentrated.

Where Brandt's *Brighton Belle* laid claim to a closeness between subject, photographer and viewer and invoked a shared popular order of humour and role-playing, Dijkstra's subjects seem to have had their social identities taken from them with their clothes. They look as if they *feel* naked. Deprived of the covering of the social pose, what selfhood remains to be visualised? And yet, in the pure studio of a beach, from which society has been bracketed out – an aesthetic device, no more – the cool, distanced scrutiny of Dijkstra's photography sees not depths beyond social roles but the depth of surface, the surface of the body. Against the standardised portrait conventions that Dijkstra has chosen to apply to all her subjects each body reveals itself as distinctive, and vulnerable – a turn of the head, a lazy eye, a few freckles or spots, an unexpected beauty. From the social emptiness of these beaches come no images of social solidarity but, surprisingly, what do begin to form are the signs of where the new beginnings of compassion might be located.

The social is shown as both diminished and yet irrepressible in Mark Power's photograph *Malin Monday 6 September 1993* (figure 28). The beach remains a public space but the public appears to have vanished from it. Instead of the rituals of group pleasure and identification we witness just two figures stranded in their privacy, enacting a rite both lonely and tender. By entering the circle the woman and her child transform the undefined place of the shoreline into a space in de Certeau's sense of a location created and recreated by people's practice, by their movements in and through it, by their inscribing their own meanings on to it (Certeau 1984: chapter 7).

The chance circle, the random flourish of the driver of some beach vehicle,

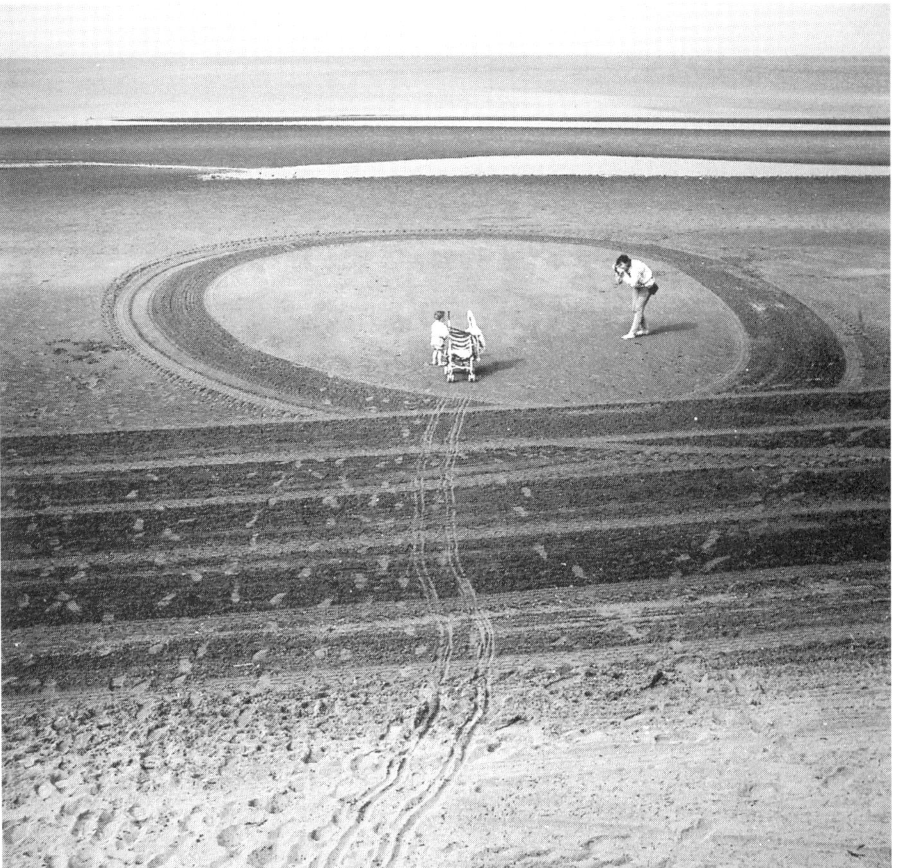

Fig. 28 Mark Power (Network), 'Malin Monday 6 September 1993'. From *The Shipping Forecast*, 1996.

encloses the intimacy that unites the two and sets it off from the beach's indeterminacy. Perhaps both the woman and the absent driver shared the same goal of writing a human signature on to the endless indifference of nature. Perhaps, like those tourists who raise their cameras in the first moments of their encounter with a famous sight, the woman takes the photograph less with the printed image in mind than with the feeling that through the act of taking a photograph she will confirm a compact with the marvellous object, her child, contain the moment as the circle contains them – and fix its presence. For an instant the space becomes sacral. Form is created from the formless, and for a while, oblivion is denied a fragment of lived time.

The intimacy of parent and child is more fortuitously linked to the stranger who described the circle. Certainly the forms left in the sand and the use made of them connect all three people. In doing so they bring human purpose, social content, to the meaningless beach.

Of course the woman's photograph will not reveal the *mise-en-scène* in which she is placed – she makes her image from within it, as part of it. It is only

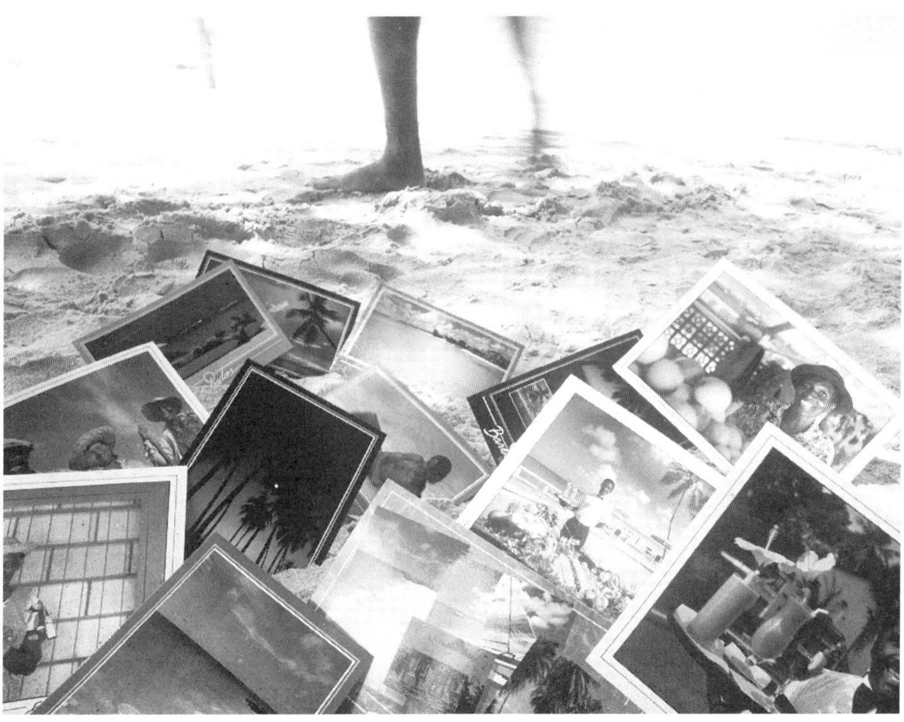

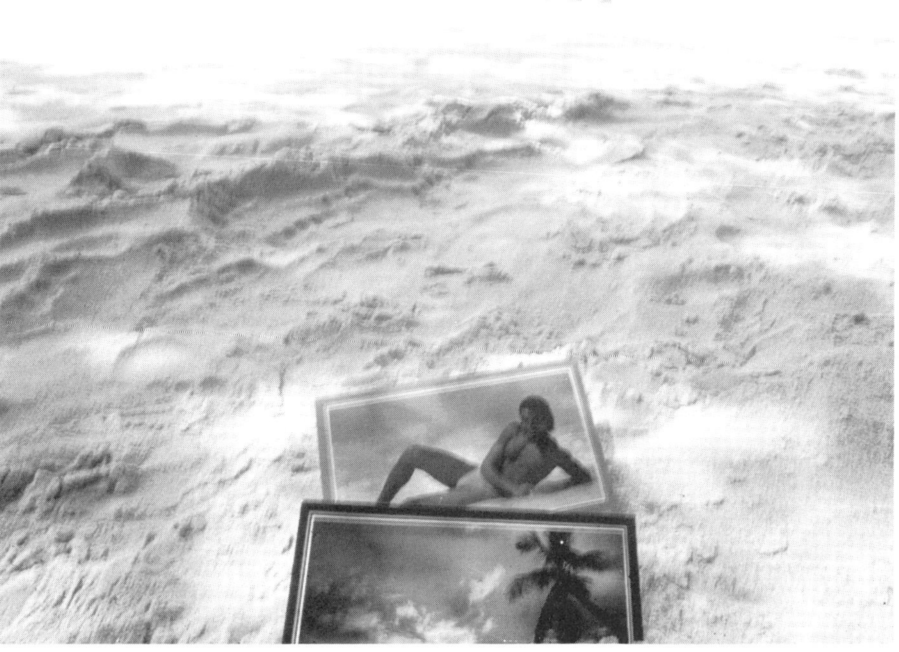

Fig. 29/30 David A. Bailey, from *From Britain or Barbados or Both?*, 1989. Original in colour.

viewable from somewhere else, in the *other* photograph – the one taken from the outside, from the discrete and dispassionate distance of the other, from the silent place of the invisible photographer – and is most likely entirely an invention of it.

In David A. Bailey's 1980s sequence *From Britain or Barbados or Both?* the Caribbean holiday beach has become a space where the complexities and particularities of the island's culture have been reduced to the types of tourism; where local identities are lost in the images and roles of waiters, maids or beach boys or 'local colour', kicked aside like the postcards and scattered by the indifference of tourists (figures 29 and 30).

This beach is a place of exclusion, of shrinking identities – a barrier to the display of selves still denied admission to the repertoire.

People continue to define themselves in the holiday and its images. The beach remains a central space for the tourist to be placed in. But while family or class may remain the ordering principle behind both their self-definition and the meanings and expectations they attach to holidays, for others it is equally age group or ethnic group, sexual orientation, subculture, taste, profession, consumer status or political tendency. A comprehensive social universe is now hard to find on one holiday beach. For this reason the most effective social photographers of the beach now draw less from the relative certainties of the documentary tradition than from the language of art photography with its capacity for accommodating irony and uncertainty, to develop the means of representing these complexities.

Note

1 In the early nineteenth century the first residence in Brighton designed for viewing the sea was built. It was an essential development in the town's evolution as a pleasure resort (Charlton 1984: 52–3).

7
Fixing Arcadia: the photographic paradise

> and we are thrown back upon the first integrity of things. (William Hazlitt, *On a Landscape of Nicolas Poussin*)

> Underneath the truly picture is a picture of the world-so-new-and-all. (Rudyard Kipling, *Just So Stories*)

Tourism exchanges all worldly denominations for the currencies of paradise. Of all the items that feature in its stock of paradisal tokens, perhaps the most common is the icon of the palm tree with its spread of familiar connotations: Orientalist Saharas, tropicalism's florid sensualities, the entangling, abundant otherness of the jungle – a sort of anti-paradise-paradise, or, more typically now, the ecological romance and nostalgia of the Amazonian rainforest (aka jungle). The palm tree additionally signifies the less arduous escapism of the hotels and star villas of the Mediterranean, southern California or Waikiki – the dream of fame and wealth and of the rituals of extreme consumption.

For those, above all, from the rainy kingdoms the palm tree stands before everything else as emblem, index and guarantor of warmth and a benevolent, if occasionally edgy, difference. To be a little more precise, it stands for 'the South', where experience deepens and the pleasure principle reigns.

Barthes finds an insistent association between the palm tree and sensual longing. In his 'autobiography' he speaks of the palm's beauty issuing from the effect of 'falling back'. It's a quality he believes it shares with writing, which he says on the book's final unnumbered page, 'one does with one's desire' (Barthes 1995: 40–1). He gives a whole page of the book over to a photograph of palm trees tossing in the wind.

The arousal of desire would seem to be the aim of a multitude of images promoting tropical island holidays in which the palm is featured. Most commonly it is shown not upright, not erect, but lounging across the frame, often heavy with fruit – as though swooning, yielding, 'falling back' across the path of the viewer; a feminised entity proposing a languorous eroticism.

The mythology of 'the South' has secreted one cluster of themes and locations more than usually freighted with paradisal meanings – the tropical

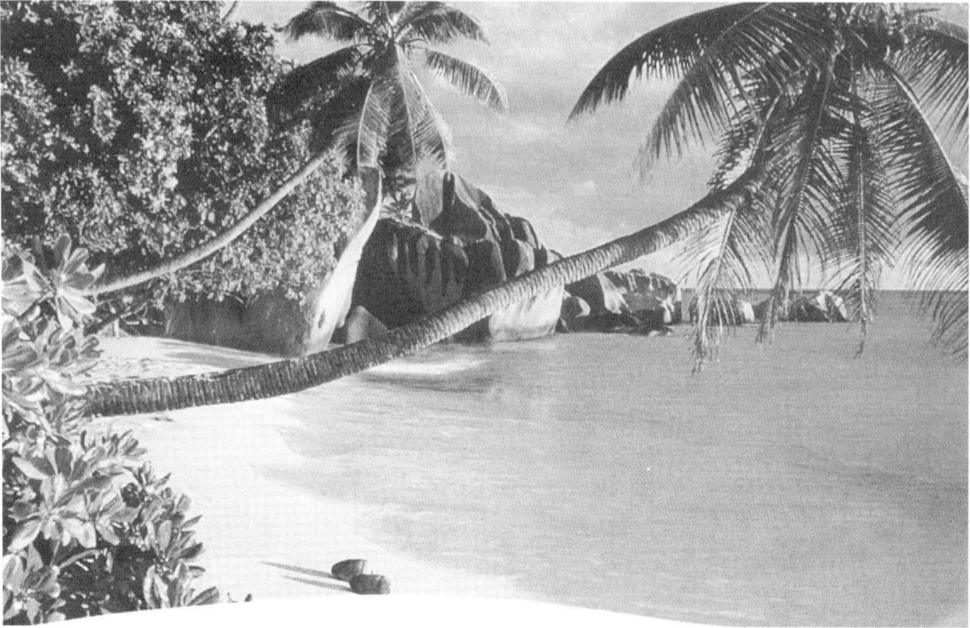

Fig. 31 Promotion for the Seychelles, 1994. Original in colour.

islands of the Pacific, the 'South Seas', with its actual and emblematic palms. 'To vast eternity's unbounded sea / Where the green islands of the happy shine', wrote James Thomson in his 1727 memorial poem for Newton.

Although it is only in recent years that long-haul tourism to this region has expanded, its link in the modern Western mind with the Edenic goes back to earlier journeys. It was being established in the written accounts and mariners' stories of the early European voyages, and in the heroic surveys and 'botanising epics' of the eighteenth and nineteenth centuries. It was reinforced by the poetic evocations of writers and artists such as Tennyson, who never went there, Baudelaire, who travelled no further than Mauritius, or Gauguin and Stevenson who did manage to become residents.

In addition to fuelling the reader's fireside reveries – adventure, barbarism, sensuality, spectacular nature – the South Seas in nineteenth-century literature served as the life-enhancing brightness which contrasted with a perceived European spiritual or aesthetic atrophy. Neither scientific methodology nor cultural distance has prevented these themes and attractions from reappearing in the products of the paradise science, anthropology and its popular adaptations.

Besides, of course, the dream-tableaux of Gauguin, traces of the link's visual ancestry can be found in earlier painters and illustrators such as John Webber and William Hodges, both of whom sailed with Cook. In Hodges's painting *Tahiti Revisited*, for example, three notions of the paradisal are present (plate 9). It is visualised equally as sensuous wonderment, noble and erotic savagery, and as a high-colour neo-Classical Arcadia – Poussin meets Salvator Rosa in the Southern Ocean.

Woven in the context of this painting's production was England's catastrophic first encounter with Tahiti which had concluded in the massacre of many natives, more through confusion than intent. Hodges's picturing is an attempt to re-present the approach to the island as a kind of sedated wonderment, free of the deranged violence which had overcome the first meeting. Tahiti was strangeness and incomprehension – a dissonance needing harmonising, a source of terrors that required calming. *Tahiti Revisited* offered the colonising sensibility a proto-Romantic Italianesque which both reproduced something of the South Sea object's fatal seduction – the excessive landscape, the otherness of the self-contained, tattooed figures indifferent to the presence of the viewer, their savage gods – while disposing it at a distance. This it achieves spatially by means of the seceded viewpoint, and temporally by displacing the island in time.

In this way Hodges produced a 'panorama of recall', to take a phrase from Iain Sinclair (*Downriver*). The painter's 'revisited' Tahiti is either an island preserved for ever in the moment just prior to first contact, or it is one already conquered, made safe, a visual feast that can no longer bite back, and yet somehow still approached eternally for the first time. Translated into an aesthetic event Tahiti can be viewed as if its purpose had always been to act as a visual device for summoning up notions and sentiments entertaining to the minds of Europeans. As in the painting's visual descendants, tourist posters, postcards, the resort itself with its themed services and entertainments, it has been made safe and made into image – made safe *by* becoming image. Tahiti is no longer quite there, neither in space nor time. It is never quite arrived at. It has become a sign of something elsewhere and of something other than itself. Here paradise is always the *prospect* of paradise.

Even though imported venereal disease, the corruption of imagined innocence and the first physical signs of the degradation of modern development had despoiled the South Seas Eden before the end of the nineteenth century, our contemporary brochures continue to present it wrapped in the old myths. It is variously a glossy perceptual feast, the home of natural societies where the gift-relationship prevails over the cash-nexus, an encounter with guileless friendship and guiltless sexuality – in essence, a place of escape from the masks and regulations, the hidden agendas and the boredom of modern life.

These were tired notions long before widespread affluence and jet travel brought mass tourism to the Pacific. In 1908 H. de Vere Stacpoole had huge success with his novel *The Blue Lagoon*, a compendium of South Seas clichés which spawned a number of musical and cinematic offspring. It provided Nathanael West with comic material for his 1931 novel *Miss Lonelyhearts*, in which the editor and hyper-cynic, Shrike, pastiches the South Seas style as follows:

> Let us now consider the South Seas:
> You live in a thatch hut with the daughter of the king, a slim young maiden in whose eye is an ancient wisdom. Her breasts are golden speckled pears, her belly a melon, and her odour is like nothing so much as a jungle fern. In the evening, on a blue lagoon, under a silvery moon, to your love you croon in the soft sylabelew and vocabelew of her langorour tongorour. (West 1957: 107–8)

However fanciful, such notions may have been the distorted products of actual encounters between the first European visitors and the inhabitants. But these voyagers did not arrive without mental luggage. Shaping the expectations of Europeans as they neared the islands of the Pacific for the first time was a congregation of mental forms and notions which together pictured Eden or, rather, a variety of Edens. Many of them continue to inform our own. They had many origins, biblical and otherwise, from the most ancient mythologies to more recent Renaissance explorations and fantasies and the fresh paradigms of eighteenth-century science.

Most held Eden to be a green, riverine and fruitful place located in the Orient, where time was suspended or had never begun, but where existence continued. The word paradise itself, rooted in the pre-Islamic Persian word *Pairidaez*, designated a walled and watered garden encircled by wilderness. This notion was later taken up and spread by Islam, manifesting itself in that analogue of heaven, the Islamic garden.

In his book *Green Imperialism* Richard H. Grove shows how, after the fifteenth century, the search for Eden remained a powerful impulse within the more obviously economic and pragmatic motivations governing European expansion. Through the seventeenth and eighteenth centuries, Grove argues, new kinds of what he calls 'Edenic Island discourses' appeared (Grove 1995: 6). They rose in part from the experience of the explorers. Tropical green islands were often the first places they landed and claimed for themselves. They provided sustenance and often safety after long and unhealthy voyages. Unsurprisingly they soon became associated with both enrichment and restoration (Grove 1995: 33).

The islands were also mental locations. Perfect, miniature worlds, they seemed to be more visible, more easily comprehended than the complicated post-Renaissance societies where the travellers had embarked. And the experience of tropical nature's astonishing abundance and the widening scientific awareness of its complex systems induced in some not only amazement but the beginnings of an ecological view of the globe. As well as real-estate, nature was becoming something to understand, to value, to conserve for its own sake – something to enjoy.

Like the ancient idea of paradise, the tropical islands were gardens surrounded by sterile emptiness, the salty wastes of the ocean. But they were grounded in a systematic order that might be comprehended. Eden was beautiful, overwhelming; yet its gardens were rational.

The scientific revolution was not unaffected by the puritan view that the greater one's knowledge of nature, the closer one's acquaintance with God.[1] As Grove reminds us, for the puritan the journey to the island might be allegorised as a voyage to redemption (Grove 1995: 4). From the fallen world disfigured by sin and deception and therefore unknowable, the pilgrim journeyed towards alternative worlds of revelation and personal salvation. Small islands had small, but, it was believed, transparent, and thus knowable social systems. The relationship between humankind and nature was harmonious, and nature displayed itself with such amplitude and concentration as to open up the observer both to wonder and to the deeper comprehension of its immanent workings. To be in those places where things were both simpler and magnified it was possible to regain the immediacy of an Edenic experience of them: a unity of seeing, feeling and knowing. Approaching the islands was like being drawn back to Eden, as if the Europeans voyaging on the vast Pacific waves were imitating the wandering soul returning to the Garden and thereby, to God, to origins.

In Romantic discourse, the islands could be made to dramatise the lonely independence of the creative self in the universe and to celebrate subjectivity, with the variety and colour, even danger of tropical plants and animals mirroring the richness of the interior life and the transforming possibilities of intensified experience.

In romanticised ethnology the islands housed a humanity still happily established closer to its collective childhood. The apparent contentment of islanders could be seen to challenge the European claim to be the more advanced, or the best adapted. Traces of this kind of thinking remain strong in Mead and Malinowski as well as in the pages and plates of *The National Geographic*. It is dramatically present in the work of Wilhelm Reich, the radical psychoanalyst who preached the overthrow of social authoritarianism through the abolition of sexual repression. His human model was built on Malinowski's study of Trobriand Island societies, interpreted by Reich as the chronicle of a sexual paradise.

Although expanded by additional material from popular fictions and entertainments, James Michener novels, *South Pacific*, *Blue Hawaii*, *Hawaii Five-O*, versions of *The Mutiny on the Bounty* and the Bounty Bar advertisements, much of the traditional Edenic lexicon recurs in tourism's palm-fringed visualisations of the South Sea experience. Their dominant key is nature – verdant, flower-decked, filled with bright birds, a blinding blue sea. The encounter promised is less with a universe of social beings than with creatures barely out of nature at all. The figures most commonly used to personify the welcoming island are children and young women, each classified as bearers of innocence and impulses close to nature, an intimacy confirmed in image and culture by their association with flowers, grass and palms. Each offer themselves and their world up to the visitor. They embody availability, they are disposed

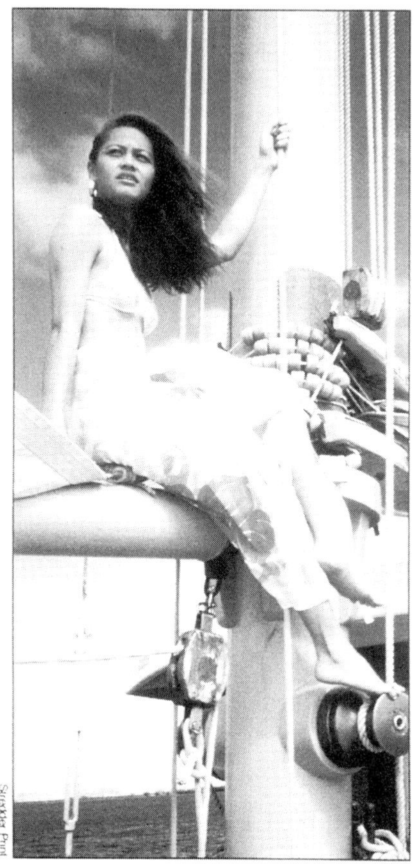

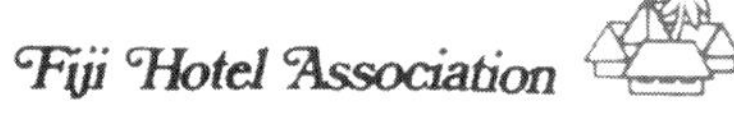

Fig. 32 Promotion for Fiji, 1994. Original in colour.

and disposable and in this they are the inheritors of a colonial contract.

Colonial power, even if transmuted, is rarely absent in such forms of the paradisal. Just as the global economy in general evolved out of the colonial system, much domestic and all 'foreign' tourism is, as Lévi-Strauss once said of anthropology, a 'child of imperialism'. Outside of Europe, there is not an inch of ground that tourists pass over which was not once crossed by explorers, soldiers and colonists. Tourist destinations are often sited in ex-colonies and offer touristic experiences which re-enact, or simulate, the colonial mode of contact with both landscape and people. The cultural features of modern tourism bear the marks of its economic ancestry. The work of imperialism metamorphoses into the dreamwork of tourism and, in at least the poorer countries, it remains an unequal exchange, a form of possession, the possession of other people's labour and resources and the possession of other people's appearances – their visibility. The view from the settler's veranda dissolves effortlessly into the view from the hotel terrace, or the tour coach window or camera viewfinder. The land and the people who work in it must still submit themselves to being looked upon – then by the acquisitive, overseeing stare of the planter with time and space in his hands; now, by the ludic, pleasuring gaze of the tourists with time and space *on* their hands.

The presence of the imperial past in the contemporary tourist 'gaze' is the subject of a photographic work of the 1980s, *Line of Sight – Crusoe's Descent*, by Olivier Richon (*Creative Camera*, November 1983), in which modern Western travellers gaze on the non-Western world with an eye still organised by the old imperial iconographies – 'imagine, dead, imagine', as Beckett phrased it (see also hooks in Grossberg et al. 1992: 343).

In this promotion for Fiji (figure 32) the phallic forms and power of the yacht belong to the explorer-tourist, positioned as masculine, traveller-transgressor, possessor and penetrator of the islands which are condensed into the body of the woman who supports herself with the mast she caresses. The image carries irresistible echoes of the old stories of Polynesian women offering themselves freely to the first European mariners. The memory of colonial consummations continue to resonate within tourism's wish fulfilments.

Another version of the South Seas rhetoric is assembled around the figure of the child. Take for example a promotional image for Vanuatu (plate 10). Here the essence of the child, inseparable from the palm matting, weaved from the same material, is proclaimed as at once nature, as eternally premodern and as product of a modern process; for both have been made, or made over, by the tourist system. They are its native commodities, its ethnic goods. More immediately they are the effect of the look of the tourist, which is a closed loop of production and consumption, a visual encounter formed by images – promotion; and images made from a visual encounter – tourist photographs.

The child's smile, as natural a bloom as the flower it is wearing, signifies an acceptance of the tourist's look. As child, it confirms the tourist's authority and renders the encounter with the Other safe, in need of no translation; for children, so the conventional wisdom has it, are 'the same the world over'. The child, cute metonym, expresses a welcoming amity which, the tourist has been told, comes naturally to these people. Post-colonial tourists can feel not only wanted but also forgiven – recognised in their innocence by the innocence of nature's child. Time has reversed here, gone back to a mythical pre-colonial era before paradise was deflowered.

> Is there no change or death in paradise?
> Does the ripe fruit never fall? Or do the boughs
> hang always heavy in that perfect sky?
> (Wallace Stevens, *Sunday Morning*)

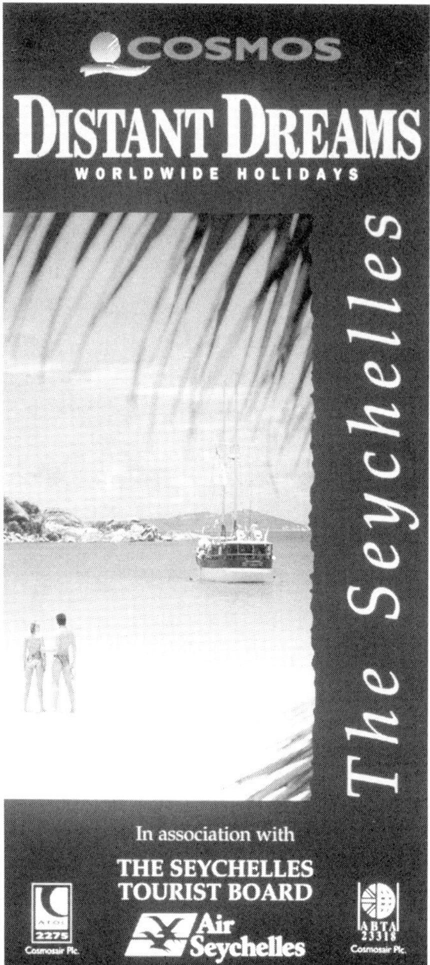

Fig. 33 Promotion for Seychelles, 1994. Original in colour.

Natural, asocial, tropical islands float outside history – on blue, semantic oceans signifying eternity. Their association with the 'childhood of the race' consolidates their appeal as a place where one can slip temporarily out of time, relieved of the burden of historical being. Lévi-Strauss characterised myths as 'machines for the abolition of time', and one of the special effects of paradise myths is the stilling of all processes of change and decay. Those which form around travel and tourism are no exception. Many of us have even fostered the conceit that travelling will preserve us from ageing itself – 'a symbolic way to stop growing old, to deny time by crossing space' writes Michel Leiris (quoted in Clifford 1988: 165). It is as if we believe that by passing through the time and history of others we'll pass out of time altogether, as if it will absolve us of its consequences, defer the arrival of death.

Through its implication with mobility and the interruption of ordinary time and routine, tourism services the same illusion. Ironically it also does so by encouraging the aspiration towards an opposed condition – the absolute stillness of the object, the lifeless thing. There is the general figure of the supine tourist, satiate, immobilised by the shock of pleasure or by scopic entrancement. There is the figure of the sunbather – an angelic form whose perfect body, nourished only by sunlight, lies fixed, preserved in a luminous, deathless zone of photographic representation.

Though based in the endless comings and goings of its clients, tourism immobilises the world, brings it to a halt as an image, a spectacle. It seizes it in the cliché, in the stereotype. Its representations suck the historical matter out of things, the better to embalm them in myth. Sometimes nothing moves and nothing ages, death's work is at once suspended and simulated. This stillness of paradise is also the stillness of death, the end of movement and of course the end of pleasure. In the image world of tourism, as in all image worlds, nothing perishes; nor does anything breath.

Time passing may have been dismissed from paradise, but tourism's Eden is always haunted by its return; as in this Seychelles promotion, figure 33.

Though staged as the original scene, it is not the picturing of the first Eden. This Adman-Adam and Eve stand on the beach as if they've just regained it; as if having departed before history began they've returned at its end, the perfect products and delegates of market society. Like Fukuyama's Last Man and Woman they stand ready to repossess the property they were once ejected from. The long trajectory through the fallen world of time and labour into which the first parents were thrown has been completed.

But these lovers have arrived by yacht. It hovers there, the great commodity, the great machine, representing both freedom and safety; both escape from the modern world and the inescapable umbilical dependence on it. The idea flatters our civilisation, and yet discomforts it. For it says that the problem of history has been solved by our kind of economy, by our kind of technology, the providers of the wealth, the power and the vehicle – all compacted into the yacht – capable of restoring us to our lost contentment on the first beach.

And yet, for these consumers in paradise there is a sense that they have nothing left to do, have nowhere else they need go – except back to production, back into time, to begin the circular journey once again.

> I don't know how humanity stands it
> with a painted paradise at the end of it
> without a painted paradise at the end of it.
> (Ezra Pound, *Canto 74*)

> as if the image launched desire beyond what it permits us to see.
> (Roland Barthes, *Camera Lucida*)

There are twin stars which across the distances of space appear as one – a single point of light and energy. Though formed from the same local matter they are distinct and their proximity only relative.

Like such stars and true to its hybrid nature, tourism's apparently singular edition of paradise reveals itself on closer approach to be made up of two quite contradictory versions: paradise as the unmediated, predominantly visual, reception of the real, and in particular of ways of life deemed more authentic than the tourist's own; and paradise as the acceptance of artifice, of the representation, of the copy. Certain kinds of tourism make clear which one is consciously in play. Ethnographic or ecological tourism would exemplify the first, a trip to Disneyland the second. In other kinds and increasingly in the minds of contemporary tourists, they are confusingly, or playfully, co-present.

Around photography the uncertainties intensify. It may be regarded as the medium which restores such lost-to-us paradisal qualities as unity, immediacy and truth. Equally it can be seen as the agent of their ruin through its generation of a confusion of multiple representations, and of an enchantment with the icon which denies the referent and defers permanently the paradisal return.

But, when associated with perspectives that link paradise to images and to the artificial – after all a walled garden is the picture of an artifice – photography is acclaimed as the formulator of tourism's simulations.

For some, this is because the notion of the deficient, fragmented and second-hand reality of images confirms the existence of the ideal qualities of a primary one, a paradise, of which they must be the shadows. Within even the cheapest Edens of the holiday world the idea of the true paradise persists; perhaps more poignantly yearned for because of the inadequacy of its representations.

In a study of documentary film, Louis Marcorelles derives the word *paradise* from the word *parada*, meaning tapestry, something woven together, that is, a fabricated imitation. In the tapestry, he writes, 'the needle knots the thread of time and reunites time and the world' (Marcorelles 1973: 128–9). The tapestry pulls things together, makes up an order. It is a visual event drawn across the dull walls of everyday life; an imaginary opening into space which overcomes the flatness and resistance of the wall; an ordered fiction where the desiring eye can wander. It represents a world where what time has scattered has been gathered in, where what was lost is redeemed.

But, seeing paradise as manifest in the tapestry affiliates it with the copy, with an apparently secondary and possibly false account of reality. It is a notion that goes against the conventional assumption that paradise and unmediated perception are interdependent.

However, as Derrida has insisted, it is the copy that invents the notion of the original and thereby precedes it. A comparable proposition is advanced in another of Michel Tournier's fables, *The Two Banquets or the Commemoration*, which recounts a competition another caliph organises to discover which of two cooks can prepare the most sublime meal. The first meal is so exquisite that many in the court urge the caliph to declare its cook the winner on the spot. However he insists they wait a week, as arranged, for the second to present his meal. It is a replication of the first in every detail of menu, appearance and taste. Fortunately the caliph recognises wisdom rather than insolence in the second cook's

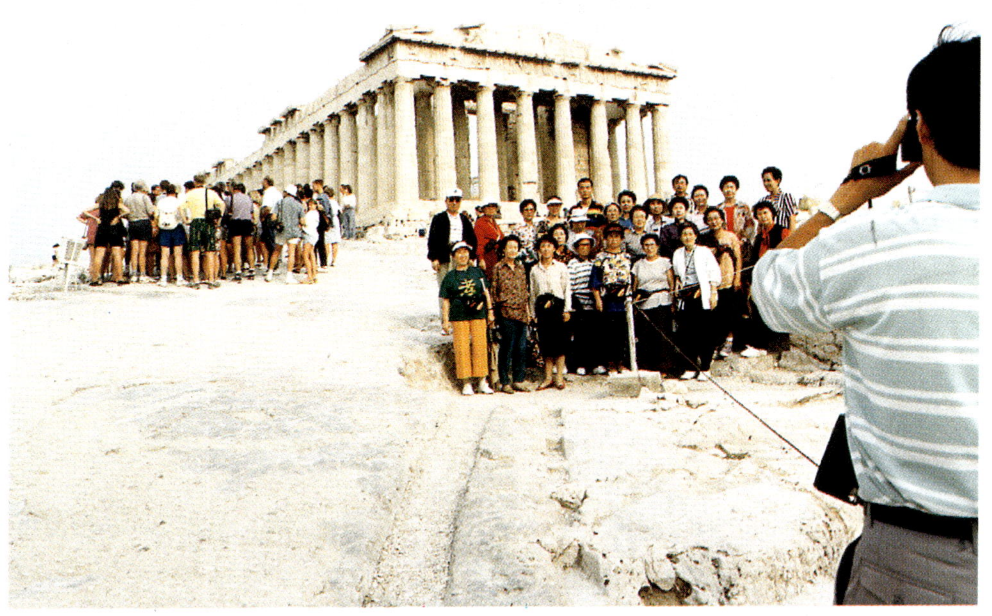

Plate 1 Martin Parr (Magnum), 'The Acropolis, Athens, Greece'. From *Small World*, 1995.

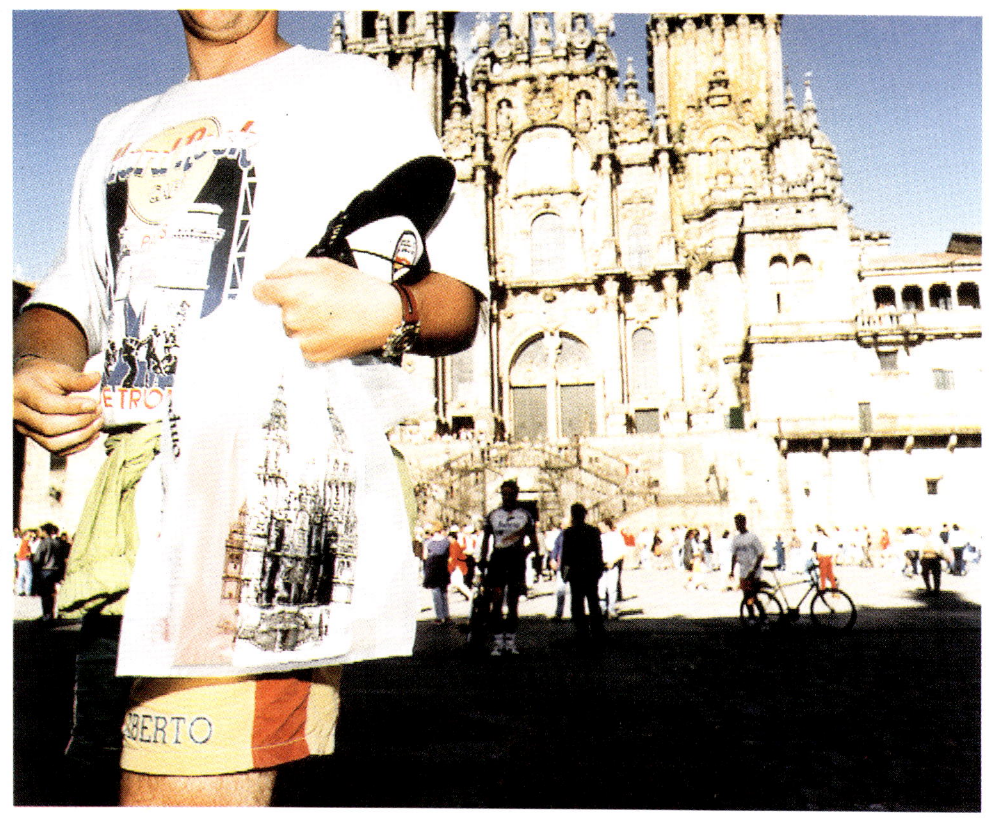

Plate 2 Martin Parr (Magnum), 'Santiago de Compostela, Spain'. From *Small World*, 1995.

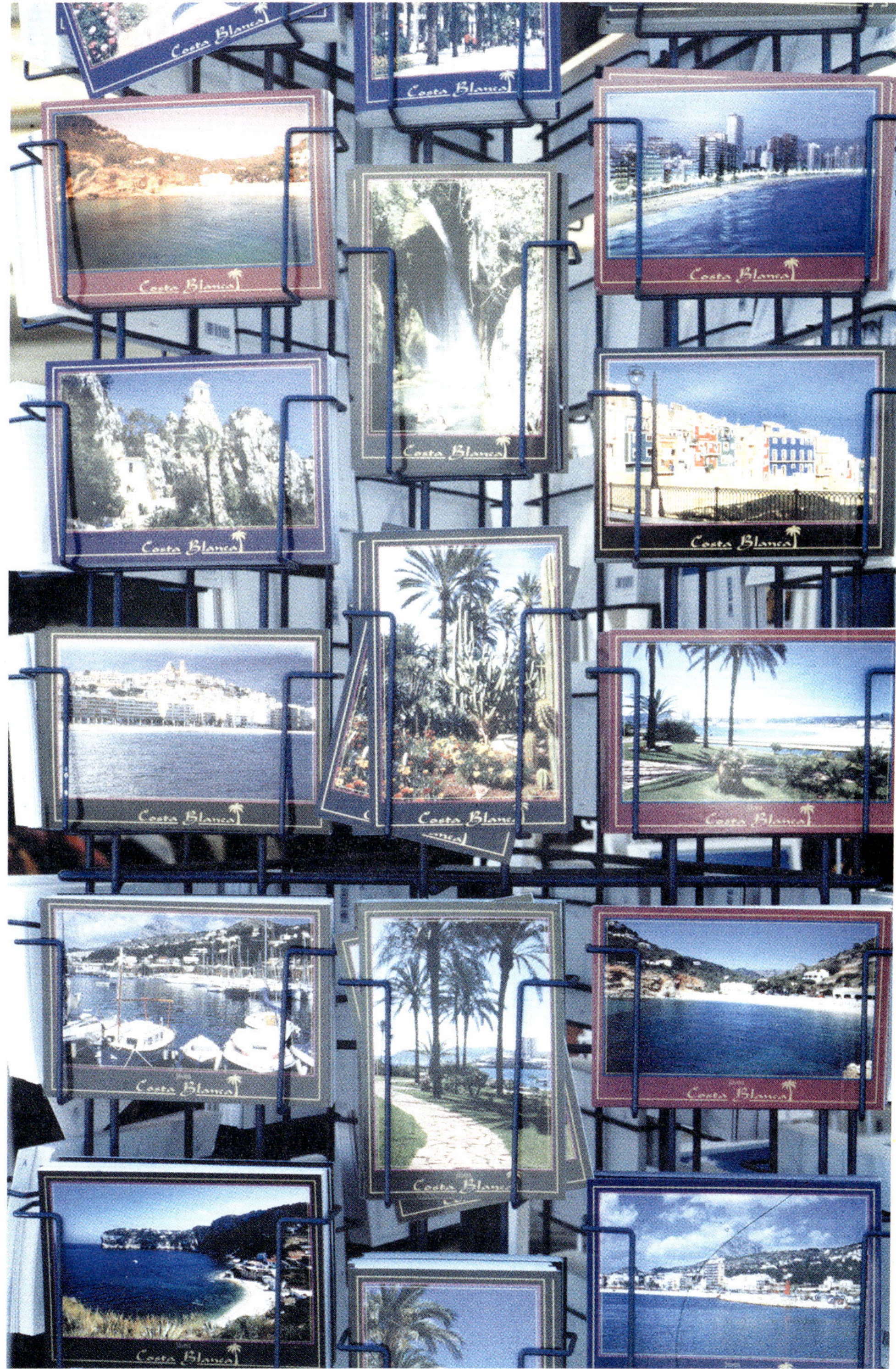

Plate 3 'Postcard Rack, Costa Blanca, Spain', 1996.

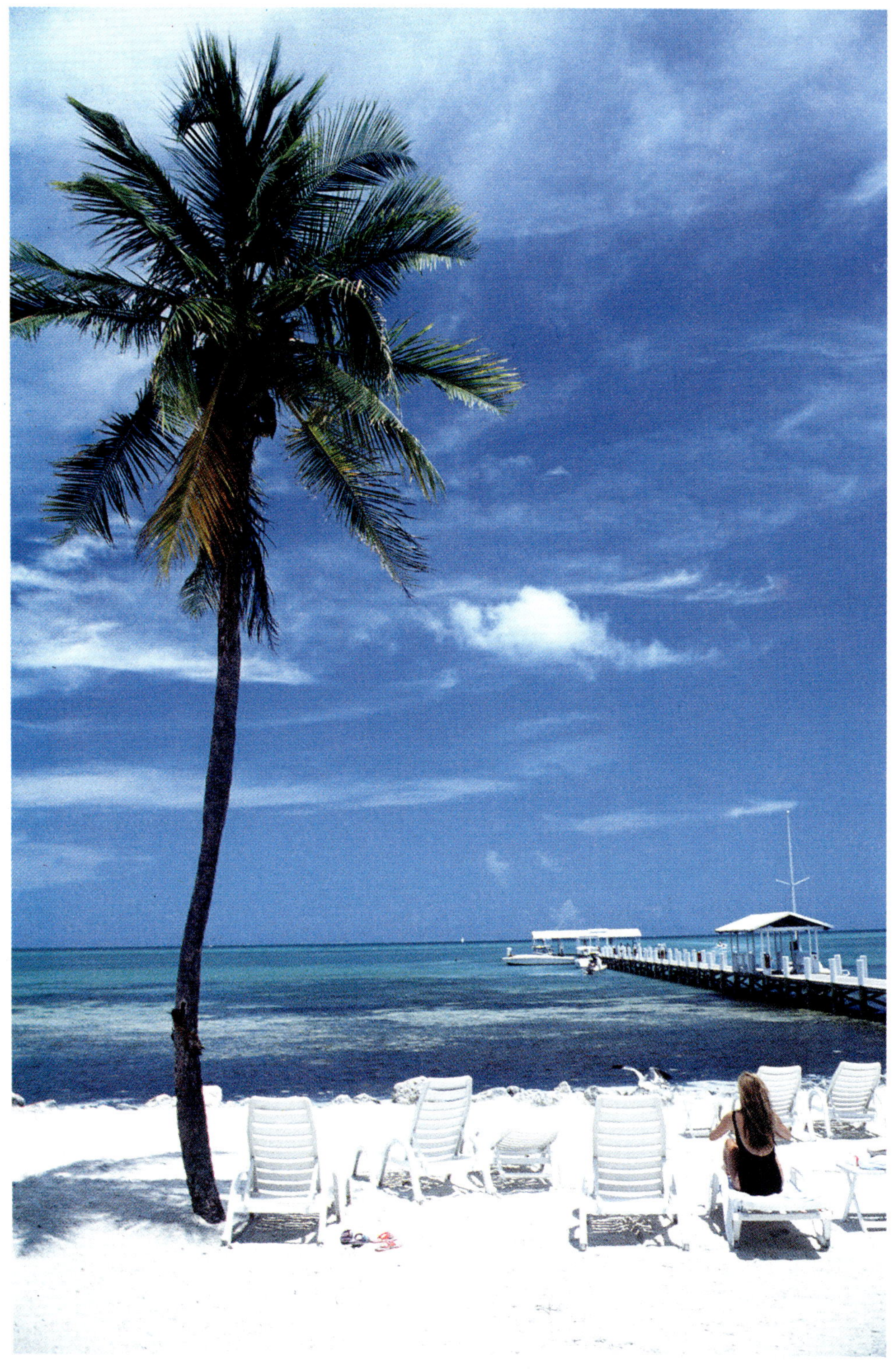

Plate 4 Mark Read, 'Isla Morada, Florida', holiday promotion, 1990s.

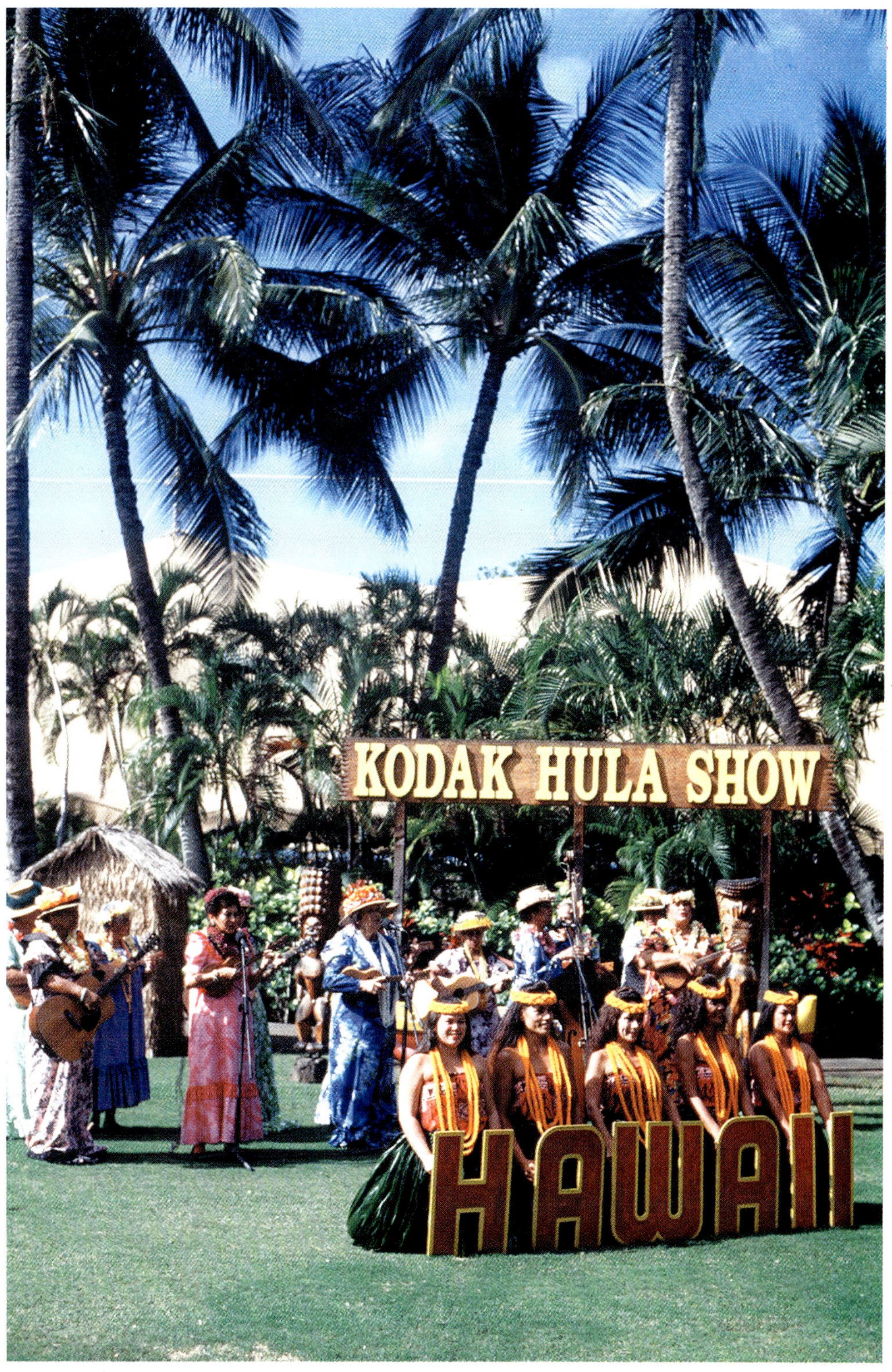

Plate 5 Mark Read, 'Kodak Hula Show, Hawaii', holiday promotion, 1990s.

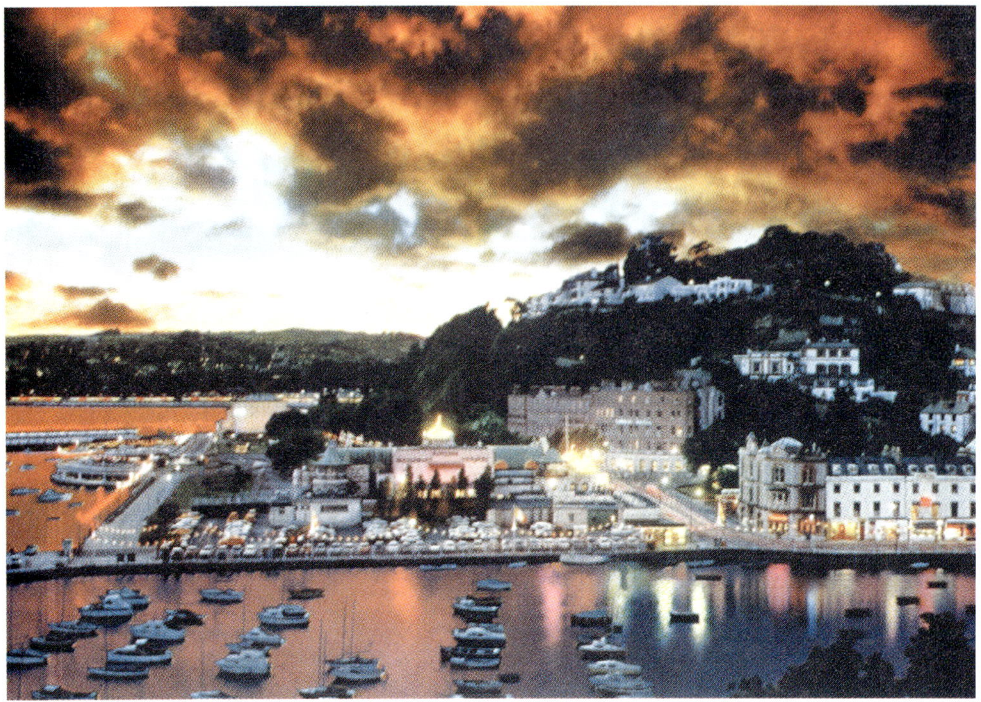

Plate 6 E. Nägele/John Hinde Studios, 'Twilight over Torquay Harbour, South Devon', 1960s.

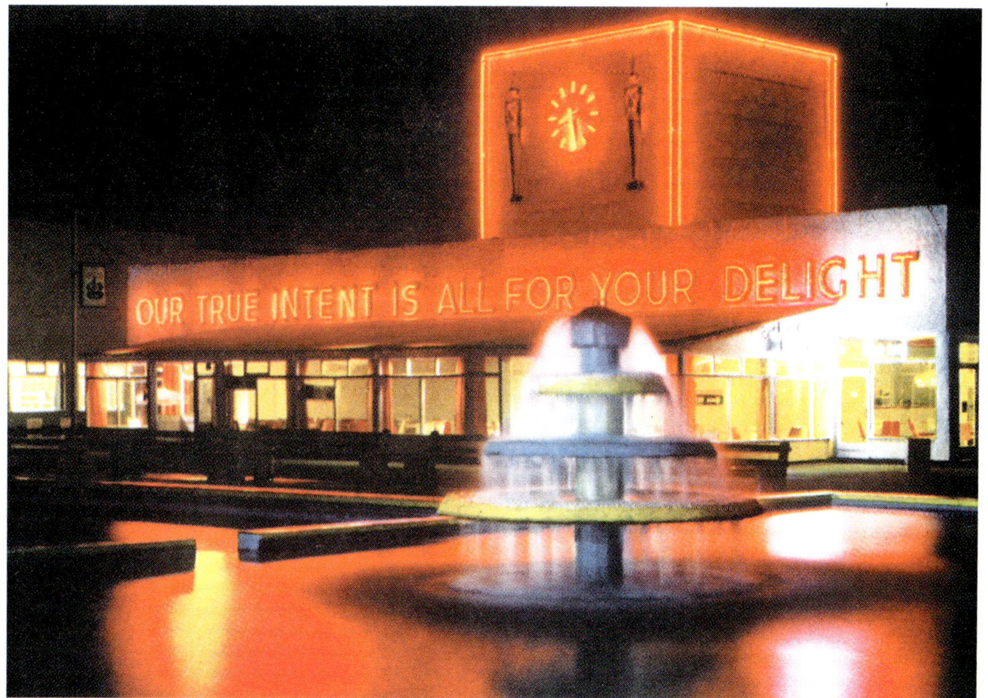

Plate 7 E. Ludwig/John Hinde Studios, 'Butlins', 1960s.

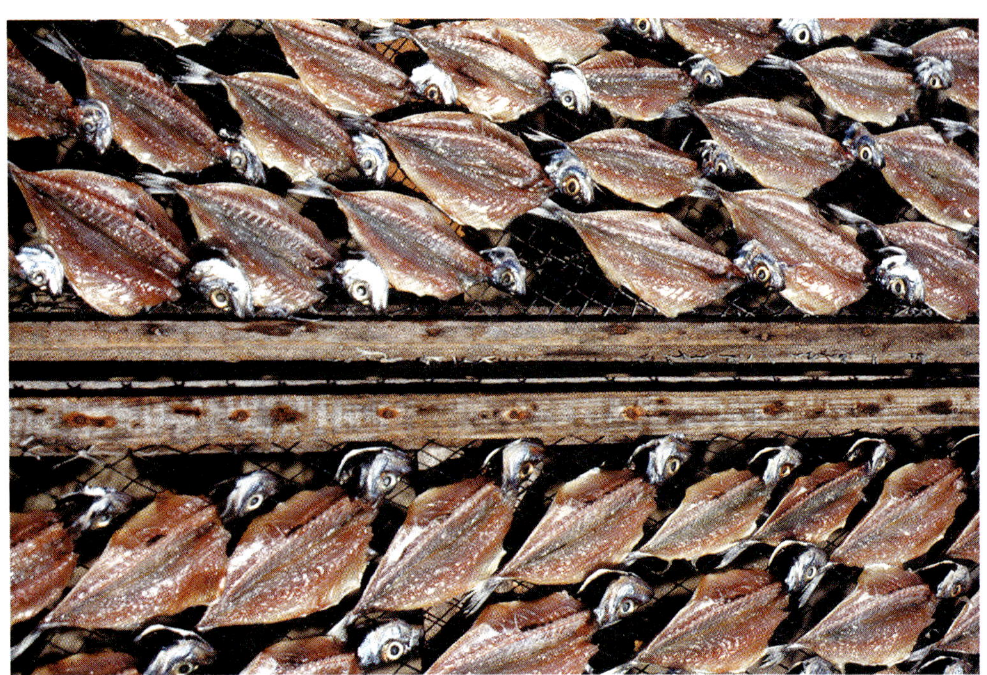

Plate 8 Mark Read, 'Fish Pattern', holiday promotion, 1990s.

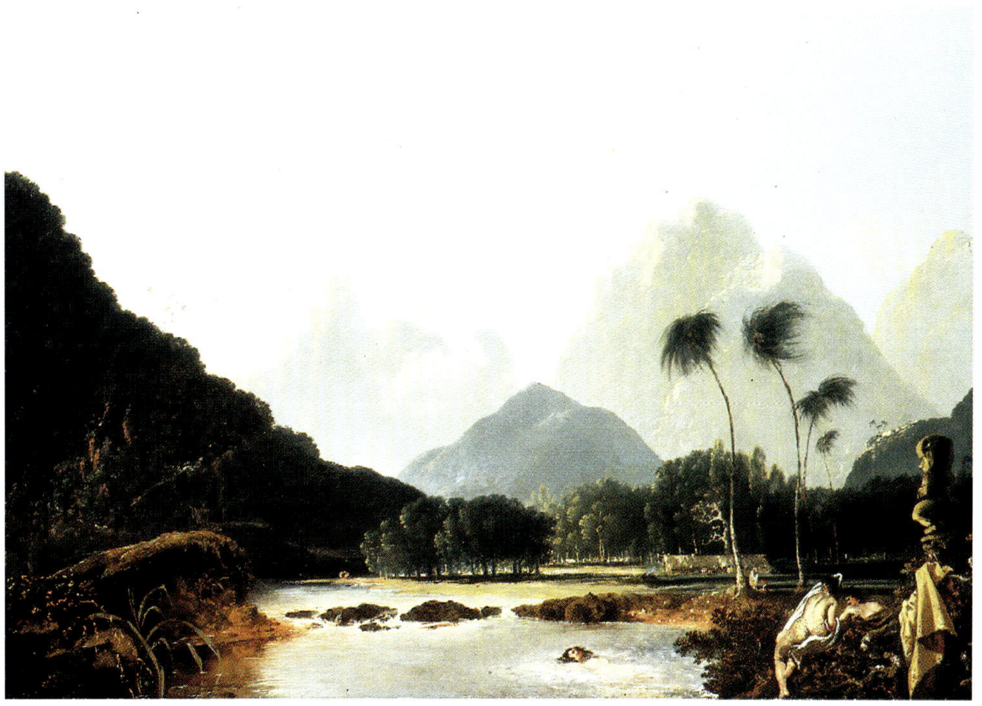

Plate 9 William Hodges, *Oateipeha Bay, Tahiti* or *Tahiti Revisited* (oil on canvas), 1776. National Maritime Museum, Greenwich.

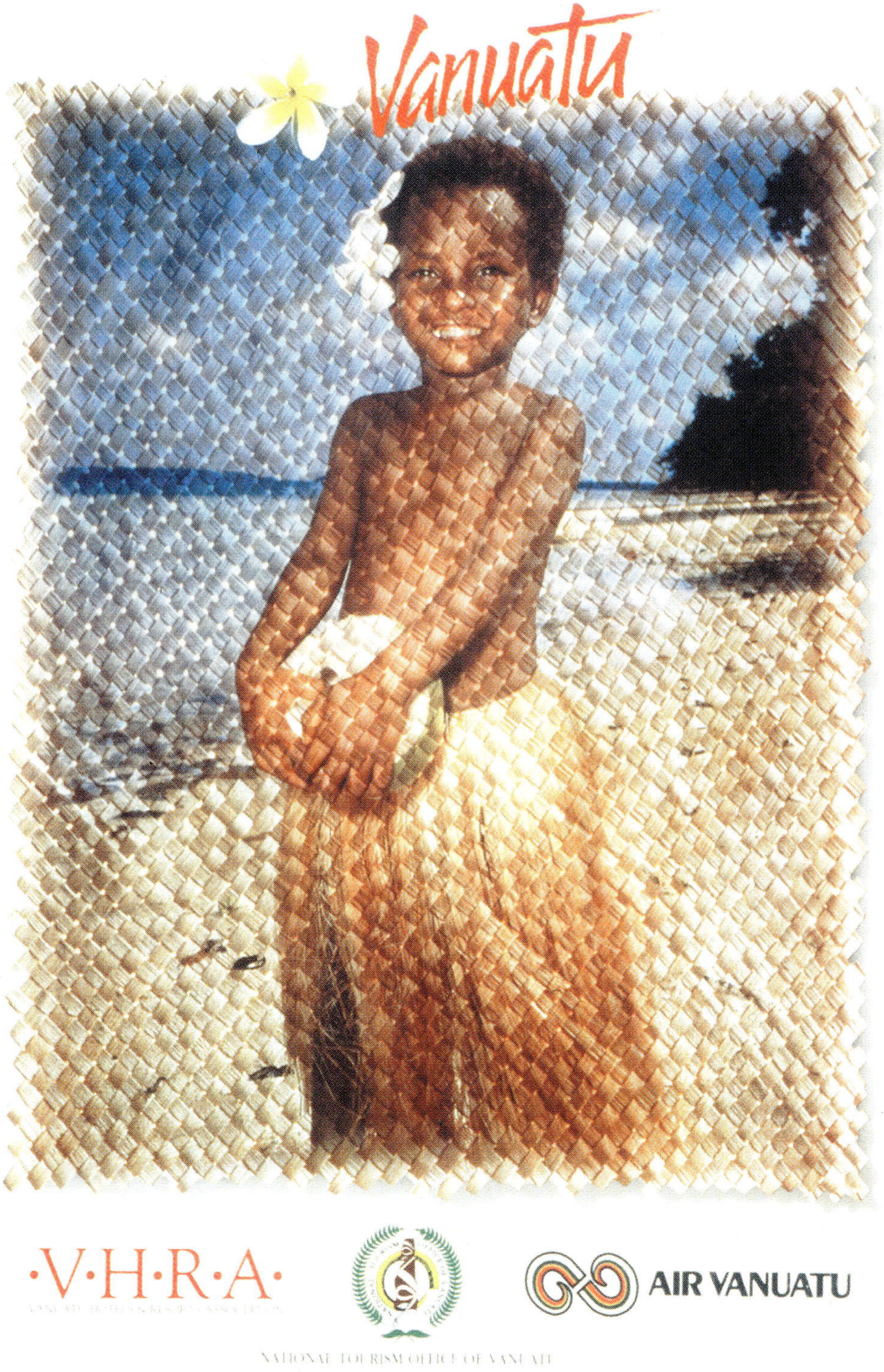

Vanuatu

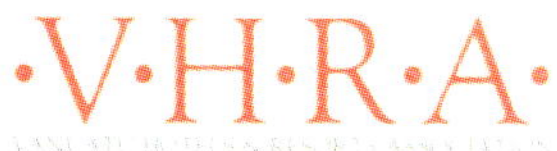

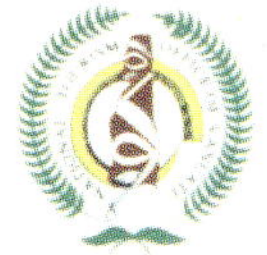

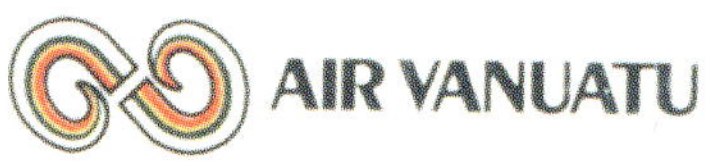

Plate 10 'The Untouched Paradise', promotion for Vanuatu, 1994.

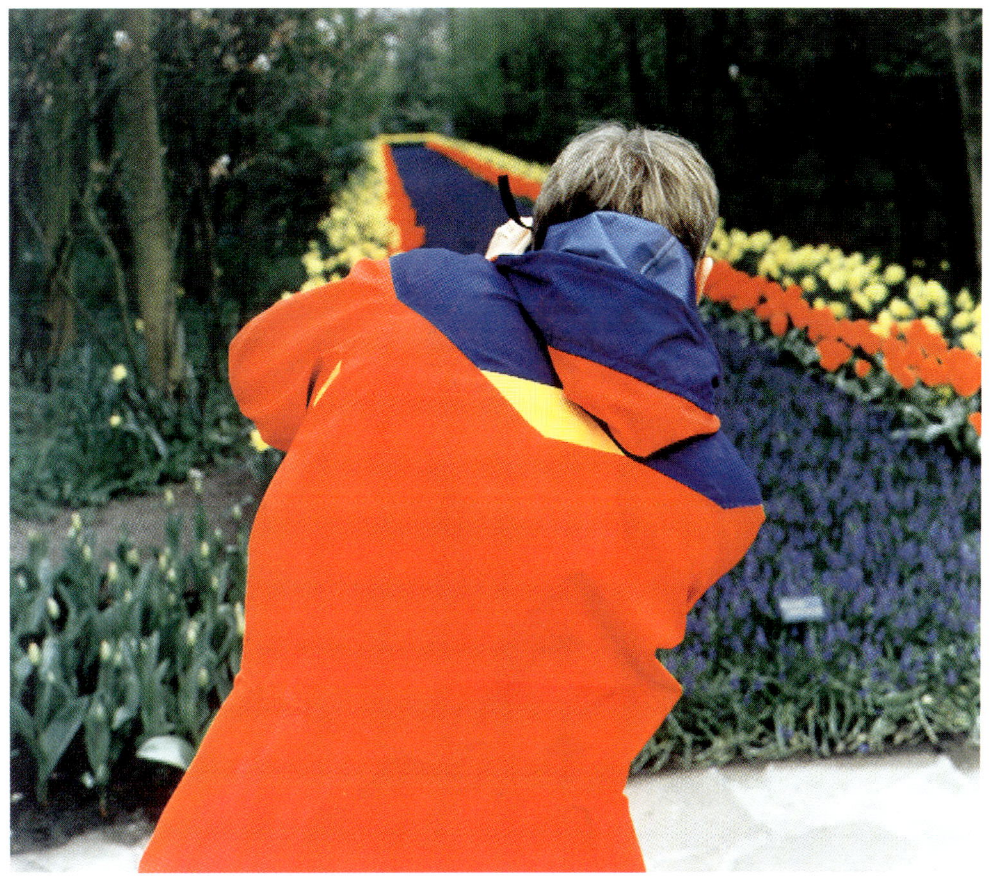

Plate 11 Martin Parr (Magnum), 'Keukenhof Gardens, Holland'. From *Small World*, 1995.

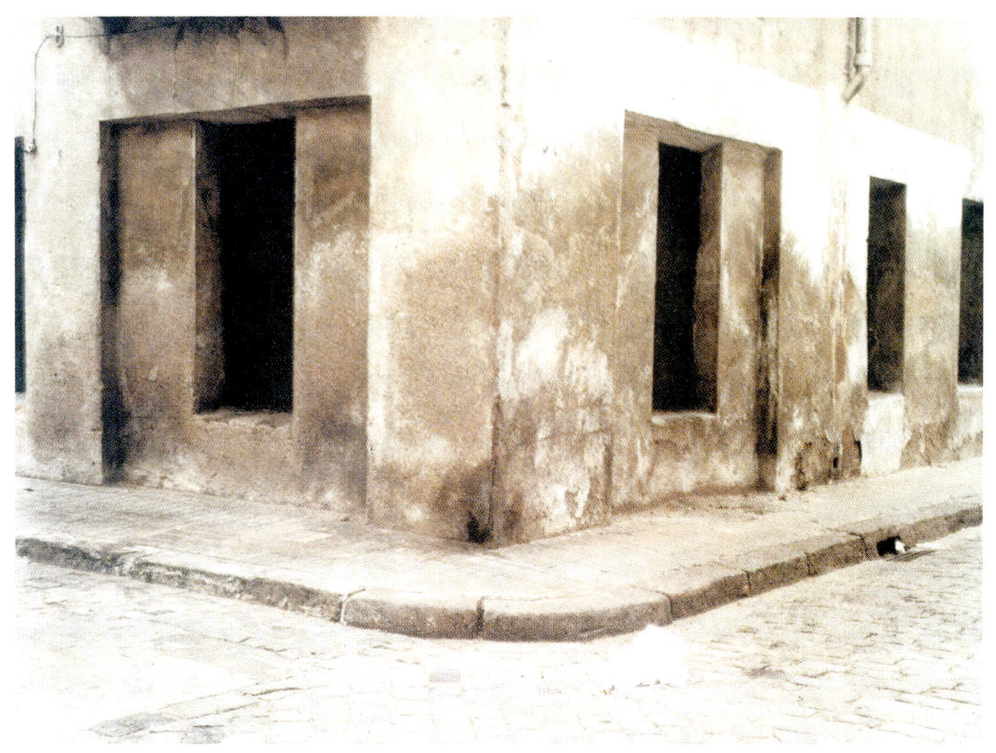

Plate 12 Humberto Rivas, 'Barcelona', 1987.

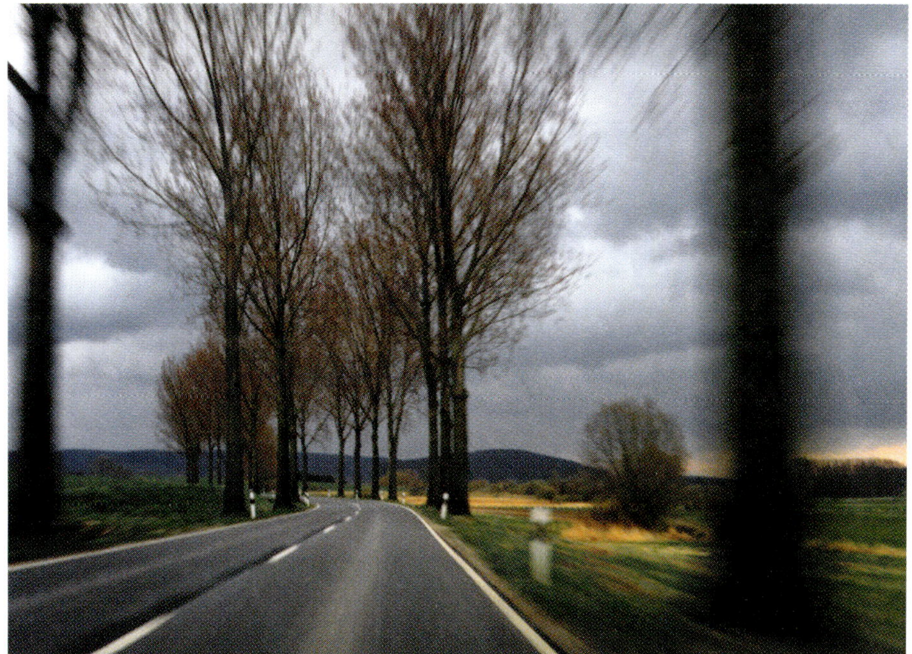

Plate 13 Jörge Sasse '5502, 1996', 1996.

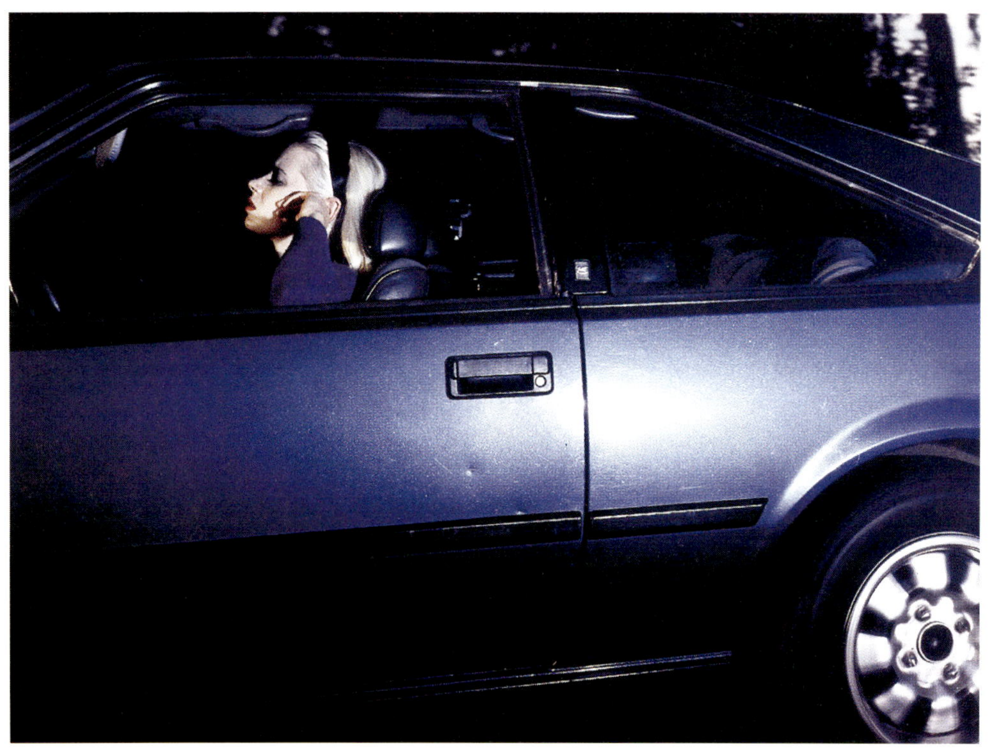

Plate 14 Andrew Bush, 'Woman Gliding Southeast at 68 mph on Highway 101 near Santa Barbara, California at 4.39 pm. Sometime in March 1990 (Listening to the Silence)', 1990.

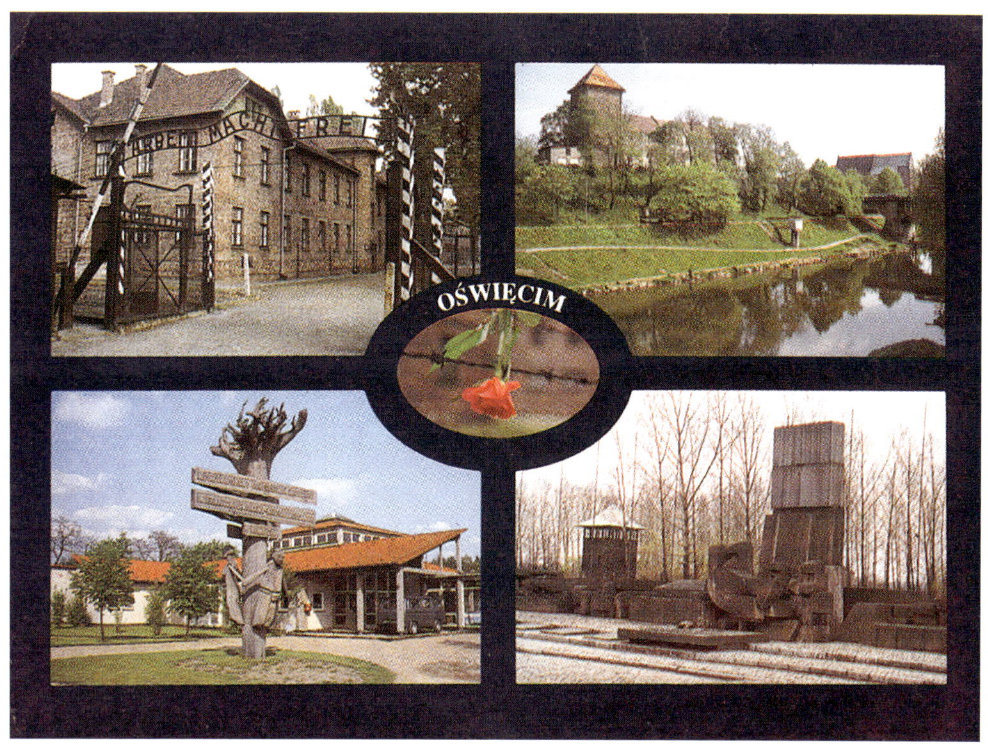

Plate 15 'Oswiecim' (Auschwitz postçard), 1994.

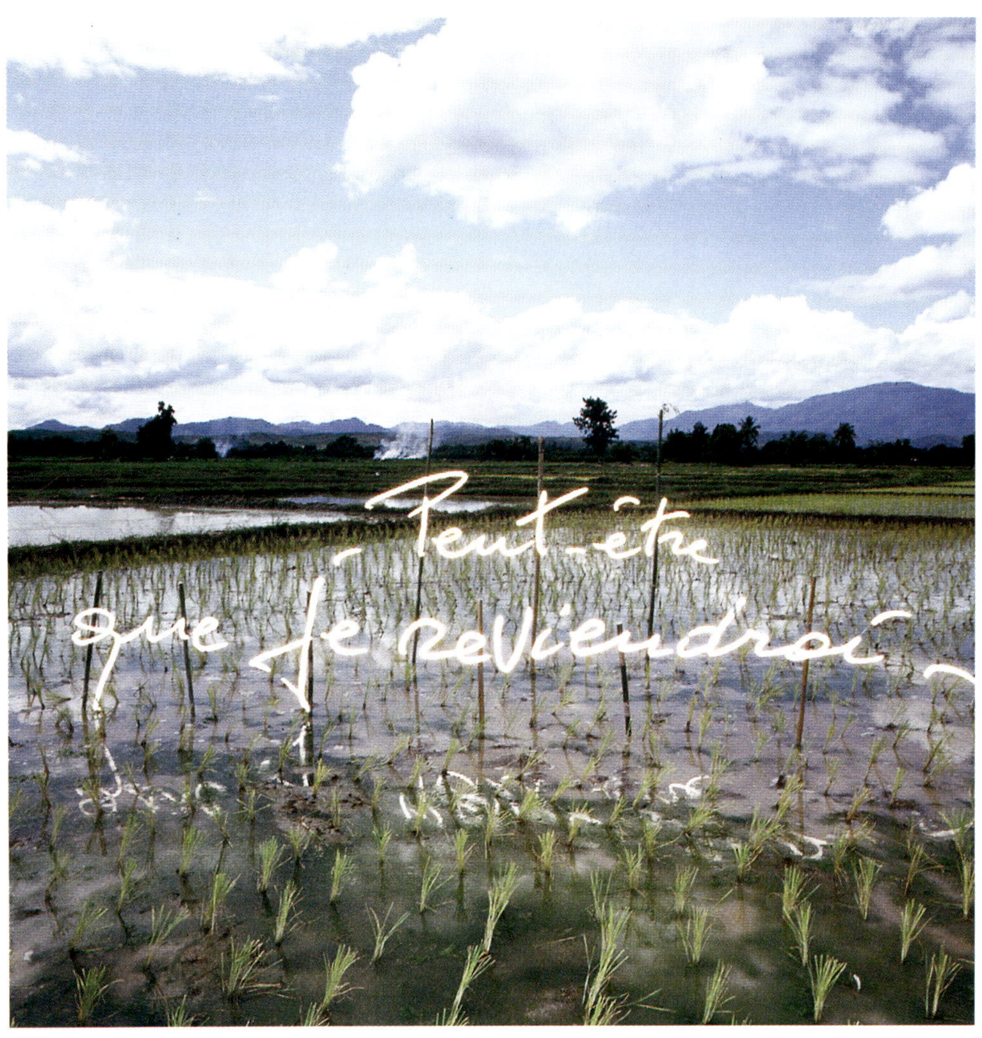

Plate 16 Bernard Faucon, 'Peut-être que je reviendrai'. From *Les Écritures 1991–93*.

gesture. His meal, he declares, had attained a 'higher dimension' than the first:

> The first banquet was an event, but the second was a commemoration and ... I wish for nothing but sacred meals. Sacred, yes, for the sacred only exists through repetition, and it gains in distinction with every repetition. (Tournier 1992: 192)

The caliph then appoints both cooks, understanding that they are equal because the sacred and thus the paradisal, the primary and perfect form, is born through the copy.

More radically, the paradisal can be found in tourism when it is at its most artificial, when its images and spectacles are the most processed, contingent and impermanent. Its refusal to be accountable to the laws of nature, the codes of realism, or to follow social imperatives represents a freedom from mastery, from the ends of others, a liberation from utility or practical application. Here *Les Enfants du paradis* have been supplanted by '*Les Enfants de la parodie*'.

Recalling the pleasure Barthes reported experiencing in Japan, as he moved unencumbered by the responsibility of meaning among the ideograms and suspirations of a language outside his competence, tourists who can celebrate the arbitrariness of tourism's fabrications disdain the attempt to fix the representation to the real (Barthes 1984). They can play among the holiday world's events, unburdened by any secure meaning or ultimate purpose, responsible for their own pleasures and interpretations.

And yet, as argued earlier, only a minority of tourists appear content to swim among tourism's bobbing signifiers, or to accept its causeless imagery without the need to establish their value. Most continue to seek, at some point in their journey, the secure ground of the real and the authentic – the hallmarks of tourism's other kind of paradise. Against its own show of play and artifice, tourism comes bearing the counter-gifts of certainty and authenticity. It offers a world experienced without intermediaries – the present of 'presence' in which desire is resolved into its object; perception into its stimulus; the sign equated with its referent. The physical and sensuous delights in which tourism implicates its clients – the feel of the warm sun on the body, the surf on the skin, the replayable beauty of the sunrise, the ecstasies of culture, the unrehearsed hospitality of hosts – return them to a supposedly lost world of connection. It is a world of touching and of being touched, which has a close kinship with our more general notions of paradise as a primal unity. Romanticism's roots are visible here, but accompanied by yearnings whose traditions long predate it.

Several of Martin Parr's photographs show tourists mimicking or otherwise mirroring the forms or colours of the object of their visit, as if by taking on its qualities they might heal the rupture between themselves and the world. Plainly, the devout pilgrims shown by Parr immersing themselves in the waters of the Sea of Galilee are engaged in a recognisable ritual of conjunction with the sacred. But the more casual and secular tourist in Parr's images seems equally prone to something similar. People pose pretending to hold up the Tower of Pisa. Others, in gestures resembling those of adulation, raise their hands to imitate the shape of the Matterhorn. In the Alps a woman clutches a bunch of Alpine flowers which by chance matches the colours of her dress. And, most surprisingly, a tourist photographs Dutch tulips clad in an anorak whose colours synchronise almost exactly with the colours and even the pattern of the flower beds. The loving click of the shutter completes the congress of photographer and photographed (plate 11).

The photograph's art of resemblance and the photographer's presence at its production make possible the ritual of fusion. They bring to mind Frazer's laws of magic: the law of similarity, under which desired effects can be brought about by imitation; and the law of contagion by which they can be produced through touching or close proximity (Frazer 1993: chapter 3, sections 1–3). The photograph, traditionally evidence of the photographer's past proximity to an object and the transference of the proximity to a viewer, imitates its object by being touched by its light. 'The visible caresses the eye', Levinas has written, 'one sees and hears like one touches' (quoted in Davies in Levin 1993: 256).

A tour-guide once told me that in his experience tourists almost invariably feel compelled to photograph the attraction within the very first moments of their arrival before it, hoping, he believed, to fix it while it still retains the charge of its first uncanny presence, before their wonder in front of the prodigiously familiar begins to fade.

Here, the photograph's function as visual record is secondary to its role in establishing the viewer's connection with it. The act of photographing has become an act necessary to the tourist's engagement with the moment when the fabulous object registers itself on the body and emotions of the visitor as a shock of recognition – and of transcendence. In such moments one seems for an instant to break through from the everyday into the timeless, from the world of perceivable phenomena into an empyrean of unchanging forms to which all attractions seem to half belong. As the inadequate trace of such a moment the actual photograph is of supplementary importance – the proof of the instant perhaps, still a memento no doubt – but a frequently incompetent documentation of what anyway is not entirely visible.

Having taken the first snaps, adds my tour-guide, most will then move directly on to the little allegories and idealising icons in the postcard rack.

Making connections and the bestowing of 'presence' are made possible by the supremacy in the tourist system of visual experience assumed to be a mode of direct and natural perception with photography as its neutral extension. Tourism promotes a mode of perception which is dematerialised, free of the flaws of transmission and the displacements of translation. By doing this tourism is able to deliver not only the pleasures of the edenic but also something of its epistemological simplicity. Empiricism typically persuades itself that knowledge can be based primarily on observation, especially visual observation. As MacCannell notes, tourism does just this. Rather than understanding or the sharing of other tongues, it expects sights. It promotes experience above comprehension, seeing over hearing (MacCannell 1976: 63–70). Tourism is empiricist heaven, and blissfully the tourist wanders there, Empiricist Royale – wide-eyed and, of course, speechless with wonder.

From the Renaissance's optical-traveller onwards, an equation has been made between individual autonomy and immediate visual experience. It has become part of the calculation in which the figure of the free modern Western individual has been computed.

There are compelling links with the foundation of our more recent modernity in the North American imaginary. There is, for instance, the image of pure seeing that Ralph Waldo Emerson draws in his essay *Nature* where he portrays it as a disembodied, 'transparent eyeball' floating, unimpeded by thought, history or social reality, through a mythically empty New World wilderness, the American paradise, already cleared, presumably, of indigenous human impediments. In his image, world and vision are born again at the beginning, each imparting to the other its edenic innocence.

Commenting on Emerson's essay, the critic James Wood writes how:

> America is thus seen as space in which the pioneers create themselves and the land anew; for the intellectual or the intellectual-traveller, it is a place to feed on cognitive novelties. But much depends on the power of the eyeball. (Wood 1995)

America, a world and a set of hopes and promises and the condition we now inhabit, was born and must be rediscovered in the eye.

By assigning a crucial position to this kind of visual experience, tourism dresses its often manipulative confections in the clothing of a non-partisan, disinterested naturalism. And, populist that it is, it concurs with every tourist's sense of reality, catering above all for his or her desire to be free of work of any kind. The modality of the visible, being ineluctable, requires no effort. In this way, tourism also once again flatters its clients, attributes effectivity to them. If seeing takes place beyond interpretation then whatever the tourist sees is valid. In tourism's mode of visual representation pure objectivity somehow makes itself compatible with the entirely subjective. To Crick's characterisation of tourism as 'Sun, Sex, Sights, Savings and Servility', one might add, 'Solipsism' (Crick 1984: 37–76). However, it is important to bear in mind that the solipsism is collective, corporate even, and that what a tourist encounters is a world already reorganised and visualised *by* tourism. In the same moment the tourist is confirmed in both the effectiveness of his or her individual perceptions and yet reassured by the discovery that they coincide with those of fellow-travellers.

But more than merely being a place where desires are gratified, tourism's paradise, in the words of Jacques Rancière, 'fulfils ... the wish of seeing things and people identical to their concept' (Rancière in Robertson et al. 1994: 35). Tourism utters its paradise into being through what George Steiner has called an

'Edenic semantics', a 'concurrence between word and object which marked language before the fall, and before the malediction of mutual incomprehensibility at Babel' (Steiner 1971: 84). Language is brought magically into the condition of divine knowledge – transparent, immediate, all-comprehending. To achieve this is to be released from something essential in the fallen human condition.

In his study of purblind artists and writers Patrick Trevor-Roper cites an ancient Egyptian creation myth which had the gods and humans being born from the head of a primary deity, the proto-God, Ptah. Humankind emerged out of the mouth, the place of language; whereas the gods were delivered, like Thoreau's America, through the eyes (Trevor-Roper 1990: 152). The creature of language, humankind cannot quite resolve comprehension and perception of the world. The world as experienced by humans must forever be deferred in interpretation, caught up in the riot and confusion of tongues, masked and delayed in representation. If paradise is an estate where things reveal themselves as they are, then those bad apples, language and writing expel us from it. It's not only tourists and the mystically minded who fear and mistrust language, especially when scripted. Following Derrida, some detect even in Lévi-Strauss a residual idealism when he expresses regret over the ruin of the natural integrities and innocence in tribal societies at the hand of writing, 'in its deferral of meaning, its undoing of the Rousseauist ideal of the community of individuals self-present to each other, it is also the loss of the reciprocal *gaze* as a form of "authentic" communicative exchange' (Arshi et al. in Robertson et al. 1994: 232).

In Eden, not only do the world and the Other have familiar faces, faces acquainted with our own, they are addressed in one universal language, a condition which Descartes thought would be indeed an 'earthly paradise' (Eco 1997: 218). Perhaps tourism with its smiling *communitas*, its planet-wide park of attractions and with, above all, its natural, transparent and therefore universal language of visual signs, has become the purveyor of that condition.

In a culture where the language of the visual continues to dominate so many of our descriptions of truth, proof and authentic experience, photographic representation retains much of its power to reassure. For many it remains the medium which supposedly bears, even bears out, an empiricism which leaves both viewers and their objects unquestioned (Jay in ICA 1986: 20–1). In this way, tourism's client and product, the traditional human subject, is able to lie in the cradle of the visual; secure there, centred and in command, at the core, at the root of its seeing, its pleasure – its paradise.

Note

1 This belief is present in André Bazin's Jansenist conception of photography and film which sees in them the means of restoring the immediate connection with God's world forfeited at the Fall.

Part IV

Twentieth-century trails

8
Neither here nor there: photographers, exiles, the faces of strangers

> Exiles light a candle
> to the Gods of place.
> (Tom Paulin, *The Other Voice*)

> The proximity of the Other is the face's meaning ... the Other becomes my neighbour precisely through the way the face summons me, calls for me, begs for me, and in so doing recalls my responsibility and calls me into question. (Emmanuel Levinas, *Ethics as First Philosophy*)

> The photographer followed the caravan on his bicycle, but never catching up as if he were going to a different festival. (Gabriel García Márquez, *Innocent Eréndira*)

Given its part in modernity's cultures with their troubled energies and agents, it should come as no surprise that photography has attracted so many exiles and emigrés into the ranks of its practitioners. Linked from its birth with professional wandering it is one of what Simmel called the 'intermediary trades', those followed typically by strangers (Simmel 1950: 401). The itinerant photographer was a common figure in the nineteenth century when smaller towns and villages rarely had fixed photographic premises. They were a feature too of seasonal and marginal events such as circuses, fairs and races – events which, like cameras, folded up and moved on. The photographer remained a travelling outsider as the medium spread into the regions beyond the metropolitan countries. Most of the early photographers of Latin America, for example, were European or North American.

But aspects of photography's own nature easily dispose it to the expression and documentation not only of dislocation but of the more profoundly uprooting and transforming condition of exile. As its statements require interpretation rather than translation, and as its evident physical mobility is almost matched by the ease with which it appears to cross cultural borders, photography is the obvious medium for those who must do the same. The fleeting, discontinuous, notational, at times provisional nature of its representations can be matched with characteristics of exile. Both intensify perceptions of the world, rendering it at once more real and more strange. And in their preoccupation with remembrance and the experience of absence, both

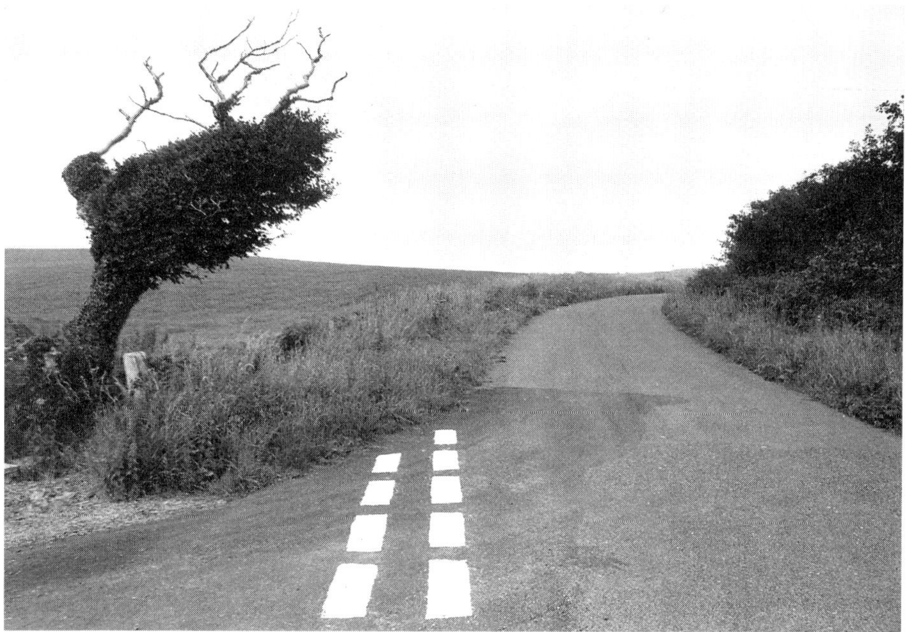

Fig. 34 Josef Koudelka (Magnum), 'England', 1978.

are associated with melancholy. Michel de Certeau maintains that *all* travel based in what he calls the, 'speculative experience of the world' is burdened with the quality of melancholy he finds in Dürer's famous engraving of the condition. It depicted, he writes, 'being outside of [these] things that stay there, detached and absolute, that leave us without having anything to do with the departure themselves: being deprived of them, surprised by their ephemeral and quiet strangeness. Astonishment and abandonment' (Certeau 1984: 111–12).

For the exile this melancholy of the traveller is compounded by the endless recall of what cannot be retrieved. It is mirrored in certain of photography's effects. In the photograph things that are gone are *still there*. We cannot live in them, cannot touch them; but we are fixed on them, unable and unwilling to renounce them. The photograph traces both our possession and our loss; it offers us access to things and bars them from us. Think of the portrayal of absence in the work of the Argentinian photographer Humberto Rivas. His empty streets and deserted rooms haunted by departures seem to picture the Spanish phrase, '*Lo noto como ido*', 'I note you as though you have gone' (plate 12).

The evidence for this is admittedly anecdotal, but photography's kinship with exile might explain the charm it appears to hold for melancholy types. An experienced student counsellor in a college teaching a range of media practice courses confided to me that of all groups it was the photographers who were by far the most prone to isolation, depression and suicidal feelings: 'All those hours alone in the dark room – cause or symptom?' she wondered.

> I sleep badly in strangers' homes
> and my own life is not near me.
> (Osip Mandelstam, *The Veronezh Notebooks*)

'Anyone', writes Edward Said, 'prevented from returning home is an exile' (Said in Ferguson et al. 1990: 362). In its most common form exile is the involuntary displacement from home or country resulting in a sense of loss and a condition of estrangement. It preoccupies our time, the era, maintains Said, 'of the refugee, the displaced person, mass immigration' (Said in Ferguson et al. 1990: 362). Clearly as a material reality exile is overwhelming. According to Amnesty International, worldwide in 1997 there were about fifteen million refugees and a further twenty million in internal exile (*Amnesty*, March/April 1997, issue 82: 4). And this is not to cite the many millions of economic emigrants and migrants moving across the world.

But the meanings attached to exile go beyond the measurement of social fact. For many it has become the defining dramatic situation and the grand metaphor of the kind of being-in-the-world that modernity has brought about.

Said identifies four distinct but related kinds of dislocation in the contemporary world. Exile itself, which he says 'originated in ... banishment'. 'Once banished', he writes, the Exile 'lives an anomalous and miserable life, with the stigma of being an outsider'. Then there is the Refugee, whose situation is linked to the politics of the modern state. Where the Exile connotes 'a touch of solitude and spirituality', the Refugee summons up the phenomenon of crowds of displaced persons. Next there is Expatriation, which is voluntary and often associated with writers and artists. They may 'share in the solitude and estrangement of exile, but they do not suffer under its rigid proscriptions'. Finally there are the Emigrés and their situation, who may share some of the Exile's uprootedness and nostalgia but their presence in a new country can be voluntary and in many instances (such as European settlers in Africa or Asia) their energies are consumed in the creation of the new identities in the nations they are inventing, which are often simulations of the old (Said in Ferguson et al. 1990: 362–3).

Said's distinctions are useful in recognising the precise motivational and situational features of displacement. In the realm of aesthetic practice they help the understanding of different responses and will be active in my discussion of work by a number of photographers positioned quite differently in terms of their relationship to exile. Although these photographers' angles of refraction into exile's substance will each measure differently, all share the understanding that the challenge of representing exile is the challenge to representation itself. For exile increases the drive for representation and at the same time reminds us of the inadequacy of all representations. A characteristic of migrants, says Salman Rushdie, is to live 'more comfortably in images, in ideas, than in places' (Rushdie 1992: 280). Exiles must hold in thought and mimesis the place they left lest it disappear and they with it. Without the space in which the self is housed, identity must be forever called back into existence, re-established in the spaces of memory and nostalgic colloquy, in the spaces of song and writing, of ritual and image. The lack of actual place is filled by a location in representation. 'It is only in the absence of the original', writes Douglas Crimp, 'that representation may take place' (Crimp 1981: 98). But, as the representations that exiles make ultimately confirm their sense of loss, they are a sort of failure.

Exile, then, is a condition which demands representation while questioning its value. For this reason aesthetic work attempting to respond to the condition faces serious challenges. However, the most interesting photography of exile turns the situation to its advantage by using such challenges as its subject matter. It does this, above all, in two ways: first, by foregrounding the subject of photographic representation itself; and second, by placing the question of what constitutes the spatial conditions of exile – the question of so-called exilic space – at the centre of its concerns. I will begin with some reflections on the question of space.

All of exile's manifestations involve a crisis in the experience and representation of space and its meanings. The violence which commonly accompanies exile is in part a spatial violence. In his essay 'Paranoiac Space' Victor Burgin quotes Elizabeth Grosz: 'It is our positioning within space, both as the point of perspectival access to space, but also as an object for others in space, that gives the subject any coherent identity' (in Taylor 1994: 236). Enforced exile seeks to murder identity by demolishing this 'positioning within space'. It destroys the *where* of self, that ecology of self and other, of objects, events and settings and the meanings and recollections that resonate through and between them. 'To emigrate', writes John Berger, 'is always to dismantle the centre of the world, and so to move into a lost, disoriented one of fragments' (Berger 1984: 57). In denying people their rights or claims to be in a specified space, exile excludes them from their own identity. Historically, following the violent exodus of whole groups, their vacated spaces are renamed, re-mapped, their traces erased. This leaves exiles with neither place of return nor of departure. In a sense their existence has become a non-possibility, for all points in space on which memory is anchored, through which the lines of a life's narrative are threaded, have vanished. Not only have the exiles' claims on a place in reality been denied, their access to the processes in which human identity is made has been blocked. To be deprived of one's space is to be deprived of the right of memory and thus of the right to selfhood.

The consciousness brought into being by these conditions exists, on one hand, in a vertigo of placelessness and near-solipsistic identification with the lost home and culture and, on the other, in a highly self-conscious, even disinterested state, having been forced to see identity, nation and space as processes, even as fictions. It is a mind as much self-distant as self-absorbed. It must live in at least two places at once: in the country of *is* and in the land of *was*. For the exile, the unity of 'nearness and distance' which Simmel found to feature in all human relations is ruptured and turned around so that the what feels closest is what is most distant, and what feels most remote is what is at hand (Simmel 1950: 402).

Most of the work I will be discussing is by photographers who are no strangers to exile. For that reason all have been familiar with the problems peculiar to its representation: how to record the content of an emptiness, how to visualise disappearance; how to give some formal coherence to the fragmentary, the incommensurable? How to objectify in the lens something which is more existential than optical; how to totalise a condition of radical incompleteness? How can one make sense of exile when speaking its fragmented speech, see a world that has grown unrecognisable?

As suggested earlier, the general response of the photographer of exile is to make sceptical use of the formal and metaphorical potential of the medium. Art generates form out of negation. It makes a second world out of the debris of the one that's been lost; one 'recuperated on a higher level of vividness and presence' as Czeslaw Milosz puts it in his introduction to Koudelka's *Exiles*. To lose a world is to become aware of the artificiality and relative nature of all worlds; is to experience their fragility, their transience.

Where talent and opportunity exist, the consequences of exile offer creative possibilities. The migrant, says Salman Rushdie, deprived of the normal components of identity (such as roots, language and social norms) is 'obliged to find new ways of describing himself, new ways of being human' (Rushdie 1992: 278). And I would add to this, new ways of seeing. The equally creative and disintegrative effects of exile reflect the antonyms which contribute to its Greek roots: one signifying disembowelling, pulling apart, the other exultation (Papastergiadis 1993). In his reflections Said reminds us that typical exiles are 'the uncountable masses for whom UN agencies have been created ... the refugee-peasants with no prospect of ever returning home' (Said in Ferguson et al. 1990: 359). He also reserves space among them to speak of the energising possibilities for seeing and making the world anew that the ruin of normality hands to the few who can take them:

> Seeing the 'entire world as a foreign land' makes possible originality of vision. Most people are principally aware of one culture, one setting, one home: Exiles are aware of at least two, and this plurality of vision gives rise to an awareness of simultaneous dimensions, an awareness that – to borrow a phrase from music – is *contrapuntal*. (Said in Ferguson et al. 1990: 366)

The photographer Mari Mahr, Hungarian by ancestry, Chilean by birth, British by residence, describes estrangement as 'the curse of the expatriate'. At the same time she identifies her expatriate's insecurity as the spur for the rule breaking and experimentation that, along with its concern with fiction and memory, distinguishes her work (Mahr 1989: 9–17).

For photographers such as Mahr 'making strange' becomes the unavoidable aesthetic response to an estranging experience. Only a familiar world can be conveyed in familiar forms. Exiles experience the world as a bad translation, its meanings misshapen, its phenomena like structureless events – *paroles* without *langue*, speech without grammar. Shared by all attempts to represent exile is the problem of representing something without the familiar contours of presence. For this reason the use of metaphor often figures strongly in such projects.

With its origins in Greek words meaning *carrying*, *transferring*, *transporting*, the metaphor is clearly a sympathetic linguistic figure for exile. The metaphor uncovers the qualities of one thing by shifting our attention to another. This displacement of meaning, this 'defamiliarisation', suggests a consonance between metaphor and migration's actual estrangements. Salman Rushdie makes much of this:

> The very word *Metaphor*, with its roots in the Greek word for bearing across, describes a sort of migration, the migration of ideas into images. Migrants – borne across humans – are metaphorical beings in their very essence. (Rushdie 1992: 278–9)

In his study of John Berger and strangerhood, Nikos Papastergiadis sees the same correspondence between these spatial shifts and transformations in the meanings and aesthetic effects of language. Exile should be considered, he argues, as a 'metaphor for the act of interpretation – as well as the journey from the familiar to the foreign' (Papastergiadis 1993: 10).

According to this view, although the in-between spaces of exile and metaphor may break up lives and sense, they are also the places where meaning and cultural practice are brokered through translation and interpretation – projects devoted in part at least to establishing equivalents and continuities, but always open to mistrust and uncertainty.

Such oppositions meet in the figure of Hermes, the patron saint of travellers, merchants and interpreters, and at the same time the saint of thieves. Hermes is a trickster figure, a transgressor, shape-shifter and border-crosser who's prepared to use violence to pass from one place, state of being or meaning to another (Kermode 1979: 1–2).

Hermes's transformations tear things up, are types of violence. Equally they are types of re-ordering, the eclipsing of one order by another or the writing of one version over another while retaining the legibility of the earlier inscription, as in the palimpsest. They are the transformations of exile, of translation and metaphorising. It would be apposite to nominate Hermes the god of a particular kind of modern artist, for it's surely not coincidental that so many writers and visual artists whose work in the era of modernism decomposed traditional form and convention, or borrowed and stole elements from inside and outside art for their work, have been exiles or emigrés, or have assumed these roles. Their acts of creative violence on the text, their hostility to monoglossia and suspicion of the stability of meaning and perception, and their engrossment in the materiality, form or language of their medium, echo much of both the anguish and rapture of exile. Some of the photographers featured here can be linked to this tradition. Others challenge it, by extending the representation of exile and migration beyond the agendas of European and North American modernism's cultural elite and yet take into their practice many of its tropes and techniques.

Writing of Koudelka, Max Kozloff notes how 'like so many others, he embraces a proposition worked out by Frank: that photography can encompass an indefinite spread of often small incidents, revealed as the consistent moral illumination of a community by an outsider' (Kozloff 1988: 103). I think this is true not simply because of photography's evident affinity with the transient and fragmentary detail. Koudelka's and Frank's ascriptions of significance to modest objects and events are the moves of the exiled mind acting out of an unsought freedom or from an unfamiliarity with the cultural order and whatever it might class as important, and thereby able to uncover its own instances of meaning.

'In the exilic plot', writes Michael Seidel, 'the extraneous becomes foundational' (quoted in Lawrence 1994: 29). The exiled artist of Western modernity assembles rather than interprets. Put another way, he or she reinterprets the world by re-assembling it from the edge of things and out of the indeterminate drift of strangers, objects and occurrences. In place of the intimate unities, the familiar absolutes of the world now out of reach, the exile has only contingencies to work with. For Richard Rorty freedom lies in 'the recognition of contingency' (Rorty 1989: 26, 46). There is no truth to be found, he insists, already-existing in the 'out there', independent of the human mind (Rorty 1989: 3, 5). While the meaning of pilgrimage and certain kinds of tourism *are* founded on the possibility of reaching such truth, the exile's life is passed in contingency, and the best work of the photographers featured here is fashioned from it. The contingent forms both its substance and subject as it documents the world as founded in a condition of *en passant*. To the discontinuous and unsettled state of exile it gives perceivable form – a visual rhetoric, a point-of-view structure, a spatial drama. But in its indifference to the monumental symmetries of pictorialist landscape or of the humanistic presences of, say, the United States government's Farm Security Administration photographs or *Life* magazine traditions, it refuses to come to rest in the consolation of some notion of stable truth pre-existing in natural forms or in the authenticity of persons. It is the still imagery of ceaseless movement, of uncompleted events unfolding in an irresolute, sceptically observed space. These are exiles' journeys, homeless by definition.

Robert Frank's *The Americans*, published in France in 1958 and in the United States a year later, is routinely proffered as an itinerary of anomic instants culled from the forlorn highways and dispirited urban spaces of the United States in the mid-1950s. The uncommon mix of irony and desolation in its emotional register and the consciously unrefined, rushed quality of its photography, described by Jno Cook as 'careless, off-angled, acompositional, grainy', has encouraged the work to be discussed as preoccupied less with American social reality than with the supposedly non-documentary concerns of photographic style and authorial expression (Cook 1982: 27). The kinds of pressure at large throughout the book's making would appear to support this. Frank's trip was fuelled by Guggenheim money, and art and authorship would have been part of the required cultural return on the Foundation's investment. Additionally a strongly formalist, anti-naturalist tendency was coming to prevail in American photographic culture at the time, associated with such figures as Minor White and Aaron Siskind, and with the journal *Aperture* which White edited. And Jack Kerouac's rhapsodic introduction links Frank to another important turn in the culture of the time – the Beat movement. This further motivates exclusively aesthetic and expressive readings of his book. For, while the Beats' writing-travelling did open on to a real America, its true purpose was the construction of an ecstatic personal geography. To the Beat movement, the journey was more egomantric allegory than social enquiry. Indeed the social was raw material to be burned up in the romancing fire of the hipster's vision.

However, Frank had connections with the Beat movement, not full kinship. Foremost he was a European; Europe had made and unmade him. His photographer's wanderings had begun there and moved on to the United States years before he ever encountered Kerouac. And like many European photographers he was marked by Parisian Surrealism. It was the Surrealist's rather than the hipster's disdain for descriptions untransformed by psychic energies that had shaped him; as had the Surrealist fondness for discovering the 'marvellous' – that release of unconscious meanings and emotions triggered by the encounter with certain external objects including the degraded and unremarked thing.

But it is a further difference from the Beats that places Frank's work beyond either expressive formalism or social documentary. While the Beats advertised their sense of internal spiritual exile, along with the shadows of the European catastrophe, Frank seems to have carried with him into the United States in 1947 much of the immigrant's traditional optimism and therefore, as Max Kozloff has noted, much of the immigrant's capacity for disappointment (Kozloff 1988: 102–3). Frank was a voluntary emigré hoping America would release him from a European purgatory. In this sense he cannot be classified as an exile; yet in another he can. He was not going back, emotionally he couldn't return. In this light the journey which produced *The Americans* can be seen as the declaration of a commitment springing from a desire to immerse himself in the country he wished to embrace.

What his images present, though, is a country where nobody seems to belong – a republic of exiles. The photographs are the condensations of both Frank's disappointment and his melancholy affiliation with America. Like the mourner who falls in love with his or her own sadness, Frank has made America both a place of loss and an object of love. Frank's exile lies in his disappointment, it governs the language of his photography – an imagery of disconnection, of non-belonging. His Americans exist in a space which, like exile, discomforts them. It cuts across them, cuts them off from each other, confines them. People appear displaced. They dream of being somewhere else or are buried in private journeys, already distant before they've departed. A black religious celebrant incants on the edge of the Mississippi – an image conjuring the Remembrance of Zion, lost African rivers, lost origins and Edens. Some are transported or consoled by the cheap beauty of the altar-like jukebox. 'Music doesn't come out in pictures', observes the photographer in García Márquez's *Innocent Eréndira*. We see their listening, but the absolute silence of the image renders them more remote than ever.

The desiring paired with Frank's disappointment reveals itself in the act of production, in the ecstasy of travel and of making images. It lies additionally in an equality the visual language bestows on its subjects. This begins in the uneasy identification that some attempt with their subjects even in the moment that the photographer's look is resisted and continues in the foregrounding of the presence and limitations of the photographer's activity.

Very few smile into Frank's lens. Some reward his intrusion with a 'who the hell are you?' glance – the couple on the grass in San Francisco, the bikers in Newburgh, New York. In these moments the photographer's strangerhood deepens, the space grows paranoid, agoraphobic. But by including these refusals of availability Frank acknowledges the autonomy of those who make them. They are not the wretched, bewildered subjects that Jacob Riis captured in his terrorising gunpowder flash. They form part of the self-distancing and irony of *The Americans*. They position the photographer firmly on the outside, in a place less of insight or omniscience than of misunderstanding, even blindness. The trope is confirmed in the images depicting people at an event the sight of which is denied the viewer by a frame which cuts them off. We cannot *see* what they are seeing and therefore cannot share their world. We must remain shut out from the events' interior meanings. The social world is not disposed to reveal itself to some transcendent viewer. It remains in the possession of its subjects.

For the spaces they reproduce and for their structures as viewed images, Frank's images can be described as analogues of the condition of exile. However, his work prompts a sceptical scrutiny of the claims of all photography and travel to offer a synoptic comprehension of the worlds they encounter. It teaches that all seeing is partial, circumscribed by self and specific location – a general insight the exile cannot avoid making.

The scepticism of *The Americans* goes further. Although there are some local patterns in its sequencing – the four consecutive images of people in cars to cite one – there is no presiding principal effectively ordering the whole, John Brunfield's exegesis notwithstanding (Brunfield 1982). Some might see the moral and political limitations of detachment revealed here. Nothing and nobody is linked to a totality or cause standing outside the representation such as a knowable social system, a desire for social reform, solidarity or even the state humanism of the type which drove the FSA photographic programme.

However, a different kind of political effect emerges from the work. A book titled *The Americans* suggests a panoptic vision; or else a set of parts in which some whole is condensed. It implies the confirmation of a whole, an 'America'.

But its aleatory form, its lack of centre, of completion or of any claim to comprehensiveness challenge the idea of a whole. Not only are the figures in *The Americans* isolated from one another, so too are the majority of photographs. It is a book of indeterminacy, of monads and nomads, which does not sum up 'America' because it implies that a singular, unified, whole 'America' does not exist. Baudrillard has said that Realism provides the simulated official order with an alibi by indicating some authentic causal 'real' lying anterior to it. The radicalism of *The Americans* was to have denied Cold War America a self-confirming image of nationhood – one that was unified, monumental, coherent and known to itself. Instead his book insinuated that America was itself a contingency.

But if, as Rorty contends, contingency is at the heart of *all* experience then the exile is not such an outsider after all. Frank then could regard himself as both observer and participant, as both the European and the American. His book concludes with a gesture that adds something beyond irony and distance, a claiming of his place in the republic of exiles. This is the group of images of his family huddled together in the car parked on the road's edge. They are ambiguous images. Taken in an uncertain light at dawn or evening, of a domestic group in a car which is both home and not home, whose fates we know something of with the hindsight of forty years. But if, at least in the photographs, they are not quite naturalised citizens of the state they might still claim citizenship of the journey. And if Frank himself does not appear in them, they nevertheless correspond to both the marginality and the intensity of his presence in America and to the coolness and intimacy of his relationship with it.

In 1968 the Czech photographer Josef Koudelka was swept into exile by the grey-green force of Soviet invasion. Some years before he'd already gone into a kind of internal exile, withdrawing from the conventional centres of national life to mix with and photograph those prototypical outsiders and wanderers, the Gypsies. In the frontality of its portraiture and its intimately framed moments of family and community – whose ties death or separation serve only to confirm – this work visualises connections, both those of the Gypsies with each other and of Koudelka's with them. Its difference from the isolates and the unresolved spaces, and the complete invisibility of Koudelka's presence in the post-1968 photography – the product of his exile – is dramatic. The Gypsies of Eastern Europe may have been besieged by an oppressive, homogenising modernity. They also presented the symptoms of future instability, shown in the photograph of the chaotic boy with the toy gun who unnerves the *mise-en-scène*, or of the man being taken off to prison. But in them it would seem that Koudelka felt he'd encountered a society still able to coincide with its own culture.

Of course, such traditional and marginal communities have long been the staple of a photography which equates the strange with the authentic. It's probably for this reason that, in the promotion and criticism of his work, Koudelka himself has at times come to feature as a premodern, pre-rational sensibility, the bringer of a truth whose authenticity is underwritten as much by his origins and the moral weight of his own exile as by the subject and consequence of his photography. He is made to emerge like some untutored hedge-poet through the Cold War mirror; out of an elsewhere, a failed modernity, and a strange rural vastness, whose unrelenting political pressures demand of the individual unambiguous moral choices, properties which amply qualify it as a source of the authentic. Against the West's sense of its privileged moral relativism and contrasting those bought-off aesthetic practices which flatter the accomplishments and self-image of its elites, Koudelka is made to stand as an 'untouchable', one who cannot be turned from his pure, ascetic and solitary path of making images which evince no interest in or even knowledge of what the modern West accepts as central.

Forced from his homeland he simply takes up his peregrinations across different zones because it comes naturally. Although the more obvious causes of his dislocation are easily established as social and historical, Koudelka is spoken of as a shamanic figure, a Tiresias with a camera, made wise in the wilderness of Eastern Europe and blind only to what is inessential. For example, David Markus writes, 'considerable mystery surrounds the life of Magnum photographer, Josef Koudelka'. Markus complicates the necessary enigma by drawing on the lexicon of religious experience when he writes of 'the haunted, hunted, hallowed world of Josef Koudelka' (Markus 1986). To this casting of Koudelka as mysterious traveller and seer Danielle Sallenave adds the part of the invoker of Kafka, the peerless fabulist and allegoriser of modern strangeness: 'the great wanderer', she writes, 'this pilgrim of remote places with the prophetic name of Josef K(oudelka)' (Sallenave 1979).

Koudelka, then, is something of an exotic cultural consumable himself – visionary vagabond, Mr Natural bearing a 'prophetic' name by force of synchrony rather than chance, standing at (unthinking) one with the truth that shines forth from his images. Koudelka himself is not without involvement in the fashioning of these mythical personae: think of the self-portrayal as 'man-who-walks' through the analogy of his feet shod in battered tramping shoes, footwear heavy with an ambulatory wisdom and Van Goghian association that no one can argue with (Koudelka 1988: 36 – further references to individual images from this edition of *Exiles* will consist solely of the illustration number); or of a traveller's simple meal served on a newspaper in the open air (Koudelka 1988: 45). Max Kozloff speaks of his 'rhetorical estrangement', of the 'solitary spirit' that 'doth protest too much' (Kozloff 1988: 102).

As Kozloff implies, Koudelka is a far more measured photographer than certain reviewers would wish to concede. And yet the book *Exiles* undoubtedly displays the architecture of a spiritual journey moving from loss towards recovery and redemption. Religious or near-religious ceremonies and gatherings recur throughout. By this, Koudelka is able to house the general themes of banishment, separation and the longing to belong in one of its most intensified forms.

The religious is present in another way. In his reflections on the figure of the stranger – in many respects interchangeable with that of the exile – Siegfried Kracauer sees it as converging with that of the detective. As the exiling or the crime has stolen meaning from the world, the most ordinary thing becomes potentially a key to unlock the mystery and retrieve it. The world, even the everyday world, is thereby transformed. It is darkened by what has assaulted it but enlivened by the possibility that all of a sudden significance might lie anywhere and in anything. 'The ordinary is what disguises the extraordinary', writes Nikos Papastergiadis in his discussion of Kracauer's essay (Papastergiadis 1993: 123). For this reason some have described detective fiction as 'religious'. During the time of the investigation anything might solve the riddle, even the grubbiest used train ticket, the smear on a glass or the unguarded facial twitch. As in religious vision the world is brightened by the immanence of meaning, by a kind of numinousness.

The visual prologue of *Exiles* consists of a single photograph of an arm wearing a wrist-watch held above a deserted and expectant Prague boulevard. On the edges one can make out a few people crouching by shop fronts. The hands of the watch indicate the precise moment in history – twenty minutes after noon – when Dubcek's democratic socialism was about to be defaced. The journey's point of departure is thus located in the ruin of political hopes and in the completion of Koudelka's personal exile. It also begins in the abolition of a certain experience of time. For it is an image of the last moment of time present, when the self with its desires, its commitment to others and to a sense of becoming, coincided with the moment, that of the Prague Spring of 1968, one of those rare moments when the small time of individual lives appears to be spliced into the grand tide of human history; when, in Seamus Heaney's words: 'hope and history rhyme' (*The Cure at Troy*). The itinerary that follows passes across a condition of time absent – an undated, disconnected and fallen world, where the joyous meeting of self and history no longer seems possible – a sequence of micro-dystopias, an anti-pilgrimage.

Koudelka's world is often cold. He prints out a dense grey light that chills even bathers in Portugal with a cold which is as existential as it is physical (54). (Note too the chilled-to-the-bone towns and the great shards of ice in his stills for the Angelopoulos film *Ulysses' Gaze*; and his study of the ice-bound Eiffel Tower.) Most of its events take place on the Outside. There are few interiors in his whole *corpus* and in *Exiles* even they are essentially exteriors – nameless, near empty public places. Locations are generally marginal: side doors, alleyways, snickets, anonymous street corners, ante-rooms, waiting rooms, wastegrounds, windswept beaches, forgotten backroads (figure 34).

Many of the journey's spaces are abject and in-between: a bleak pissoir lined with shabby, hunched figures or a concrete walkway scrawled with furious sex graffiti. Its fellow-travellers are the old and lonely, the very young, the crippled and injured, the poor, the marginal, the mentally disturbed, joyless devotees, solitary, abused animals. Looks between people fail to connect as if they inhabit different worlds, or share neither medium nor language to transmit them. In

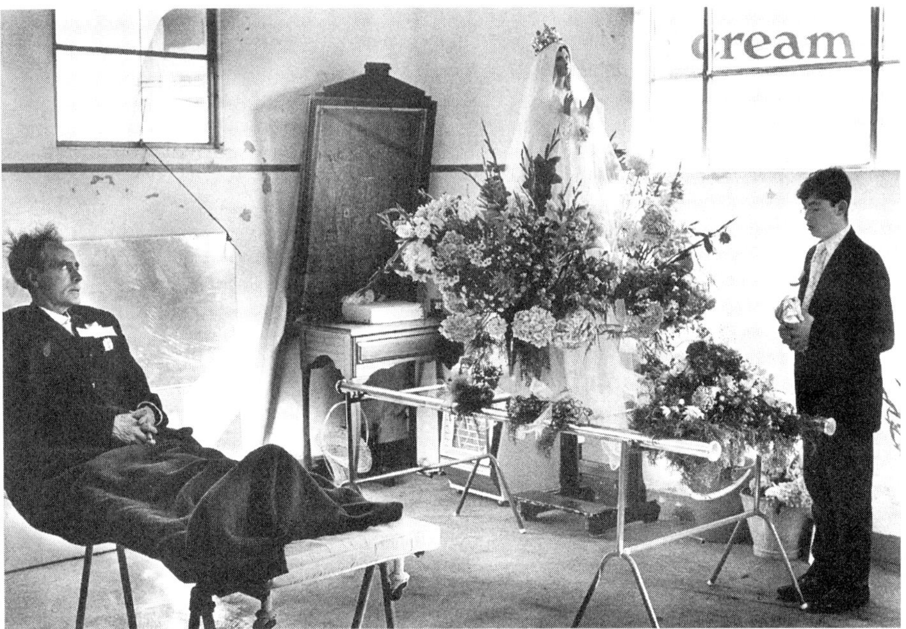

Fig. 35 Josef Koudelka (Magnum), 'Ireland', 1971.

Koudelka this is where the greatest distances lie – between faces.

Yet the book appears to chart a course out of these states of exile. It opens in images of loneliness, fragmentation and paralysis but appears to offer two modes of slipping away. First, by coming to rest in the serene quietism of an aesthetic order without human reference – the cool forms in the empty restaurant interior (57), the abstract composition implied by the dispositions of wire and hunks of marble encountered in a quarry used by sculptors (55). And, second, in the figuring of spiritual transcendence. In a book whose first photographic sequence is preceded by Hugo's lines 'Exile is not a material thing, / it is a spiritual thing', the viewer might reasonably feel invited to read the closing image of a curious wave-form on the otherwise still ocean surface as an index of the presence of some immanent shaping spirit – as an almost Wordsworthian trope.

Perhaps this is what Max Kozloff has in mind when he writes of 'that redemptive zone where Koudelka wanders' (Kozloff 1988: 103). Perhaps this is the quality in Koudelka's work that attracts those who see in it more than the registration of the doubt and separation brought on by exile. As I have said, religious signs and suggestions recur throughout *Exiles*. But their presence serves only to reinstate the universality of doubt. Those images that touch on religious practice show people more paralysed than transported by it. They present us with the fragments or out-takes of ceremonies; the parts before or after their culminations, as if Koudelka believes we can never reach or return to the moment when the ceremony gathered everything in – or as if he suspects it never really took place. There is the bored boy dressed as an angel on a stationary bike too weighed down by the quotidian fact of his humdrum vehicle and his scuffed running shoes to take off. The wings seem like heavy redundancies, the paraphernalia of a belief system that no longer works (3). There is the disabled man before or after a religious procession who stares from his margin across to the youth at his (figure 35). The man has been put out of the way to wait with the Madonna statue and bits of unused furniture in the corner of some public hall.His look seeks connection, perhaps signals sorrow or illicit desire. Outside the window can be seen the word 'cream' – or perhaps it is part of the word 'scream' (29).

Then there is the agony and achievement of the three men who've reached the summit of Ireland's hill of Calvary at Craighpatrick, some of it on their knees. But their craggy religiosity is undercut by people in the background devoting themselves to the afternoon's secular distractions of a nice view and by the fact that they have nowhere else to go but down (31). Once more the time of vision has passed. In another context there is the couple consoling each other on the emptying site of a rock festival, abandoned to litter and wind. They look as though they've just lost paradise (49). Again, we have arrived too late for the ceremony, we stand outside the vision, for ever 'after the Fall'.

Two photographs of children provide Koudelka with his most subversive picturings of the religious performance. One shows a small boy kissing a larger-than-life statue of the Virgin or St Anne, her mother, at, I think, one of the Stations of the Cross in Lourdes. At a site dedicated to illness and death the naughty boy reveals the lively desire to end the primary post-Oedipal exile in a permanent, even physical unity with the lost loved maternal body of past and future (35). It is a component of the religious impulse rarely acknowledged within religion's official expressions. The kiss confirms the boy's desire but also the sepulchral chill of the religious representation.

By chance another boy who looks on disapprovingly is barefoot – many walk the Lourdes 'Calvary' in this way. His unshod feet summon up the shade of Oedipus himself, whose name, we might recall, was translated as 'swollen feet'.

The other photograph is not included in *Exiles*. Taken in France in 1973, it is a rear view of a man praying at a monument. Alongside him and facing the camera a boy, perhaps the child of the man, secretly pulls an ugly face (Koudelka 1984: 34). As in so many of Koudelka's images selves are haunted, passed or shadowed by their others, their opposites, or by what threatens to deny their projects. The boy's gargoyle features may be no more than the expression of a delinquent boredom. Yet, in the context they register as a negating scepticism which supplants the beatified (or complacent) face of devotion, the face we cannot see. The little grotesquerie introduces into the ceremonies of belief and connection a dark, carnivalising laughter that proposes things as chaotic and meaningless. Is the praying father, betrayed by the ridicule of the son, just mumbling into the void? Here it is the adults who are innocent.

If the possibility of religious or Romantic or artistic redemption *is* raised in some of Koudelka's photographs it is thrown down in most. The exile may be a victim, confused and powerless, but his or her weakness can be attended by the cunning and undermining insights of the trickster, the Hermes who must thrive in the in-between, in the condition of unstable dualism, transience and discontinuity; who understands that most journeys end in the failure to arrive – concluding, instead, in loss, misrecognition and disappointment.

Doubt is registered not only in the imaginary dramas he constructs, but in the use of the medium's own characteristics. For example, in the image of wire and marble referred to earlier (55), the realism of the photograph becomes the source of its incredulity. A tension develops between the notion that behind the chaos of things lies an immanent order for which the artist finds formal equivalences, and the countering fact that the composition is no more than the framing of what remains resolutely a pile of fortuitously arranged wire and rubble.

Doubt and uncertainty are given form in the strange and condensed quality of the images. Some are like trailers for dreams. Freud regarded the sense of unreality or of the 'uncanny' ('*unheimlich*', literally unhomely) that travel can produce as a form of protection through displacement. The particular feelings of strangeness experienced in certain places serve to distract the traveller from the painful associations and repressed material such as the guilt or regret at the leaving, the loss or the rejection of home or family they call up.[1] If Koudelka's images can be described as metaphors of exile in general, the source of their metaphorical power lies in the trauma of his own particular dislocation. The creation of metaphor can be a means of releasing such distress through the process of representation. More precisely, given that the metaphor operates by replacing one thing with another, the process can act to displace the pain of which it is the expression.

As I noted earlier, Said sees the exile's loss of his or her 'natural' world resulting in things being taken over by the magnified, uncanny quality of fiction. In *Exiles* this takes the form of its 'stories' becoming frozen into metaphors. Narrative, journey, destination and closure have all become unviable. Rather than raising the expectation of what follows, the images induce the enquiry, 'What do they stand for?' And the answer is likely to be 'absence', one brought about by the loss of the exile's territories of space and meaning. The metaphor compounds the sense of absence by its displacement effect and by being the mark of the exile's melancholy gesture. In his discussion of metaphor Richard Rorty, *pace* Donald Davidson, writes that it

> does not express something which previously existed, although, of course it is *caused* by something that previously existed. For Freud, this cause is not the recollection of another world but rather some particular obsession-gathering cathexis of some particular person or object or word early in life. (Rorty 1989: 36)

The metaphor then stands less for some recognisable or recoverable external terrain than for the interior geography of the traveller. If this is the case, Koudelka's representations need to be seen not as the alien's interestingly out-of-kilter viewpoint on a given, stable world, one familiar to insiders, but as re-descriptions and therefore re-inventions of the world. His representations ask us to accept that the worlds we all *experience* are built out of metaphors whose non-metaphorical origins and causes we cannot be sure of retrieving. Meaning itself is homeless. In a sense it is exiled. Our world is debatable, there is always a gap between the world and our representations of it. In short, the world we live in is unsettled. There are journeys not destinations – the metaphors move on.

Regarded in this way, *Exiles* opens no roads, proposes no return routes – to neither history nor paradise. If it does offer redemption it lies nowhere else than in the work itself – in the ecstasies of making images, in the 'consolation of photography'.

But Koudelka is a photographer, and the photographic image diverges in its behaviour from that of the metaphor as described by Rorty, by its facility for being at once metaphor and at the same time the trace of the metaphor's cause, the trace of the scene of its origin. Photography operates in the space where the symbolic and the real are required to converse as if they were distinct modalities. The poetics of Koudelka's photography may be the precipitation of his personal obsession and solitude. But at the same time his work lays us open to the sad, imperfect world that determines it. To that extent he remains a documentary photographer who requires us to face the world we are passing through, the exiling world for which we are responsible.

Writing of *Reflections on Exile*, Caren Kaplan upbraids Edward Said for what she regards as the essay's citing then abandoning of dislocation as 'a global phenomenon'. She complains that Said returns to a mystified figure – the solitary exile. Rather than elucidating the modes of representation that arise in an age of refugees, immigrants and the homeless, Said returns to a figure more closely associated with classical Western traditions as well as modernist myths of authorship. (Kaplan 1996: 120)

What makes Kaplan's objections redundant is Said's extended attempt at precisely such an elucidation in his book with Jean Mohr on the Palestinians, *After the Last Sky*, published in 1986, barely two years after *Reflections* (Said 1986). The book is neither a photographic essay, nor an illustrated text. Nor is it a series of photographs 'explained' by a writer. It is what we might still call a materialist document in that photographic practice and a politically engaged theoretical inquiry into the actualities it discloses rest on a belief that only through the establishment of historical truth can human dialogue and progressive social change become possible. It identifies exile as a loss of both history and visibility and above all as a loss of meaning. The book's aim is to help the restoration of all three by drawing the reader and viewer into a particular way of looking at the book's images and of linking them to the realities they indicate. It is an approach which understands that inscribed in the perceivable arrangements of the social world is a language in which history, social and political practices and the interior motivations of people are speaking. It demands of the reader and viewer both comprehension and an intensity of involvement with the faces and situations of the Palestinians – that is, empathy.

In this we can detect the influence of John Berger, aspects of whose work Said admires and with whom Mohr has collaborated. Berger conceives of empathy as more a question of methodology than sensitivity. For example, in his essay on August Sander, 'The Suit and the Photograph', he cites with evident approval an observation concerning Sander's work made by Walter Benjamin that could as easily describe Said's and Mohr's practice. Benjamin writes of Sander's 'delicate form of the empirical which identifies itself so intimately with its object that it becomes theory' (Berger 1980: 28). Here the very act of representation demands some sort movement beyond the perspective of the subject towards that of the object of their interest. Commenting on this, Nicos Papastergiadis argues that Berger's use of empathy does not bring about the observer's disappearance into the object. Instead it can create new and more reciprocal positions for observers and observed, speakers and listeners in what Papastergiadis calls 'the dialogue with the excluded' in which the different ways people are placed by history can be communicated (Papastergiadis 1993: 160). By this token the purpose of representation should not be the production of a neutral, unpositioned truth, but the building of dialogue; the creation of accounts that are multiply voiced, located within but also between subject positions.

Of course the fact of Said's personal implication in the Palestinian tragedy is central. His own exile in the Palestinian diaspora is the instrument on which the book's themes of exile are replayed. Both knowledge and acquaintance attune him to the cultural signals and historical resonances the photographs pick up.

But Said is an exile not a refugee. His citizenship of the United States and academic tenure mean that he is also a privileged and distanced outsider. This distance is augmented by Israeli restrictions at the time of developing the book which prevented him visiting the camps. Thus his reflections must perforce set out as responses to Jean Mohr's photographs, themselves the mediations of a Swiss who, though sympathetic, cannot share Palestinian traditions or privations and who speaks little Arabic. Consequently the text becomes a struggle to abolish distances: those between Said himself and the out-of-reach compatriots in Israel or Israel-Palestine; those between the book's metropolitan public and the Palestinians in general, who remain estranged from themselves by loss of homeland and centuries of distorting orientalising; and that between writing and photography.

At certain points Said mobilises his local knowledge and acts as a friendly guide to an unfamiliar region. At others he draws back, searching for those points at which the visual structure of the photographs translate into the spatial politics of the subjects. At times his writing method recalls surrealist techniques of releasing poetic meaning from the objects discovered by the photographer, using it both to multiply and to specify their connotations. At others, he

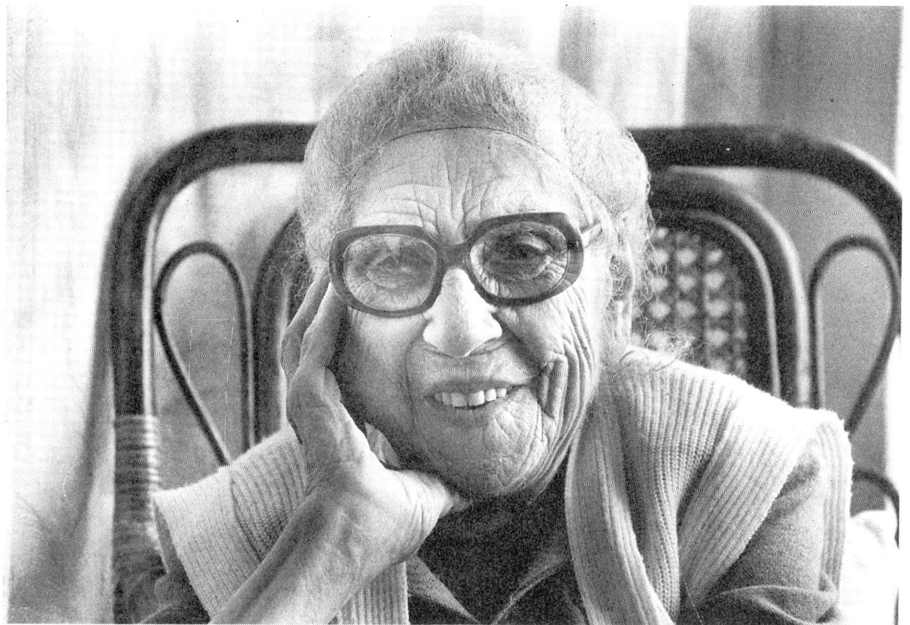

Fig. 36 Jean Mohr, 'Amman, Mrs Farraj', 1984.

resembles the analyser of aerial photographs; here scrutinising cultural and political patterns, forcing intelligence from Mohr's images – the histories and meanings that lie within the events and conditions they depict. This calls to mind the Lukácsian concept of the 'partisanship of reality', which regards the appearances and structures of the social world as the external expressions of the historical and ideological forces that produced them. In this light history, the residues and results of socially positioned human practice, is observable, representable and can be made coherent (Lukács 1971).

Whatever form his intervention takes, Said establishes himself as in-between, as mediator, interpreter or translator – as one who can transform the mute phenomena of the photograph into *figures* that articulate the shifting complexities of the Palestinian condition.

His location is important. *After the Last Sky* is a reading of exile and at the same time an exile's reading. There are moments when Said seems to be looking for his own face, for some bridge to connect what he sees with his own story as a Palestinian. For example, he discovers he is looking into the eyes of an old woman he and his family had known forty years previously whom Mohr had by chance photographed (figure 36). The diaspora had determined their actual separation. A photograph has now returned her to consciousness. It is only a virtual reunion, but perhaps one that will initiate for Said some kind of modest redemption in which a mere image becomes the representation of a lived existence that once touched his own. 'Exile', he writes, 'is a series of portraits without names, without contexts. Images that are largely unexplained, nameless, mute' (Said 1986: 12 – subsequent references to this work will consist of a page number only). This person's name, he informs us, is Mrs Farraj (85).

But the problems of visibility and comprehension are not entirely the expressions of Said's own situation. For reasons noted earlier, exile is a difficult condition to represent. It is made more resistant by exiles having learned to dissemble, or to reveal themselves sparingly, obliquely. If they are refugees any assertion of personal or cultural presence is likely to be denied by whoever has power over them. Said remarks on how the Israeli authorities classify certain Palestinians as 'present-absentees' – there and not there. For such exiles the photograph that figures most commonly in their lives is the one that appears on the identity pass. As part of the specular weaponry of the controlling authorities, it functions less to represent them than to fix them, to *get* a fix on them, to hold them in place. It's a photography that does not so much see, as *over*see. Thus the Palestinians are overlooked and the mechanism that renders them visible also causes them to disappear.

In this context the question 'What do I see?' is political. This is demonstrated by Said's discussion of a close-up facial portrait of an ageing Arab man. He is wearing a pair of glasses with one shattered lens (the photograph also appeared on the cover of the first edition). Said issues the caveat that his interpretations spring from objects in an image rather than from the being of the man himself. 'The blotch', he writes, 'is on the lens, not in him' (128). Nevertheless he identifies this portrait of impaired, imbalanced vision, with its suggestions of the precariousness, poverty and even violence that surround the life of this man, as displaying motifs which correspond to an imbalance and contradiction in the lives and perceptions of all such Palestinians (128).

The face is open and direct and at the same time closed in. It engages clearly with our looking and yet is purblind. It expresses cheer and yet seems to have been struck by violence, by an assault on its own looking. Is this the mark of fortitude or of the failure of experience to register itself; that is, of an unlearning passivity? 'No matter how clearly he sees (or is seen),' Said writes, 'there is always going to be some interference in vision, as well as some disturbance for whoever looks at him'. The face is only partly recognisable; the seeing is incomplete, it is blocked (129). As a degree of mirroring takes place in the contemplation of any photograph, metropolitan readers and viewers might sense that reflected here are also the common flaws in their own seeing – more often oversight than insight.

The theme of a face made up of non-synchronous elements, of split vision, of an absence of visual resolution is translated by Said into the notion that imbalance and loss of focus afflict the general historical and existential condition of Palestinians for themselves and for others. Theirs is an existence and way of seeing dishevelled by the refugees' road of exile along which they must always fail to meet themselves or be recognisable to others. 'As if having taken on our Palestinian identity in the world', Said concludes, 'we have not completely brought into harmony the wildness and disorganization of our

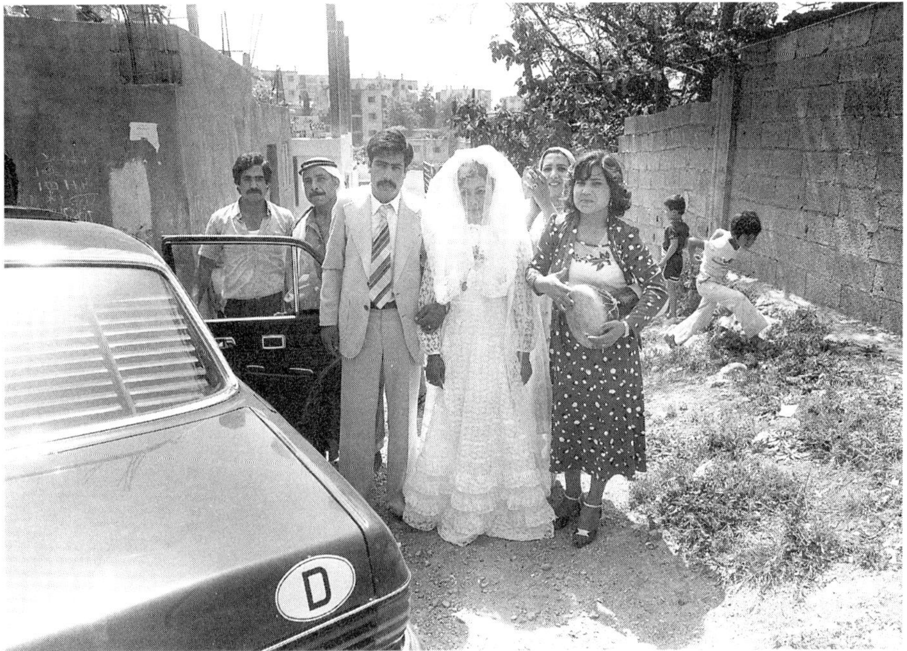

Fig. 37 Jean Mohr, 'Badawi Camp, Tripoli', 1983.

history with our declared and apparently coherent political, social, and cultural personality' (129).

The thought is echoed later in his reflections on the photograph of a scarecrow: a figure constructed from an array of odds and ends, a made-up creature not unlike the jumble of identities that Palestinians are forced to wear, or the bricolage and improvisation that necessity imposes on their lives.

Said devotes much of his attention to the way these conditions are experienced as a spatial predicament. It is for this reason they are appropriate subjects of photographic scrutiny; and the writing vocalises what the photographs spatialise.

The first sentence of the first chapter contains the word *space*:

> Caught in a meagre, anonymous space outside a drab Arab city, outside a refugee camp, outside the crushing time of one disaster after another, a wedding party stands, surprised, sad, slightly uncomfortable. (11)

These words open Said's reflections on a photograph of a Tripoli wedding group (figure 37) where space is degraded, temporary, unimportant and nameless – and 'outside' everything else. Other than the group's ordering of itself into the conventional pose, the gathering seems breathless and at the edges, discordant. And cutting across the foreground space, the Mercedes rudely

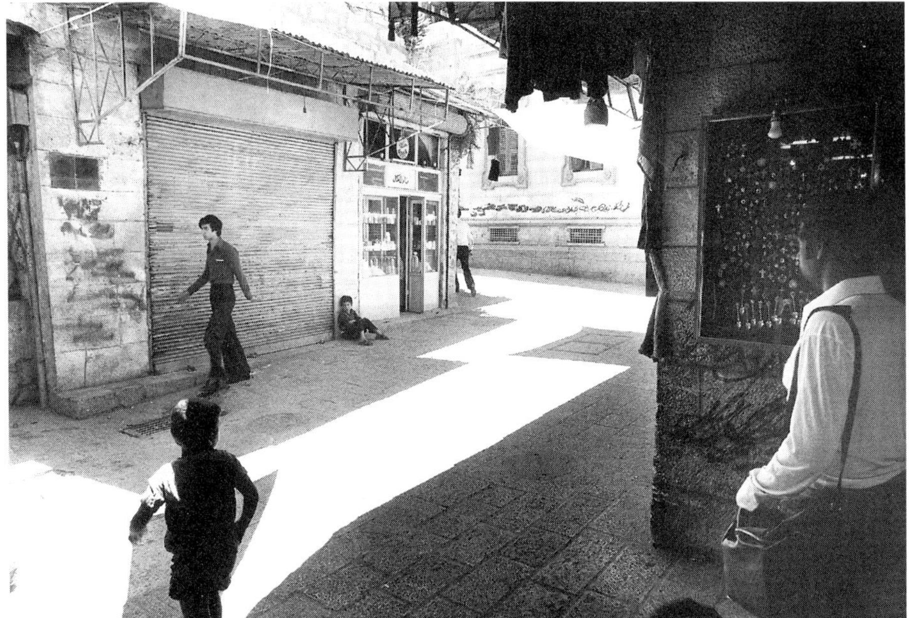

Fig. 38 Jean Mohr, 'Jerusalem Snapshots', 1979.

interrupts the plane of the newly weds, undermining the rituals of unity and completing the air of destabilisation that inhabits the scene. It suggests that there are other more important places to be than this.

The story of the Palestinian condition cannot, Said tells us, be told smoothly but only as a series of 'occurrences and coincidences' (30). If so, in the snapshot it receives its most expressive form. Mohr's three studies of Arab sections in Nazareth and Jerusalem are described in this way (figure 38).

They depict a social condition which has no centre, has nowhere to be. Read metonymically, the images show social life as disassembled, fleeting, random, and taking place in peripheral spaces – at the mouths of alleyways, on street corners. People are waiting for something to happen; or they chase after the event. Stateless people live in permanent contingency. Their reality is generated elsewhere.

Said sees Palestinian interiors offering little more sense of belonging. In part, he points out, this is explained by the fact that they've been investigated or violated by outsiders for centuries. In part it is because the domestic space is ultimately incapable of overcoming the sense that Palestinians are never quite at home. Once again the grammar of space – here the arrangements of forms, objects and people – betrays their condition.

Two interiors by Mohr reveal dwelling places where, according to Said's reading, nothing belongs (13). Figures are positioned near the door as though for ever about to depart. Diagonal lines on the wall conflict with the lens-distorted horizontals and verticals of the door. The wide angle also makes the floors appear to drop away. These visual anxieties generate a sense of unease

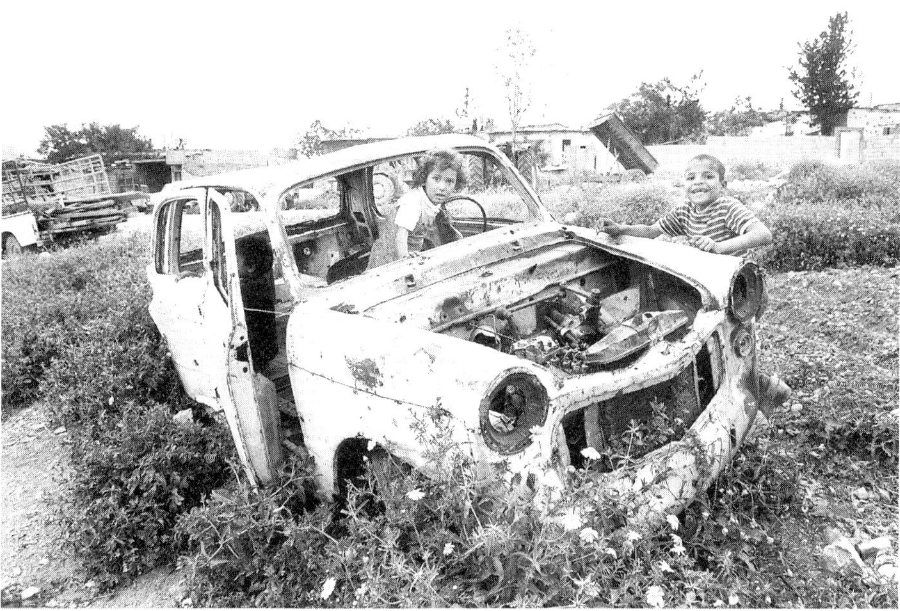

Fig. 39 Jean Mohr, 'Tyre, Bourj el-Shemali Camp, South Lebanon', 1983.

and insecurity. In them Said perceives further symptoms of more profound dislocations:

> The angles are all wrong. Lines supposed to decorate a wall instead form an imperfectly assembled box in which we have been put ... all at once it is our transience and impermanence that our visibility expresses. (12)

Even in the images of the homes of the ostensibly well off, stocked with enough weight of possessions and comestibles to keep the lightest of dwellings on the ground, Said detects overstatement, a masking of insecurity. As with the splendid interiors of Romany caravans such cluttered opulence stands against the impoverished external space over which they are permitted no claim. Said's writing takes the still images of apparently settled people and finds portraits of those who in their being have never found rest; who are still travelling (60 and photograph *Nazareth*, 1979).

But it is a travelling that has broken down, come apart, like the long-wrecked car played in by children in Mohr's study (figure 39). Said pulls alongside it with his ruminations on the traditions of broken and failed narratives in Palestinian literature and makes the incapacity of one vehicle to reach any destination analogous to the failure of another to reach a conclusion. 'We ... ride conveyances without movement or power', he writes (21).

The photograph is not used here as a source of symbolism. Rather it is accepted as the depiction of a particular and actual event but one charged with a force of connotation that permits the writer to read from it a *motif* that runs through the wider history and culture of the Palestinians. On the page accompanying the photograph Said observes that 'since our history is forbidden, narratives are rare; the story of origins, of home, of nation is underground. When it appears it is broken, often wayward and meandering in the extreme' (20).

In another context the evocation of split-ended postmodern narratives that never reach home might be read as the celebration of some modish nomadism. Here, though, the fragmentary and the discontinuous are marks of disablement. This is dramatised in what Said describes as 'the almost metaphysical impossibility of representing the present' (38); it materialises with most force as the deep instability of lives and structures in the refugee camps. The photograph of one such settlement at Ein-el-Hilwé, a dusty pile of half-demolished, half-built breeze block and corrugated iron shelters, is captioned: 'Time passes: destruction, reconstruction, redestruction' (39). And if, as Pierre Janet has said, humanity is created in narrative, the fragmentary and the discontinuous are impediments to the production of identity itself (quoted in Certeau 1984: 27).

With photographers such as Frank and Koudelka the distance of exile becomes the subject matter of their work and the apparel of their artistic persona. They seek less to change the world than to make poetry out of it. This distinguishes them from Mohr and Said whose intention is plainly the overcoming of the distances that exile has brought about both within and between individuals and the reform of the way in which metropolitan readers and viewers apprehend the Third World or any marginalised Other.

The focus of *After the Last Sky* progressively shifts from the exile as object to the exile as subject. A preponderance of portraits towards the end of the book indicates this evolution. They show a variety of social identities which share in common the sense that they are all directors of their own space, of their own image. This is not only because some are successful professionals but as they are likely to fill the frame with their presence, or choose to smile, hold the eye of the photographer, or to be absorbed in their occupations and thereby demonstrate their independence of the representation. But while the attractive vibrancy of the often young faces contrast the sometimes paralysing ambiguities in many of the earlier photographs, the text recalls us to the fact that these are only 'vulnerable' triumphs. They are, it reads, 'a hint of the provisional success and momentary flair that many of us have developed in our lives' (165). Around these instants of energy and hope still cling the debilitating uncertainties of exile. Perhaps they are wish-fulfilment – photographs taken on a conditional setting.

However, the book concludes in movement as it begins to form a last step towards the visual and phenomenological viewpoint of the Other, beyond even the 'dialogic ethnography' which James Clifford calls for, and suggests that this will be the direction in which future reflections and representations in general will need to move. Two small children photograph the photographer and Said comments, 'we too are looking, we too are scrutinising, assessing, judging. We are more than someone's object' (166).

By urging the relocation of the reader's and viewer's point of contact at the other side of the representation, on the side of the Other, *After the Last Sky* designates a position, a space beyond the reach of both its own voice and its own operations. As the issue of space is central to the condition of exile, the place in and from where one speaks is central to the way it is represented. It is especially important in the case of the post-colonial subject. Writing on the nature of this subject's discourse Homi Bhabha emphasises the importance not only of 'what is said, but [of] where it is said. Not simply the logic of articulation but the topos of enunciation' (Bhabha 1994: 162). This 'enunciation' is almost invariably located in a space filled by the distance of exile, the inheritance of travelling or estrangement. For whether or not a migrant, he or she is always an exile by virtue of having still to endure the psychic and symbolic depredations and the territorial removals and restrictions introduced by colonialism which may have long made their own cultural *habitus*, what Fanon termed, 'uninhabitable'.

It is therefore no surprise that a clustering of the issues of identity, space and mobility is common in the photographic practice being developed out of this condition. The condition's complexity and the uncertainty it produces have determined that such practice is highly reflexive. Some photographers remain committed to the belief that the documentary photograph can still deliver appropriate representations. But even this work reveals a formal self-consciousness. Take, for example, the Mexican photographer, Eniac Martínez. His primary purpose is the documentation of migrant workers as they travel through Mexico and into the United States. Yet he employs the sort of decentred space and ambiguous iconography more commonly associated with European and North American art photography. But what in those traditions might be taken as an overriding concern with form as 'bracketing out' the social is, in Latin American art, more likely to be the mark of a desire to find more effective correspondences to a complex and sometimes mysterious social reality, one made more so for people who often do not speak Spanish let alone English. Martínez's images are less representations of the social world than of the social world *experienced*. They reflect the desire common in Latin America, objectified for much of its history in the systems and perspectives of others, to show the world according to its own experience of itself.

Ironically the world which Martínez does bring to light often dominates the migrants by the alien weight of its objects as well as its ambiguity. They poise precariously over them, shove them aside or constrict their movement. They themselves must act like objects, pushed and pulled by economic forces and patterns of investment or decline. In one of his photographs, for example, a Mixtec woman is pressed to the bottom of the picture by the weight of redundant industrial plant in the shape of an enormous battered and rusted metal globe. The object seems to embody a whole condition, a whole world of industrial failure and unemployment edging the woman out of her life space.

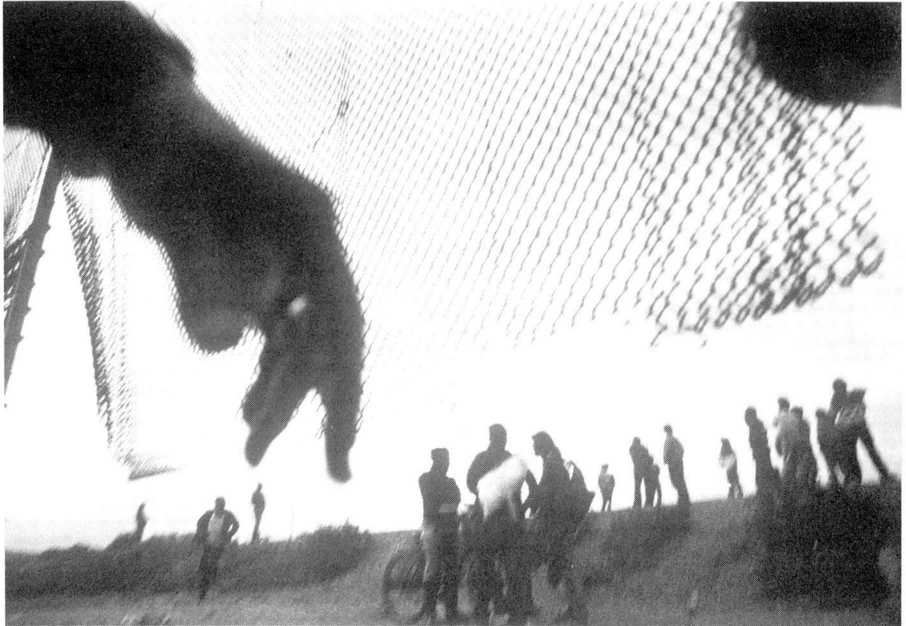

Fig. 40 Eniac Martínez, 'La Vieja Reja en El Bordo', Tijuana, Mexico, 1991.

Martínez's images visualise the migrant's life as a constant switching between inertia and activity. Migrants must learn to act out passivity and wait – for money, for papers, for transport, for a job selection, and for a chance to cross over the border into the United States (figure 40).

In his El Bordo photograph, anonymous figures wait in the twilight for the darkness that will conceal the crossing. They seem equally static and restless. The fence has been breached but continues to dominate the scene like a metal shutter or portcullis, retaining its power to imprison and exclude. And the uncertain meaning of the hand, which may or may not be forming a gesture, places a disturbance in the way of seeing as both a visual interruption and a source of semiological uncertainty. Whatever it may be thought to signify – the cutting of the fence, victory, peace, or the head of a snake about to strike, the hand of a policeman or nothing – and all these suggestions have been made – it remains there, the obdurate presence of uncertainty and anxiety. It evokes the anamorphic skull which blurs the foreground of Holbein's painting *The Ambassadors*.

In moves which both echo and contrast those of European and North American modernism and postmodernism from John Heartfield to Sherry Levine, many Third World photographers or artists using photography have come to deny the single photographic image with its realist assertions a dominant place in their work. Many have taken the view that photographic realism gives the appearance of fixity to what is unresolved; and that the single image imposes a seamless, singular unity onto syncretic realities. For these reasons it is felt increasingly to be incapable of giving form to the displacements and absences and the contradictory cultural grammars of exile and the post-colonial condition. Some, such as the Chilean critics Ronald Kay and Nelly Richard, even regard the medium and its effects as inseparable from colonial and neo-colonial domination present and past (Merewether 1987: 66).

Nevertheless, whether it is ironised, reworked or forced to share the aesthetic space with other forms, the photographic image retains a significant presence in a great deal of Third World aesthetic visual practice. Its relative cheapness, its accessibility and mobility make it attractive in impoverished circumstances. Its realism, however sceptically viewed, maintains a link with the social process which the pressure of events makes undeniable. For example, in the period following Pinochet's 1973 *coup d'état* in Chile, photography was incorporated into avant-garde works the better to denounce an unacceptable reality because, Nelly Richard informs us, 'it enabled the work to present its relation to the context by turning all signs of reality into evidence or the *proof* of its accusations' (Richard 1986: 35). At the same time, as the prominent discourse of social representation after the written document, it has become the object of critiques and revisions which form the central activity of works by artists wishing to reorder the received picture of their world. Additionally, a medium which embodies both the persistence *and* the fragility of memory, and which deals in both appearance and disappearance, is clearly of great import in a region where these issues have a tragic relevance. Lorca's words come to mind: 'la eternidad vulnerable de las fotografías' / 'the fragile eternity of photographs' (*Infancia y Muerte*).

In such work, space and mobility frequently constitute more than its authorial, textual, political and cultural concerns. In some instances the actual itineraries followed by the aesthetic object itself as it crosses the international art system's archipelago of galleries and museums, or its relocations in social and cultural space, are taken up as part of the work itself – as part of its meanings and affects and of its material body and presence – as the condition of its performance. This is more than an attempt to take things beyond the interior orders of the work or the gallery; although by doing so such work parts company with the cool and apolitical steps of North American postmodernists. It foregrounds the view that, like the exile, the work is for ever unfinished, beyond itself, and that its meaning is not established or guaranteed in one centre or from one perspective. Like the exile the work travels but has no final destination, no ultimate meaning. Its existence is produced out of its travelling, and its meanings are as much a reflection on the spaces and locations it passes through as they are the result of what occurs within its own aesthetic borders. These ideas are not new. But the contexts of their realisation are. Through translating them into new kinds of material poetry, then introducing them and their disrupting energies into significant social and cultural spaces, they are regenerated, impassioned by their engagement with those in extreme situations.

The protean, shifting, character of such work puts into aesthetic form the

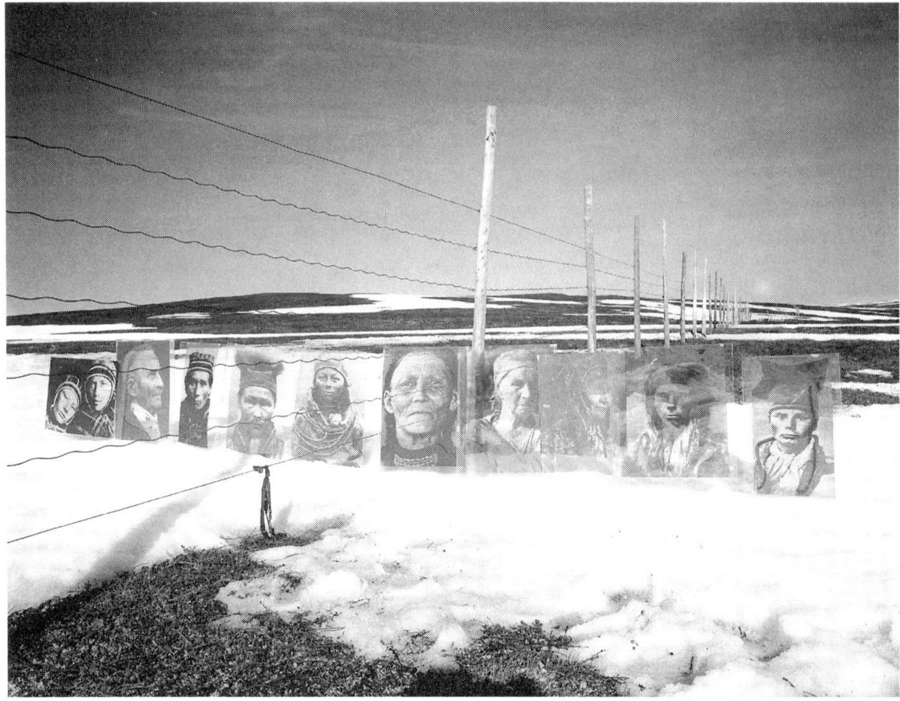

Fig. 41 Jorma Puranen, 'Untitled' (gelatin-silver print). From the series *Imaginary Homecoming*, 1991.

desire to challenge ideologies which hold some centre to be the sole or privileged source of originality and authority; to be the point at which the order of space itself is secured. The most potent and pervasive form of this comes of course in the form of the mental secretions of the imperialist order and the global system evolved from it, with their arrangement of the world into central and peripheral zones, and their corresponding hierarchies.

The Finnish photographer Jorma Puranen is not himself of the Third World. However his work on the plight of a semi-nomadic minority people, the Sámi, who live at Europe's social and geographical edge in the Arctic, operates along these lines. Puranen rephotographed anthropological images of the Sámi made mostly in the 1880s. He printed them on large transparent Plexiglas screens, then transported them to and literally placed them in the same landscapes through which these people had once moved and from where their likenesses had been extracted by a photographic practice shadowing the nation-state's policy of cultural homogenisation (figures 41 and 42). As the Sámi became objects of ethnographic science they became the objects of the state in its desire to settle them and incorporate them into the modern nation's cultural and geographical territories.

The work attempts to repossess the actual space of its subjects, shifting the term *site-specific* from an aesthetic to a political register. The literalness of the gesture is offset by the haunting, memorialising affect – the cold, blue light

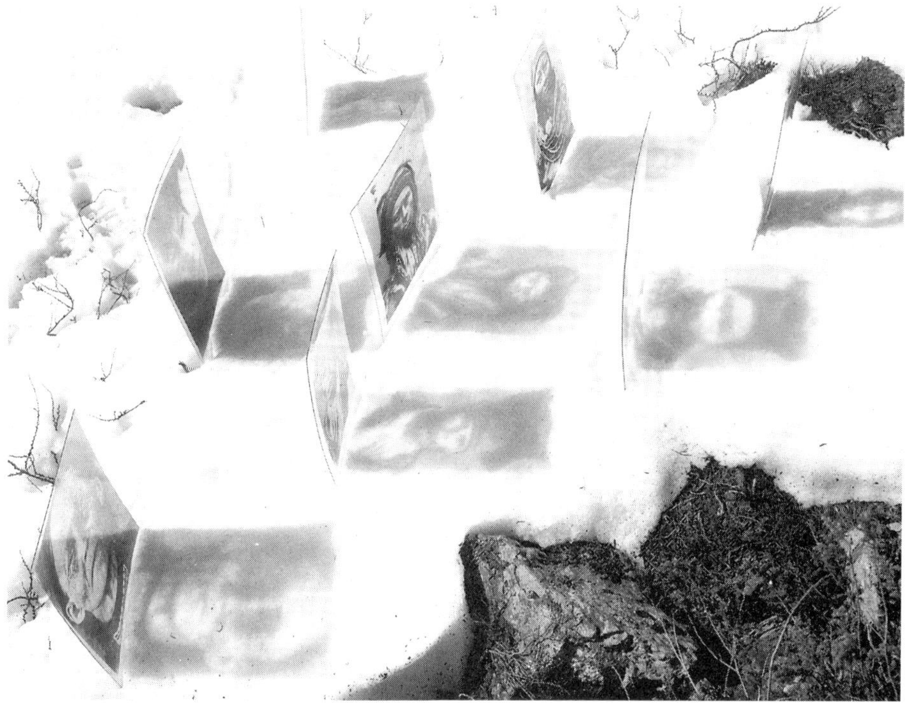

Fig. 42 Jorma Puranen, 'Untitled' (gelatin-silver print). From the series *Imaginary Homecoming*, 1991.

glowing on the snow, the faces of the dead – in which the restoration of the Sámis' presence confirms their disappearance, and yet at the same time reunites their faces with their landscapes in an act of reclamation (figures 41 and 42).

For a travelling culture with a fluid conception of space, the enforced accumulation of its faces at a fixed centre such as an ethnographic archive, amounted to a declaration of war on its cultural logic. The nationalising function of the original imagery also contained the fear and fascination settled peoples have often feel in relation to nomads. They seem to them to personify an enviable freedom outside social constraints and yet, in their unknowability and their silent challenge to property and social order, appear to embody chaos.

These acts of symbolic possession represented a form of symbolic exile for the Sámi which Puranen's work attempts to reverse. In Michel Tournier's novel *The Golden Droplet* the Islamic calligrapher teaches that 'the image is always retrospective. It is a mirror turned towards the past' (Tournier 1988: 179). By placing them in the landscape of the present, Puranen, like the Shaman pursuing and retrieving lost souls, seeks to release memory from the archives. He shows, too, how the 'wilderness' is an historical, even political, as well as spatial entity. Finally, his work advocates a continued presence for the Sámi on their ancestral ground.

One of the most elaborated instances of this kind of practice is to be found in

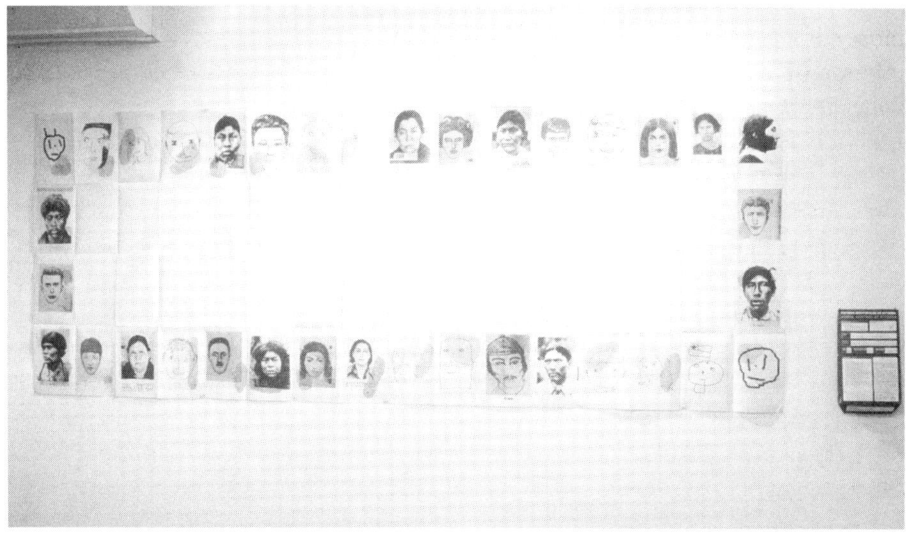

Fig. 43 Eugenio Dittborn, '13th History of the Human Face' (the Portals of H)', *Airmail Painting # 95*, 1991. Installation at the New Museum New York City, 1997.

the *Airmail Paintings* which the Chilean artist Eugenio Dittborn produced in the 1980s and 1990s. One typical example incorporates a number of face drawings made by a young child, the reproductions of Chilean police mug-shots of petty criminals of the 1930s rescued from old crime magazines, and anthropological photographic portraits of indigenous people from Chile's far south made by a German anthropologist in the 1920s. These elements are photo-silkscreened on to non-woven fabric then stitched roughly on to large sheets of the same material in alternating columns, producing the appearance of a catalogue of confused classifications (figure 43). When in transit or for some other reason not on display the sheets are folded up.

In its form and material, Dittborn's art analogises aspects of Latin America's condition. His own aesthetic choices and self-definition mirror the terms it imposes on the artist. The use of found photographs denotes his engagement with the often overwhelming social and historical realities of his world and the work's indifference to personal expression. But he waives the title 'photographer'. 'I am not a photographer', he says, 'I work *with* photographs printed in magazines, newspapers, catalogues and books ... I collect, I recreate and reconnect in diverse modes' (in Merewether 1987: 72). In this way he pictures the artist as a non-specialist bricoleur; an aesthetic rag-picker at work on Latin America's rubbish heaps, foraging in its abandoned archives, one who does not so much originate as rearrange in order to make visible what the dominant order of representation has repressed.

Dittborn employs materials and procedures such as forensic and ethnographic photography, images cut from crime magazines, stitching, reprographics, re-photography, and childrens' drawing still regarded by the more conservative traditions of fine art as impoverished, marginal, second-hand, inferior or merely *applied*. In choosing to work in these ways he allows the wider issue of his country's cultural and political subordination to appear. Like Latin America in general, Chile was in part invented as a dependent periphery of Europe. Its culture was seen by Europe, if seen at all, as an inferior, junior copy; or as a mimicking of its own. For most of its history Chile's models of truth and value have been formulated and confirmed elsewhere – at the centre, in European or North American mentalities and institutions or in their local agencies and outposts.

Against this Dittborn poses a sombre carnival of mixed and multiple forms and improvisations – unstable assemblies which defy the apparently unified axioms and representations of the official order. His work embodies and thereby accepts, even celebrates, the precarious – an important word for Dittborn – and often shambolic but fertile hybridity that typifies so many of Latin America's cultures.

The approach is not uncommon among the varieties of cultural resistance in Latin America. More directly, it reflects Chile's post-1973 *avanzada* (avant-garde), and the postmodern cultural politics of the influential Chilean journal *Revista de Critica Cultural* edited by Nelly Richard, with its championing of the marginal and the heterogeneous against oppressing centres, totalities and essentialisms that preach false purities.[2] It echoes similar themes present in the work of the Chilean social theorist, Benjamin Arditti. Arditti argues that the social formation is an ever unresolved struggle between two dimensions within itself. On the one hand is *Society*, a totalising project whose aim is to unify the social world 'in the name of a single "rationality"' (Colas 1994: 15). On the other hand is what Arditti terms the *Social*, which is everything and everyone that *Society* cannot contain, cannot quite control or which it wishes to exclude: minorities, dissidents, deviants, underclasses, criminals, even cultural avant-gardes (Colas 1994: 15; Lechner 1987). Any form of social objectification, of which the anthropological and police photographs are instances, is 'political ... and must bear the traces of the acts of exclusion which govern its constitution' (Mouffe in Robertson et al. 1994: 106). It can be regarded as an example of *Society* shutting out the *Social*.

The politics of the *Airmail Paintings* lie most crucially in the unwrapping and denunciation of this process. It is in Dittborn's use of travelling and in his work's uncovering of particular effects and meanings of space that this politics is uniquely placed.

In his work travelling means a number of things: the transportation of the art works; their material instability; the spatial dispersals of colonialism and Third World migration; the movement that disturbs, or returns to life, that which has become fixed and dead, that 'makes strange' our inert perceptions of things; the transitional character of all cultural and social orders; the movement of the past into the present that photography effects; the movement that restores communication and the possibility of social dialogue.

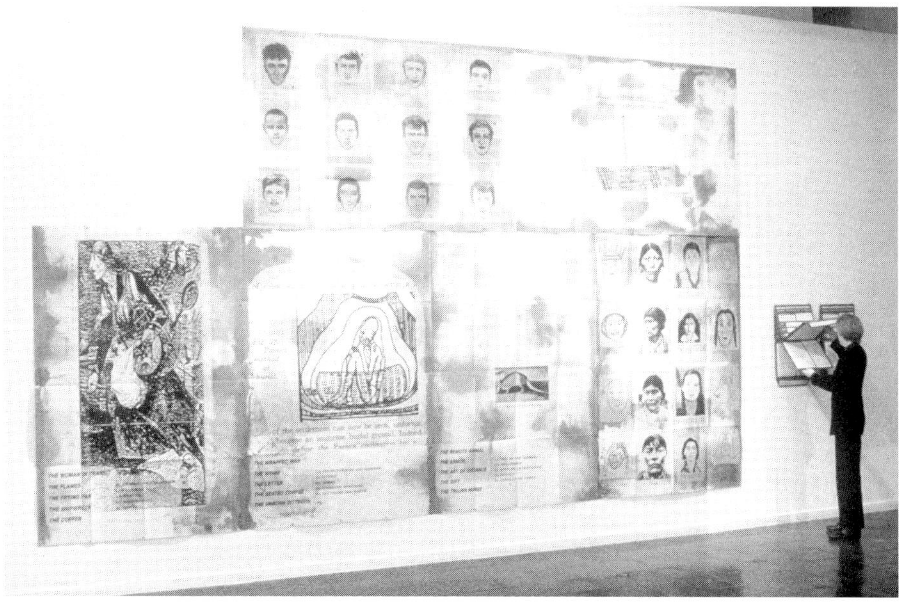

Fig. 44 Eugenio Dittborn, '16th History of the Human Face (to Besiege)', *Airmail Painting # 99* (paint, stitching, photo-silkscreen, non-woven fabric), 1991. 2.1 x 5.6 m.

In the *Airmail Paintings* movement is written on to the physical body of the work itself. By displaying both the creases and folds which form on the works as they are opened and closed before and after each show and the stamps, frankings and customs tabs which adhere like barnacles to their jumbo-sized envelopes – also exhibited – the *Airmail Paintings* incorporate, in Guy Brett's words, 'into their artistic structure their own process of travelling' (Brett 1990: 6). And the 'Travelling', insists Dittborn, is 'the political statement of my paintings. And the folds, the unfolding of that politics' (Dittborn 1993: 20).

As it travels through the art system the work continues to evolve as an aesthetic object in terms both of its material form and of a politics of culture it reveals. Being in part the traces of the handlings of gallery staff, the folds, for example, represent the gallery's influence in the work's making, in its actual substance. Like the postal, customs and insurance systems and the political and bureaucratic orders they are part of, the galleries are identified as moments in the work's continuous origination, as being among the multiple locations of its authorship.

However, it is the insistent and more desperate politics of Latin America's past and present that cuts across all other meanings. In forcing associations across time and space, in bringing movement to the stasis of fear and amnesia that Chile became in the 1970s and 1980s, Dittborn is attempting quite literally to return dead realities to life, to unblock the roads of communication.

Like most works in the series, *Airmail Painting # 99* features the images of those who've left little presence in Chile's official histories – the indigenous and the systematically deprived. They were often the same people. Dittborn soon noticed that most of the thieves and burglars whose police photographs he was reproducing were 'transplanted and impoverished peasants'. He also observes that the process of social and geographical dislocation they'd been caught up was itself, like photography and criminology, a product of modernity (Dittborn and Merino in Dittborn 1993: 13). The exiling of such groups from the national picture enforced by the interred visibility of police files and anthroplogists' cards – simply modern forms of a practice prevalent since the Conquest – is overturned by Dittborn, if only in the realm of representation. As he says: 'their looks continue travelling, but they are no longer looking' (Dittborn and Merino in Dittborn 1993: 13). Dittborn unburies their images and sends them travelling, dispatches them into social space where the meanings they generate concerning history, national identity and oppression can be revived.

There is a nice irony in Dittborn's use of the postal service. The post was an institution which assisted in the birth of both the nation state and the private citizen. It represented the interface of state and individual, public communication and private opinion (Bennington in Bhabha 1991). To use the post to transmit the visual traces of those who were denied rights of citizenship as part of the process of founding and evolving the nation satirises the nation-state's claims to universality and inclusion on which its legitimacy rests.

It is only the novelist who can reconstruct Macondo from its own dust and ashes in *One Hundred Years of Solitude*. In the case of the *Airmail Paintings* it is the trickster, photo-bricoleur, the ransacker of the distant and degraded parts of culture who brings to light the nation's repressed histories, amplifies the stammer in the uttering of its narratives. Dittborn speaks of his fascination with the way the dead or the lost leave traces: in an African mask, the last gift of his dead sister; a pre-Columbian mummy; a Celt cured for centuries in bog chemicals; nineteenth-century English sailors preserved in the Canadian permafrost; and by photography itself, likened to mummification in a manner akin to Bazin's comparison of its imagery to the death mask. Dittborn sees the recording or mummifying action of photography as both a mechanism of oppression and the means of its unmasking. Although many of the visual elements in the *Airmail* series are not photographic, the whole project *is* – either in practice or spirit. In method and in political and cultural meanings, it is based in the essentially photographic effects of conserving, copying and reproduction.

The general theme of the past's persistence leads Dittborn to reflect on how its injustices are continuous with those of the present – haunting it, maybe prefiguring it. He has pointed out that his work travels in time as well as space. Photographic bodies and faces from different epochs assemble in what he describes as a 'temporal hybridization' (Dittborn and Merino in Dittborn 1993: 17). To travel in the past is to discover the face of the present folded into it.

This gives force to the links between the *Airmail Paintings* and more recent events in Chile. While the faces of the indigenous, the poor and the delinquent are the ostensible subjects of Dittborn's project, they might also be said to function like the manifest content of a dream. They carry meanings in and of themselves and at the same time serve both to evoke and to disguise a latent subject too disturbing or perilous to be released. For rising up from within the faces of the *Airmail Paintings* are those of the 'disappeared' of the Pinochet years. The association is irresistible, and confirmed by his use in a work entitled *Liquid Ashes*, made in 1992 when it had become possible in Chile to refer to such events less obliquely than before. He uses a newspaper photograph and story concerning the discovery of the corpses of those allegedly murdered by Pinochet's agents and preserved by chance for seventeen years in the chemical deserts of northern Chile.

Disappearance, used extensively in the 'dirty wars' in the Southern Cone during the 1970s and 1980s, is a form of exile; the experience of the exile of others, rather than of their deaths. Much of its cruelty lies in the retention of all knowledge concerning their fate. It punishes through the anguish of uncertainty. The familiar characteristics of exile appear in the unexplained absence, in the empty but unrelenting visibility of those who will almost certainly never be seen again. As with the exile the 'disappeared' are deprived of identity, of any clear status of being. Neither dead nor alive, neither absent nor present they are in-betweens. And, like the exile, they are deprived of a territory which, for the dead, means a burial ground, a place where they are known to lie.

As different epochs coincide in *The Airmail Paintings*, the 'disappeared' of the 1970s and 1980s unfold to reveal those of the 1930s, the 1830s or indeed of the 1520s, when the conquistador Alvarado first appeared in the region; and back again, a *continuous representation* of conquest and exile – the folding away, the vanishing into blindness and silence of those barred from the New World being prepared.

By incorporating 'travelling' so literally into his work Dittborn returns this history to its global stage. Many of the metropolitan centres to which it is dispatched were the sources of the colonial and post-colonial system in which Chile was created. The historical amnesia of the Latin American elites concerning their foundational violence and the centuries of internal exile to which they consigned whole communities in their populations is merely a local inflection of a defective global speech in which Latin America itself has been demoted – deferred into remoteness and insignificance, into a solitude as much structural as psychological. The arrival of Dittborn's work at these centres, and the marks that these centres leave on the work like fingerprints recalls their implication in, their making of, this history. Now metropolitan gallery visitors desire the art of the margins because of some supposed loss of their own sense of authenticity, when in the past they were happy to sup on its resources while remaining unmoved by its meanings.

Imperial centres had part of their beings in their peripheries – in the sources of wealth that made their dominance possible. But the fact that their identity was in a sense situated beyond itself, implicated in and dependent on the distant and on the Other, was something imperialist cultures found difficult to acknowledge. Through the killing of difference, and of the realities of colonised peoples, it sought to deny it. The figure of Jemmy Button, whose portrait appears in *Airmail Paintings* numbers 49 and 76, signals this directly. As readers of Darwin will know, he was a native of Tierra del Fuego who, with two compatriots, was purchased and 'adopted' in 1829 by Fitzroy, an English naval officer and later captain on a maritime expedition. Fitzroy dressed him up and had him made over into a Victorian gentleman in England. It was the English who dubbed him Button, the price paid for him, thus initiating the process of exile by unnaming him and burying his identity. A text running alongside his portrait in *Airmail Painting* 49 describes him as 'exiliado fueguino jemmy button' ('exiled Fuegian Jemmy Button'). Four years later he was returned to the South on Darwin's ship *The Beagle* and, to the astonishment of the English, he reverted overnight to his former way of life (Browne 1995: 268–9).

Two themes haunt this episode from an Anglo-Chilean past. First, the European need to obliterate otherness by replacing the Fuegan's identity with a simulation of their own; and second, the nature of the resulting creation, Jemmy Button as a lay figure, a transitional selfhood with neither home nor clear place of origin. His was an in-between identity, but one also possessed of agency – for he made his decision to hand back the role and the fancy dress to its makers. With hindsight it is possible to regard him as the prototype of a subjectivity that imperialism would make widespread and which has now become a kind of normality. It is akin to the condition and identity which post-colonial studies identifies as 'the subaltern'. As Homi Bhabha shows, in discovering the language and form of expression true to itself the 'subaltern' has no choice but to be transgressive, subversive of the colonial structures and values that brought it into being. It amounts to turning the language of mastery which invented it and yet made its existence impossible, against the process of mastering. It required and continues to require the production of 'other spaces of subaltern signification' (Bhabha 1994: 162).

In one of these 'other spaces' – Dittborn's *Airmail Paintings* – the laws of the physics of culture are overturned. Jemmy Button, from the most remote 'edge' of an empire, little more than a note in the margin of Darwin's biography and one of a million lives at once invented and fragmented in the force fields of Europe's expansion, appears for a moment at the centre of things. In an inversion of the received pattern of history Dittborn's imagery ends Jemmy Button's exile. It has him reappear as one of a set of figures, in principle infinite, whose faces and stories need to be uncovered for truly post-colonial subjectivities to become imaginable.

The work makes it clear that there is no resorting to a weaponry of counter-essences. Its presiding metaphor of travel connotes the restless translations and metamorphoses of journeys. Its uncentred and inconclusive language and foregrounding of material methods makes it plain that Dittborn's Jemmy Button is no less an invention than Fitzroy's. He was processed by Dittborn out of a series of copyings: the photo-silkscreen of a photograph in a book of an engraving of an original drawing by an English naval officer made over a century and a half earlier. However, although uncertainty prevails in the work, it is and remains focused on history. Once again, we can see the isomorphism in the relationship between Dittborn's methods and Latin America's cultural situation – until recently, at least, a copying of a Europe that was the foundation and source of originality and authenticity (see Richard in Beverley et al. 1995: 220).

In the post-colonial epoch when societies have been attempting to synthesise identities out of the colonial inheritance, copying has become a defiant choice. What was once a weakness has become celebrated as an advantage. Copying as imitation is being replaced by copying as reworking, as the re-interpretation and recirculation of images and texts. If identity can found itself on the absence of foundation, then the copy becomes more than imitation and can be proclaimed as the pre-condition for origination. Dittborn's work and Latin America are both copy and original, made and re-made, both self and other. The continuous travelling of the *Airmail Paintings* both expresses and confirms this. That is to say, they are both here and there, both of and beyond themselves. Cultural remoteness becomes replaced with a co-presence of distinct cultural languages, a coincidence of difference. Through making these aesthetic events present in London, Birmingham, New York, Berlin, Osaka or Milan, audiences are invited or seduced into internalising the same fragmentations, dispersals and painful contradictions within the work and to understand that they were always there within them and their own societies and part of their own foundation.

In a few of his *Airmail Paintings* Dittborn lays among his clues, fragments and rejected faces an image of a house, or of Noah's Ark or some other shelter. But they are simple, sentimental, even childish renderings – the diagram, the patchwork picture (*arpillera*) or the child's drawing. And for these reasons they suggest the idea or the fantasy of a house, not a house that can be lived in. Or they evoke the nostalgic recollection of a home that is irrecoverable. And yet, while both the textual meanings of the series and the art objects themselves are intended to remain unsettled, perhaps Dittborn has sent them on a journey which, like all journeys, is looking for a home. By being sent beyond itself Chile might not only see itself and be seen better, but also might find itself more at home in the world.

Art cannot eradicate the material facts of exile. It can bear witness to their existence. Of all forms photography accomplishes this with most effect. But aesthetic practice in general can go further. By transmuting the negation and hunger of exile into an object, a performance, a text, a set of images, it introduces into the world something that wasn't there before. In making something out of a condition that had made lives almost impossible to live in, the principle that exile can not only be overcome but can be the source of new cultural forms, even new ways of living freely, is given a palpable existence.

Photographic practice has contributed to these possibilities. It confronts the viewer with the truth of exile's frozen existences. Yet, through the critique and overcoming of its own limitations as a medium, it also unfixes itself from that truth and suggests the possibility of moving beyond it.

Notes

1 For reflections on Freud's thinking on travel see Porter 1991: chapter 7.

2 An extended discussion of these questions can be found in Beverley et al. 1995.

9
Disappearance: twentieth-century photography, art and travelling

> You have to travel ... not to acquire a more informed vision of the world – there is no universality anymore, no possible synthesis of experience, nor even ... is there any pleasure of an 'aesthetic' or 'picturesque' variety to be had from travel. (Jean Baudrillard, *Cool Memories*, 1990)

At the close of the twentieth century the futures of familiar modes of both photography and travelling are being thrown into doubt by a speeding-up of social and technological developments underway since its outset. The emerging condition is emblematised concisely by one of Jörge Sasse's digital photographs titled, '5502, 1996' (plate 13).

When a photograph is titled with a computer logging number we are being told what not to expect. In Sasse's road image, there is no presence traced or expressed. No journey is being recalled. We share nobody's point of view. Given Sasse's general working methods, even the base image would have been serendipitous, and any reference, personal or otherwise, was further attenuated in the process of scanning the image, of translating it into digital information for the generation of new picture species. Its origins lie not in subjectivity but in the domain of digitalised image-processing. These origins are displayed in its pixilated flat-depth. The slight fuzzing which renders forms indistinct or generalised reduces further any traditional depth illusion and ensures the unreachability of objects or figures. We focus then on the formal relations on the *surface*. We know that, as with all digitalised representations, the presences in the picture exist solely in the present of the viewer and have no origin in the past of an image. Yet, this image seems to be generating time by adding speed to sight and to be carrying us into a space which moves ahead of us – a space that never was – towards events that will never take place. The beauty of the work lies in its having created an absolute visual present which owes nothing to and is not displaced into anything that lies before or after it – neither history nor memory, neither distance nor the real. John Berger maintains there is no meaning without narrative (Berger and Mohr 1982: 89). Sasse's image is free of any such unfolding. It is meaningless. But that is the source of its still sublimity.

These contradictory qualities in Sasse's work mirror themes in the general culture at the close of the twentieth century concerning the transformation of both photography and journeys. The flood of photographic images grows in power and dimension and yet the medium is, we are told, about to disappear or metamorphose into the digitalised unfamiliar. More people travel further and more often than ever before and yet the 'death of distance' at the hand of super-velocity electronic transmission has been announced (Cairncross 1997). As a consequence, travel will become for many increasingly stationary and virtual. Christopher Pinney writes, 'we have replaced the ascendancy granted in the nineteenth and twentieth centuries to distance/time with the ascendence of the "*distance/speed* of the electronic picture factories"' (Pinney citing Virilio in Taylor 1994: 420).

These changes are being determined by more than the force of transforming technologies. Contributing pressures come also from economic, political and cultural restructurings in the world and from mutations in theory concerned with them. The aim of this chapter is to follow the continuing interdependence of photography and travel as it has evolved since 1900. Discussion will be restricted to photographic practice which understands travel and mobility as among modernity's central themes and metaphors and seeks to develop new visual languages in which to embody them.

Modern movements

> A space of time, filled, always filled with moving. (Gertrude Stein)
>
> Artists ... do not show space, they create it. (Henri Lefebvre)

Movement as a phenomenon in its own right had become a significant object of photographic attention before the end of the nineteenth century. The work of Muybridge and Marey had opened up an 'optical unconscious' by making visible the structures of human and animal locomotion using what were, in hindsight, proto-cinematic means – sequenced photographs which visually dissected a brief movement such as somebody jumping and displaying it as a series of stalled micro-events – as if the elements of movement were themselves unmoving. Observation here was conducted from positions resolutely external to the object and the presence of the observer was suppressed.

In the same period and during the near half-century which preceded it journeys of dramatically enhanced speeds and extended range became common as more and more travelling was mechanised. Yet the style of the photography of travel remained mostly undisturbed – a fixed positivist stare. While there exist thousands of photographs of trains, sailing ships and steamships, early automobiles and aircraft, until after about 1910 few are formed in a visual language able to express the nature of modern travel – its dynamism, its reshaping of visual perception, its sudden dislocations and multiple coincidences, its associated mentalities and sensibilities. Travel was commonly represented but not in an aesthetic form that was itself a product of travelling.

Aaron Scharf has shown how European painting rather than photography attempted to discover ways of visualising the changing experience of movement. Monet, for one, exploited as aesthetic virtues the deficiencies of the camera in its depiction of movement by taking the blurred and ghostly forms of photographed street figures, those mid-century products of slow shutters and sluggish emulsions, and translated them into painterly smears to notate the energies of the boulevards. Another instance was Seurat's Marey-influenced work such as his studies of the visual-temporal traces of movement, *Le Chahut* for example (Scharf 1974: 230–1).

Of course, the visualisation of movement alone does not represent even a *formal* equivalence of travel. But out of this wider project which concerned itself with notating or anatomising movement came work in which we can witness the attempt to embody in visual form a consciousness and a way of seeing becoming transformed by travel's contemporary modes; that is, to resolve travel's objects *and* subjects. Prior to Cubism, the attempt is most developed in Degas's depictions of spaces as restless, full of unconcluded encounters, their visual energy gathering at the margins of the frame. In his spaces things are forever poised to move on to the next moment, to the next chance configuration of people and objects, to the next arrangement of space (Scharf 1974: 196).

Degas depicted inhabited or experienced spaces. This above all is what links him to the evolution of a visual language of travel. In order both to document and to express from within the kind of space that corresponded to the *habitus*, not simply of the modern traveller but of an extensive, emerging cultural condition more and more deeply formed by travelling, the photographer needed to absorb the lesson of Degas and others – that space has a subject; and yet to take on and take further the lesson of Muybridge and Marey: that movement has a objective structure that can be documented. More than this, photographers themselves needed to become travellers, whether of the quotidian or the remote, whose ways of seeing and aesthetic practice would also become in some sense modes of travelling.

However it seems to have needed more than the cumulative experience of modern life or the influence of pre-Cubist painting to transform photographers and their practice. The new photographic language did not begin to emerge until the meaning or at least the tenor of the scientific, philosophical and aesthetic revolutions of the period from about 1900 to 1916 had been assimilated; until a new intellectual order and '*structure of feeling*' began to form.

Through the din sent up by shifting paradigms in the early years of the twentieth century could be heard voices which, though distinctive, shared one conviction:

that the old separations of subject and object prevailing in science and philosophy and the stability and security which rested on them were illusory and needed to be abandoned. In 1913 Husserl would propose that 'an act of consciousness and its object are but the subjective and objective parts of the same thing' (see Kern 1983: 205; Derrida 1973: 18–24).

Descriptions of space and time which held them to be absolute, objective and static were undermined by a range of alternative pictures where they appeared fluid, heterogeneous and significantly determined by the perceptual structures, behaviour and purposes of participants and observers.

Einstein famously saw space as the product of the relative speed and positions of objects, and also regarded many of the qualities and activities of objects as the consequences of observation. By 1916 he had given up on the term 'space' as signifying an already given, objective and inactive dimension or context, preferring instead to see it as an *event* dependent on precise but impermanent conditions and conjunctions.

While this same period can be made to present different features expressing the promotion or imposition of unwavering order, clarity, certainty and unity, it was overwhelmingly the fluid and relativist characteristics of the former picture that became most thoroughly installed in the thinking and practices of the artistic avant-gardes. A number of things appeared to coincide with their own concerns or most excited their imaginations. They were fascinated by the question of how the observer's relative position or mode of enquiry effects the nature and behaviour of the object; by how the observer becomes part of the observed. Their work absorbed the understanding of time and space as coterminous. Above all, they accepted the central importance of movement in the essential activity of both matter and its observation – a principle implicit in all the others.

The Cubists were the first to give aesthetic existence to these ideas. In 1911 the painter Jean Metzinger, who with Albert Gleizes produced the Cubist movement's first theoretical work, characterised the Cubist painter as a mobile consciousness, moving around the object, synthesising it from 'successive aspects'. The picture, they announced, now reigned in time as well as space using the 'free, variable system of [Picasso's] perspective' (Metzinger 1911: 18; see also Golding 1968: 11; and Kern 1983: 145).

At the same time the Italian brothers Anton Giulio and Arturo Bragaglia initiated Futurist *Photodynamism*, a practice committed to the production of what the former proclaimed as the 'transcendental photograph of movement' (Bragaglia in Philips 1989: 293). Photodynamism would push photographic practice beyond the individual photograph, and beyond both Marey's chronophotography and the cinema, all of which were denounced for merely reproducing particular states or stages of movement and thereby draining movement of its force.

Instead, their work aimed to portray the fullest trajectory of a movement comprising all its intervening stages, by layering numerous exposures of its evolution through time, one over the other. As the progressive superimpositions degraded the representational image the object gradually decomposed into abstract forms – curving tracks of light, clouds of glowing radiation – analogous, supposedly, to restless sub-atomic elements and pure energy.

In the familiar Nietzschean–Bergsonian voice of Futurism, Bragaglia heroises movement as a destructive-creative and idealising force which escapes the given and the particular through its violent transformations of matter, by its releasing of the energy imprisoned in static forms: 'We seek the pure essence of things: pure movement: and we prefer to see everything in slow motion' (Bragaglia in Philips 1989: 293).

In practices such as Photodynamism and later investigations by Moholy-Nagy and others time materialises into near abstract photographic forms, objects which invent new spatialities, visualising the inseparability of space and time.

However, Futurism's spaces rage and resound with forces and forms which expel all subjectivity, expressing a species of anti-humanism which can easily slide into the totalitarian as was to be demonstrated later by the movement's political choices. For this reason its contribution to a photographic aesthetics of travel is limited. The depiction of human mobility requires the incorporation of the effects of subjectivity – travelling implies a traveller.

Laszlo Moholy-Nagy's work was comparably experimental, and frequently abstract and similarly preoccupied with time, space and movement. It sought, in his words, the 'activisation of space' through the application of 'the dynamic principle in art' (Moholy-Nagy 1922 in Passuth 1985: 290). But his work did not function to disbar the subjective from its representations. Rather it was informed by the more dialectical awareness of how motorised travel and mechanised visual systems were transforming the nature of human perception and the human physical experience of being in the world. The effects on modern life of increasing mobility, speed, the constantly changing viewpoints, and new visualising technologies dominate his 1943 article 'Space-Time and the Photographer'.

> Space-Time is now the new basis on which the edifice of future thoughts and works should be built. Contemporary arts, rapid changes in our surroundings through inventions, motorization, radio and television, electronic action, records of light phenomena, and speed are helping us to sense its existence and significance. (Moholy-Nagy in Passuth 1985: 351)

The body and the eye remodelled by the pace and mobility of the machine inspire many of Moholy-Nagy's photo-graphics. They are taken up with speed, with lines of force which shoot across the empty white spaces of the new designed environment. They show the fusion of the human with the mechanical. There is his rider and motorbike, for example, pictured as evolved into a single body – a mechanised subject, a subjectivised machine. They lean on the curve, liberated by speed from gravity's inertia. Other works employ photographic superimposition and cameraless photograms to act as the photographic 'synonyms' of events in which different spaces and times coincide as, he says, they do in dreams, in the reflections of city traffic, in shop windows, and in travelling (Moholy-Nagy (1943) in Passuth 1985: 351).

His work is a quest for an aesthetics incorporating machine vision – the products of cameras independent of the eye. Often the camera is established spatially and optically beyond it in travelling devices producing images that are fast, crystalline, microscopic, galactic or aviatory. But Moholy-Nagy is interested in the production of new visual subjectivities out of these objective phenomena. However altered, even decentred the human presence becomes in his work, its spaces remain for the most part inhabited, or in some way grounded in or forming the ground of changing human perception and aesthetic practice. In this respect it is linked with Manet and Degas and Cubism, and with applications of photography in which 'the temporality of the camera's eye was tied to a recognition of the mobility of being, to movement in the world' (Lury 1998: 162).

Moholy-Nagy's conviction that speed, the mobile technological environment and new visualising mechanisms were seriously altering human perceptions is open to doubt. Patrick Maynard, for one, is unconvinced, insisting there is little evidence for it. 'Like cubism', he writes, 'the "new vision" somewhat shifted people's tolerance and expectation regarding *images* – but that is quite a different issue' (Maynard 1997: 196–7). What is more certain is that Moholy-Nagy's work realises in terms of perceivable (predominantly visual) aesthetic events a series of transformed conceptions concerning the nature of time and space and the new environment and how they are experienced. It reproduces the world not simply as it is seen but as it has been re-conceived.

Presenting its object as the product of an assembly of moving viewpoints, Cubism and its many heirs were displaying an understanding of space as the product of a relationship between a space and an observer – space as a practice. In a Cubist work each perspective constructs a different space and therefore a different object. A Cubist work is a multiplicity of events as, too, is the activity of its viewer, obliged by the contradicting forms to move around and take up various positions in relation to the picture and thereby become more consciously implicated in its construction as well as radically subject to its effects.

Some eighty years later Braque's and Picasso's experiments retained sufficient power to move David Hockney to apply the same formal principles to the photographic representation not so much of space but of how the experience and possibly the structure of space is conditioned by the way we travel through it.

In 1986 Hockney put together one of his photo-collages, or 'joiners', titled *Pearblossom Highway*. It might be described as a 'road photograph'. It depicts a crossroads in the desert an hour or so by car out of Los Angeles. While it bears some resemblance to an image keyed around one viewpoint located at a fixed position in a single moment, it's soon clear that the picture is made up of maybe three or four hundred separate, overlapping photographs amounting to a continuous survey of the space around the crossroads but carried out over several days and taken from different angles and at varying distances from objects. Like an easel painting the picture is built up from many visual instances of time and space which relate to each other but, like buckled plates, refuse to fit. This intentional 'failure' to resolve the parts into a unified whole represents an aesthetic itinerary – the process of picture-making as it developed through time and space. Hockney recalls how he made exposures at various points along the road, drove through and around the area as both driver and passenger each with different options for looking. As driver he was governed by the need to keep his eyes on the road, to check the signs. As passenger he was able to cast his eyes around at his leisure. Hockey also walked the area, moved very close to certain objects, shot some from above, some from far off, used a ladder to photograph road signs straight on – the better to reproduce fully their iconic impact (Hockney 1988: 147–61).

Pearblossom Highway visualises place as a synthesis of *experienced* space-time; as space that has been entered, passed through, viewed and reviewed, recalled and thought about; as the accumulated *movements* of a viewing, reflecting and moving subject. It is the record of space as *travelling*, as in some part subjective, as something put together. The recourse to photographic collage dramatises the inadequacy of the camera's optical realism for representing lived space, designed as it is to visualise the space from the viewpoint of some static, absolute and universal individual, an abstraction which cleanses the picture of the effects of any actual viewer's presence and suppresses the role of movement in the making of space. Hockney could have painted the scene but this would have failed to make the point. The effect of the temporal discontinuities introduced by the many bits of spatialised time – the individual photographs – would have been lost. So too would have Hockney's desire to carry his challenge to visual realism beyond the concerns of fine art by means of a practical critique of the photograph – 'fooling the machine' through collage – a medium even now widely accepted as a master template of visual experience in general (Hockney 1988: 161). Hockney insists that we don't experience space as camera vision; and given that he sees the real being in and part of a moving, shifting, active human consciousness, and not exclusively 'visual', the orthodox use of the camera and its imagery for making analogies of the real is clearly pointless.

In many respects *Pearblossom Highway* reprises the aesthetics and phenomenology of the early twentieth century. But Hockney's use of the singular coincidence in photography of both spatiality and temporality accomplishes something new.

In 'The Rhetoric of the Image' Barthes described photography as 'a new space-time category, spatial immediacy and temporal anteriority, the photograph being an illogical conjunction between the *here-now* and the *there-then*' (Barthes 1977: 44). In Hockney's joiner the conjunction becomes a polarity, or many polarities active both within and between the many photographs that constitute it. They generate what is equivalent to a kinetic energy driving the viewer's visual engagement. The eyes are drawn through the desert. They flicker from space to space; they cut suddenly from vague horizon to emphatic close-up. They move from moment to moment, through the time that, citing an idea of Estelle Jussim, photography has made 'transparent' (Jussim 1989: 50).

Made up of stills that are never at rest, *Pearblossom Highway* is a road that can be seen only by travelling it – a journey which, of course, takes time. As Doreen Massey has written, 'space is not static, nor time spaceless' (in Keith and Pile 1993: 155).

The surrealist tour guide

> Photography, which had grown out of traveling, now fueled it. (Peter Galassi on Cartier-Bresson)

Of all the aesthetic currents live in the first decades of the twentieth century only Surrealism comes close to the Cubists in its lasting influence over subsequent practice. For the photography of travel it holds a double significance. First its commitment to freeing the photograph from reference introduced uncertainty and therefore movement into the process of photographic meaning. Second, Surrealism celebrated travel as creative and experimental in its own right, as an activity which could serve the movement's cultural politics.

Surrealist photography generally favoured the use of techniques that doubled, multiplied, fragmented or mounted a physical assault on the representational image: double exposure, solarisation, combination printing, photo-collage, the stressing or partial melting of the negative. Their function was to bring about the destruction, no less, of photographic realism in so far as it rested on the claim that the unique and unified single image is a direct transference of the real and filled with its presence.

In an essay on Surrealism and photography Rosalind Krauss shows how, by introducing the effects of doubling and spacing into the image, reality is convulsed from within. The dominance of the original is brought down by the 'multiple representations in "one" image', and presence is 'transmuted into succession'. The image begins to take on something like the sequential characteristics of writing with its effect of forever deferring the real. As a result meaning becomes liberated from the real's domination: 'through duplication, it opens the original to the effects of difference, of deferral, of one-thing-after-another' (Krauss 1986: 28).

Through such blows against the single meaning founded upon some transcendent authority – the real, the grammatical – and by releasing the elements of the work to produce stray and limitless meanings and affects,

Surrealism wished to bring to cultural forms the restlessness of the world and have them reflect desire's endless journey towards the thing it loves. After all, it was to the triumph of desire that Surrealism had dedicated itself (Nadeau 1973: 207).

For the Surrealists travel was a method, a means of smoking out the unconscious, forcing it to reveal its presence in the daylight, in the street, if only travellers could lay themselves open to the unexpected encounter with whoever or whatever might trigger its arousal. But more than simply pleasuring its subjects, the surrealist journey conveyed them towards an encounter with some kind of otherness which might also destabilise and transform them.

Surrealist travelling was lived collage, cultural subversion. Journeys would provide experiences and material to be laid alongside and relativise, ironise and even contaminate the cultural forms and norms of a European culture so secure in its sense of singularity and cultural supremacy. The surrealist traveller wandered the world as though it was a vast flea market (see also James Clifford's discussion of 'ethnographic surrealists' in Clifford 1988: 133–4).

By the early 1930s the surrealist journeys had become the key to the young Cartier-Bresson's photographic approach. His work consistently uses the risks and possibilities in the encounter between the stranger-photographer and stranger-subjects as a source of aesthetic and moral power. The photographer frequently confronts his subjects face-on, at times venturing well into their dramatic space, forcing their response.

And yet his work abounds with the faces of the self-contained who look away, or haven't even noticed – indifferent to the traveller's intrusion, to his anguished curiosity. They speak of an irreducible remoteness in others, or of their refusal to give themselves finally to the undivided outsider – an independence of being which Surrealism heroised.

The journeys were the key also to his photographic language, the translation of the conditions of travelling into visual form. The surrealist strategies which Peter Galassi maintains Cartier-Bresson's depends on are themselves akin to or even derived from the effects and opportunities furnished by travelling (Galassi 1987: 35). Galassi cites the use of the *juxtapositioning* of things to bring about associative effects. Outside the collage-maker's studio, the photographer discovers or invents such contiguities through walking, driving, wandering – that is he or she reframes the world by travelling it.

Cartier-Bresson's work also employs the surrealist method of *dépaysement*, the dislocation of things and people from their 'expected spatial or narrative context', in order to 'release hidden poetic force' (Galassi 1987: 35). The word itself means to be removed, perhaps even wrenched from one's country (*pays*) or from home, from the familiar – to be, that is, in the condition of a traveller in which the everyday becomes strange and the strange everyday.

The original French title for his collection *The Decisive Moment* was *Images à la sauvette*, images made 'on the run', 'in haste' – a far more accurate designation. Yet his work is almost invariably spoken of as the uncovering of the essential beneath the impermanent – while change, chance, and the arbitrary all remain its central qualities. The moment in his images when forms miraculously rhyme with each other seems to embody principles of unity and necessity, bringing to them at times a near-Classical stillness. But it is also the moment prior to the unravelling of form when the principle of chaos reasserts itself. Things and the photographer move on. Such a moment is an event, a chance occurrence made more likely by travelling. The unity is not discovered but created. Cartier-Bresson is Plato *and* Heraclitus. The beauty of his work is a stoical and occasionally melancholy one. It rises from the tension between the moment of formal coherence and its death, a death once imminent in the event that has left its trace as an immanence within the photograph.

The 1934 portrayal of the two prostitutes in Mexico City's Calle Cuauhtemoctzin, to select a widely known image, takes a subject with traditional associations in the culture of masculine travelling. It shows the sexualised female figure who sells pleasure and connotes danger; who stands in certain abject and exotic spaces of the outside against the figure of the domestic female located in some form of domestic or familiar interior. The sex trade is of course traditionally associated with travel and migration, with roads, ports, areas around railway stations, lorry stops, hotels.

In one sense the two figures can be grouped with the drifting objects and other cultural flotsam which the Surrealists and Cartier-Bresson found so charming: the tailor's dummies, shop window mannequins, the sprawled drunk who's acquired a porcupine crest, the man whose head has transformed into a knotted curtain, all of them like characters in some parallel world of fictions. One of the women resembles a ship's figurehead you might come across in a coastal antique shop, the other some discarded sentimental portrait.

However, the two women are also presented in the condition of their trade – at once framed, displayed and imprisoned in the half-doors. One composes herself as object within the frame like, as they say, a picture – something good to look at, something for sale. The other makes herself proud beyond the frame, protrudes towards the client-photographer. The two are non-identical twins – passive and active, painting and drama. But both these acts of self-presentation are front performances which, while proffering intimacy, serve to withhold it more completely.

The spatial and photographic arrangements of the image are indispensable to the plausibility of this reading. Since the picture has been shot at an angle slightly oblique to the women, the viewer's relationship to them is off-key, uneasy. It also puts the woman on the right, who looks at us directly, just beyond the depth of field and thus slightly out of focus, more distant. Her companion is closer to the lens and sharply focused but her eyes are almost closed and our attention becomes concentrated on the carefully made-up face. The closer and clearer she has got the more like a mask she has become, and in this respect, at least, the more impenetrable.

The uneven range of focus and formal imbalances, the imperfections of images made *à la sauvette*, are the emblems of the photography of the passer-by, the traveller. They also mark something of the nature of the male photographer's relationship to these women – a man whose look they attempt to control, the carrier of a look their material existence depends upon.

But the unresolved structure of the image which makes the women not quite visually possessible by the viewer's look underwrites their own play with availability. The image is structured around an encounter centred on the male look. But it is not reducible to it. However circumscribed their existence may have been the women keep hold of their otherness; they represent an energy that flows from the other side of the image by determining something of both the performance and the *mise-en-scène*. The transience of masculine presence here, the man's passing, is as much an expression of his inability to control things fully as it is the mark of his privilege to be able to move on.

Highways and drivers

> Panoramic perception no longer belongs to the same space as the perceived objects: the traveller sees ... *through* the apparatus which moves him through the world. That machine and the motion it creates become integrated into his visual perception: thus he can only see things in motion. (Wolfgang Schivelbusch quoted in Dimendberg, *The Will to Motorization*, 1995)

> The unique spatialities created by technology. (Stephen Kern, *The Culture of Time and Space*, 1983)

While noting how a landscape becomes fragmented when viewed from a speeding train or car, Léger sees its gaining in 'synthetic value' what it has lost in 'descriptive value' (Léger 1973: 11). The truth of this observation seems borne out in the work of certain contemporary and near-contemporary photographers exploiting the possibilities for producing aesthetic form that car travel introduced. There are two types of such work: that based on the visual-photographic results of car travel and speed; and that concerned with the changes in the social spaces we inhabit determined by the car economy. Among the former is an imagery which remains descriptive but whose aesthetic force is achieved by the exploitation of the random juxtapositions that the passing car brings about and the photographer chooses to fix on for their synthesis of form or meaning. The method echoes that of the Surrealists while dispensing with their political project – replacing revolutionary negation with the relativism of liberal irony.

An example is Joel Meyerowitz's 1966 car windscreen view of a low-flying

Pan Am Jetliner passing over an elephant made of concrete piping near Heathrow Airport. Though an instrumental element in the unextraordinary urban world, the moving car becomes the vehicle of transforming perceptions; initiator of representations and metamorphosis and of motoring as an aesthetic exercise. The constant movement and alterations in point of view transforms the ordinary journey into an encounter with an infinity of possible ironies, aesthetic or comic effects, even modest subversions of the environment's dull utilitarian purposes.

The photograph confirms what the car has made possible. But it is the photographer, the mental traveller, who recognises the conceptual relations in these incidental covenants between things. It's the image, the framing in particular, that renders them essential.

Like Meyerowitz's, Lee Friedlander's photography from cars might be termed descriptive, yet in it not only has actuality become an enigma, but looking itself has become a form of puzzlement. Within the apparent confusion of a visual world divided and fragmented by frames and reflections, street furniture, architecture and monuments are the mirrored details of the photographer's eyes, face, camera. They mark visualising acts which are no longer the invisible sources of the imagery but divided from themselves and become objects or elements within it, part of the world seen, part of the composition. If the world and vision do have meaning, whether social or metaphysical, this artist does not offer himself as their interpreter. The self-portraits of the bleary-eyed motel traveller, dishevelled and disengaged, seem to make this clear and encourage the acceptance of John Szarkowski's promotion of his work in the 1960s as compelled by the will to form rather than to inform or reform (Szarkowski, introducing the *New Documents* exhibition 1967; cited in Rosler 1981: 78). The world's purpose is to end up in a photograph and the road's mess of stimuli – the highway's montage – are welcome acquisitions, raw material for the photographer. Friedlander's unblinking, protuberant eyes in the self-portraits speak of a permanently unimpressed yet insatiable visuality. They are the eyes of a certain type of traveller, one at once uninvolved and ravenous for experience. This detached intensity, the tangle of things in his photographs and their use of unremarkable, even banal items and places permits the joy of image-making, of transmuting motoring into iconography to take place without the distraction of other issues.

Yet from out of all this Friedlander established a language that is at once busy and poised. Formal continuities appear in his 'road' work. There are the passing coincidences of form, the cut *within* the frame and the multiple framings. There are the mirrors which create a temporal and spatial sequence in the still image by making the preceding event approaching in the windscreen, and the receding event diminishing in the rear-view mirror, coincide as a single visual event. In this way the spatial and temporal condition of the driver is precisely rendered. There is the blurred form played dissonantly against the sharp detail which often stands out in the image like a face or some curious

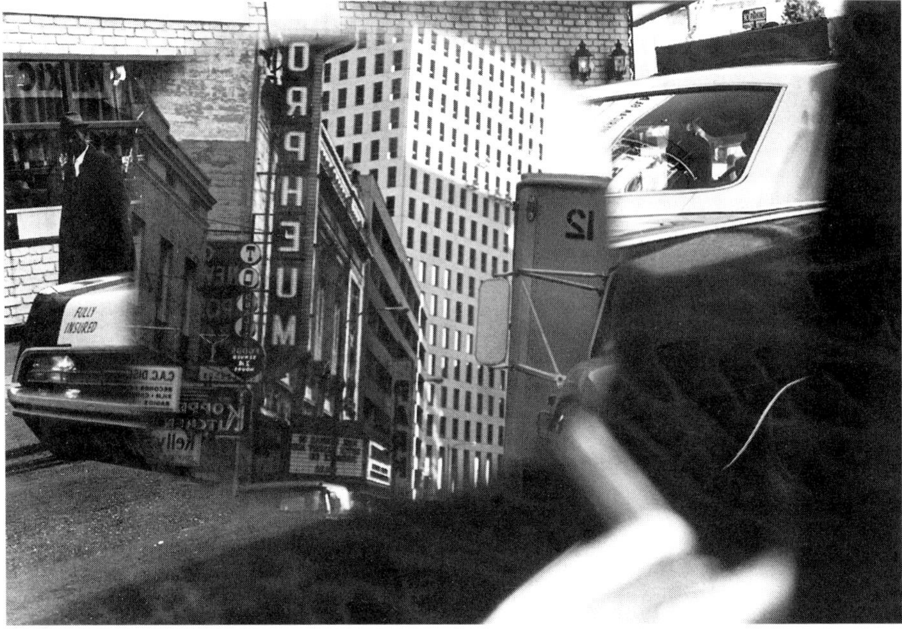

Fig. 45 Lee Friedlander, 'New Orleans' (gelatin-silver print), 1969.

uncompleted incident glimpsed along the road as you pass which remains impressed insistently on the memory, held out of time.

Through its use of insignificant objects in making significant form Friedlander's art remains modernist – located outside its material in the transcendent place of the aesthetic. But there exist other dimensions to his work which Szarkowski's personal-formal characterisation ignores. First, his work offers a visual phenomenology of car travelling. Second, as we shall see below, his work can be linked both to what we have learned to call the postmodern and to an aesthetic practice that permits us to see more fully characteristics of the contemporary social world.

Other photographers have used the car as an aesthetic device in a more concentrated way. With some it becomes almost an optical instrument which radically alters our perceptions. Their view of driving corresponds more closely to both Schivelbusch's and Léger's descriptions.

Their work is produced variously: by a dramatic registration of speed on the emulsion; by creating a series of framings and reframings; from continuous or intermittent shooting through the car windows or off its mirrors; or by introducing into the image the body or shadow of the car in movement. The car becomes both object in and creator of photographic space; both extension of the camera and definer of its limits.

One example of the latter is Ikko's (Ikko Narahara) 1970s photograph of a limousine's speed-stretched silhouette ploughing up streaks of light as it races

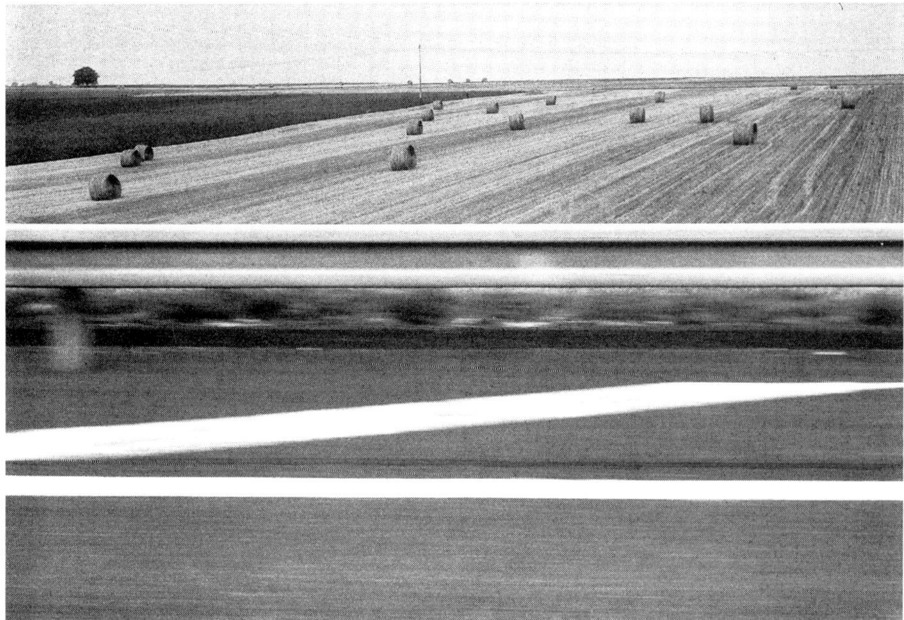

Fig. 46 Patrick Zachmann (Magnum), 'France autoroutes', 1982.

across the floor of the Arizona desert. The luminous energy and the escape of the driverless shadow from its cause (the actual car) express the curiously detached, hypnotised excitement and ambiguous freedom of surrendering to an impersonal process induced by driving fast through the night on the long western freeways (Ikko 1975; Ikko 1978). Think of those set, wordless, faces in Robert Frank's image numbered 73 in *The Americans* titled *US 91, Leaving Blackfoot, Idaho.* (For some other photographers of the American highway see Green 1984: 178–80 and Jussim and Lindquist-Cock 1985: 104–22.)

Patrick Zachmann's studies made on French motorways reveal a set of fixed physical and spatial environments that have been created by the road system – the motorway, its installations, bridges, toll booth architectures and so forth. They also present the fluid perceptual space contingent upon the car's direction and speed, weather conditions and the car window the viewer is using. The sequence from which this still is taken (figure 46) recalls Reyner Banham's observation that the space viewed through the windscreen of a moving car is panoramic while that viewed through the side windows is parallax. Zachmann's sequence cuts from the nearside and offside world with its strata of relative speeds – from the streaming foreground out to the fixed horizon – to the apparently still road ahead. (A triptych from this series appears in Magnum 1996: 83.)

Here Zachmann incorporates into his imagery both the thing and, as Mallarmé preferred in painting, the effect it produces – space as a consequence of relative speed and position.

Fig. 47 Alexander and Susan Maris, 'Momentum # 7' (selenium-toned gelatin-silver print), 1995. 9 x 4 cm.

'Descriptive value' is entirely abolished in a series of photographs titled *Momenta* exhibited at London's Lisson Gallery in 1996 by the Glasgow-based artists Alexander and Susan Maris. The pair have travelled Europe by motorbike photographing at speed from the pillion with exposure times of between four and fifteen seconds. The result is the complete dematerialisation of the solid urban and suburban scenes before the camera and their transmutation into a series of foggy, diaphanous 'imaginary landscapes' suggesting the presence of mountains and oceans (figure 47).

The piece amounts to a destruction of the visible but not in the tradition of Expressionism. For not only do the Marises demote the place of subjectivity in the making of these images by giving in to the process, albeit a chosen one – the fast bike and the gaping shutter – they also had them exhibited inside thickly glassed vitrines which rendered them and their makers more out of reach.

Furthermore, *Momenta* questions the continuance of human presence in general. The Marises have expressed their hostility towards the denatured contemporary world. Like Wim Wenders's glum protagonist in his film *Alice in the Cities* who endlessly produces polaroids to 'blow everything away' he can't stand as he motors across the United States, the Marises combine light and speed to 'blow away' time present and its appearances. They sublimate it in the light of their travelling and replace it with what they have described as the deep geological time of the pre-human past and of the distant future beyond humanity's disappearance – movement, light, mountains, water, weather. Alexander Maris describes how their images of 'the monotonous urbanality which imprisons us, begin to reveal the primeval seascapes and storms which will inevitably replace the conurbation from which they are invoked' (letter to the author February 28 1998). These time-conscious photographers, integrated with vehicle and camera, form a space-time travelling machine – passing time passing.

Through the 1960s and early 1970s Ed Ruscha, an artist working in California, produced twelve books each containing a set of photographs reflecting one theme bearing titles such as: *Twenty Six Gasoline Stations*, 1962, *Some Los Angeles Apartments*, 1965, *Thirty Four Parking Lots*, 1967, *Every Building on Sunset Strip*, 1968, *A Few Palm Trees*, 1971. Laid out equal size and up to eight per page, the images were notable for their seriality, their flat, anti-expressive, stock-shop zero-degree of photography style. Like the Pop and Conceptual art work of the time, they were taken up with concerns such as repetition, minimalism, visual banality, surface, process and mass production which for the most part bracketed out the social.[1]

And yet they index something of the social spaces and sensibilities that concern us here. To begin with, roads and cars feature importantly in many of them. The environment that provided Ruscha with his themes was a product of motoring – the gas stations and car parks of course – but also the spread out, linear and centreless city of Los Angeles itself. And motoring is inscribed in Ruscha's visual language. The repetition of forms reflects the serial production, design and sheer numbers of automobiles, as it does the repetitious journeys made on the standardised national road systems.[2]

Linear development along highways also becomes a key formal figure. The flatness in his photographs, both in style and in the sense of space – the preponderance of the horizontal – has turned up an aesthetic quite distinct from that of European traditions of the picturesque with their portentous grandeurs of height and depth and recessions of forms. Ruscha's photographs are depthless landscapes. They symbolise nothing behind or before themselves. Signs on a flat surface (the parking lots were shot from the air) – they signify only each other: another gas station, another car park along the same road. Reality has become syndicated, a relay.

In both form and subject, Ruscha's sets offer a particular manifestation of a social spatiality emerging in Western capitalist countries since the Second World War, above all in the United States. Fredric Jameson has described it as a process of 'despatialisation' associated with the general appearance of the postmodern order in which landscape is flattened out by the effects of capitalist market forces and rearranged into 'a grid of identical parcels' and exposed 'to the dynamic of a market that now reorganizes space in terms of identical value' (Jameson 1994: 25; see also O'Connor 1997: 257). Edward Dimendberg names the resulting condition 'centrifugal space' where the dense clustering of the traditional metropolitan areas is replaced by 'dispersed settlements and a shift from urban verticality to the horizontal sprawl of suburbs and larger territorial units'. And the 'preeminent centrifugal space of the twentieth century', he adds, is the highway (Dimendberg 1995: 92–3).

In spite of reservations about over-reflective theories of art and culture, when we review Ruscha's work in the light of such theories of modern capitalism's spatialities the apparent isomorphism between the social and the aesthetic is striking. Ruscha's sets are similarly managed under a centrifugal principle. With the exception of the *Sunset Boulevard* group, the number and order of subjects in each are arbitrary, and their locations unspecified. There is no beginning or end, and no centre. And spatial homogenisation receives its equivalence in the visual monotony and repetition of subject matter. Ruscha's places look much the same as each other and in a sense they are the same place – products and spatial instances of the economic system globalising and reproducing itself through space, abolishing the differences between places. In spite of the best mythologising efforts of image-makers the gas station with its glowing pump heads, to take one heavily romanced item on the American road, is no longer a Romantic beacon marking the path of redemptive escape but rather an object of nostalgic longing, a piece of charming Americana, as many now would conclude there is nowhere left to escape to. More than in Ruscha's 1960s the gas station is now simply the standardised distribution point of an oil corporation, the confirmation of dominant capital's ubiquity.

If the postmodern spatial economy can be traced in Ruscha's themes and visual structures, its renowned depersonalising effects are manifested in his work's cool, even blank, neutrality. But this is not to imply that work which does seek to evolve a photography of contemporary spaces and travelling while accepting the impossibility of panoptic or transcendent viewpoints must fail inevitably to enable critical insights in its viewers. To return to Lee Friedlander: although his images plainly are not intended to raise any moral or political fervour, their visually unsettled events nevertheless serve to portray America as a series of unresolvable contradictions and isolated fragments. These are not merely the effects of the car-bound photographer's perception. The centrality of the road, of cars and mobility to American life, and photography's mixture of the fixed and the fleeting, makes this perceptual modality especially appropriate for its visual representation. In an effect reminiscent of Charles Ives's two bands passing as they play different tunes, Friedlander's small towns with their monuments and ceremonies, flags and churches – all emblems of order, tradition and stability – are disrupted, driven through, by the equally American phenomena of transience, haste, redevelopment, removal and speed.

Distractedness and isolation seem also to afflict the drivers photographed by Andrew Bush on the California freeways. His pictures of estrangement call up the faces Walker Evans fished from New York's subway fifty years earlier or Geoff Stern's grab portraits of passengers on the London Tube of the 1980s. In a comparable series Martin Parr's British motorists are identified as social beings in so far as they see their social status mediated and their aspirations declared by the cars they drive. But where Parr's brand-loyal British are privatised, Bush's Californians are unknowable. They seem to have purchased the freedom of car travel at the expense of inhabiting an irreducible loneliness. The distance between them and the viewer is existential not spatial. Like the dead, they are unreachable, cannot be spoken with. The photographer can do no more than record them, catalogue their strangeness – and imagine them (plate 14).

While they are formal inventions, modulating between repetition and variation, these studies of motorised subjects can be viewed also as portrayals of social being. As Raymond Williams pointed out, 'traffic is not only a technique; it is a form of consciousness and a form of social relations ... [the] mode of relationship embodied in the modern car [is]: private, enclosed, an individual vehicle in a pressing and merely aggregated common flow ... we pursue our ultimately separate ways but in a common mode' (William 1975: 356).

In a series of photographs exhibited in New York in 1993 under the title *In the Place of the Public*, some of which appeared four years later in the Photographers' Gallery (London) exhibition *Airport*, Martha Rosler takes the spaces and systems of international airports and air travel as both method and metaphor of global capitalism. In her catalogue essay she identifies the role of jet transportation in the creation of a system of traveller-consumer throughput and standardised abstract space determined primarily by corporate interests and functioning to further corporate goals and reproduce its hierarchies.

Her photographs of concourses, flight desks, transitways, departure lounges and the rest seem to concur with the striplit, 'Alphaville' abstractions of her subject matter. Perhaps the only worrying thing about this dead time and blank space is the lack of people.

It is the phrases scattered on the walls around the photographs but not anchored to any image in particular that introduce disturbance into the pictures. They float in and over them like unsettling thoughts and begin to counter the overcontrolled wordless perfection of these spaces:

white noise hiss ø a hospital regime bright
image of displacement ø vagina or birth canal? ø
imperceptible airflow ø capital costs ø institutional
facade ø blind turns ø there are only no
fragments when there is no whole ø destinations always
approached never achieved ø brightly lit atrium ø.

Nothing in Rosler's work goes without saying. Much of it dwells on how visual arrangements can function to repress language or how language can be made to repress meaning. The effect of these words is to press us to reinspect the images, to see that their emptiness is itself the content to which the hypervisibility of airport design and procedure blinds us. For besides their obvious functions, airports produce emptiness and non-experience; they depersonalise, dislocate, displace, suspend us between things, disavow our anxiety, act like sensory deprivation chambers, render us submissive and evacuate us along the channels of the global system. Paul Virilio has said that the faster we communicate the more static we become. Air travel is the fastest mode of mass travel. Yet for most of the time it is an experience of stasis – of waiting in the white squares, restrained in metal tubes. There is no speed in Rosler's airports, no kinesis of any kind. It is the 'rustle of language' against the silence of the image, the anarchy of words against the tyranny of the visual, that forces them to reveal where they are taking us. Yet, as in Rosler's earlier work, the negation of the visual also requires the production of another image – Rosler's dissident visualisations.

Diasporas

> Travel is not a word that can be easily evoked to talk about the Middle Passage, the Trail of Tears, the landings of the Chinese immigrants at Ellis Island, the forced relocation of Japanese-Americans, the plight of the homeless. (bell hooks, *Representing Whiteness in the Black Imagination*, 1992)

> – My heart hurts Rabbi
> – I have troubles
> perhaps Rabbi Nachman
> could give advice
> but how could I find him
> among so many ashes
> (Zbigniew Herbert, *Mr Cogito Seeks Advice*)

As we have seen, as late as the 1960s some photographers in Europe and North America were still able to associate the journey with transcendence, self-creation, access to the Other or as instigator of aesthetic innovation. Yet, in the same decade developments were taking place which would render such associations if not obsolete then hard to maintain. Some of this was indicated in Ruscha's work and later confirmed in that of Rosler.

Of course, since the late 1950s, the further compression of time and space brought about by faster and spreading communications and the multiplication of capitalist economies brought about crucial changes in the nature of both travel and representation (Harvey in Bird et al. 1993). But for some time prior to this, the modernist romance with travelling was already being undone. Its imagined road was becoming blocked by the jostling ghosts of two major historical events, the histories that trailed behind them and the moral and intellectual consequences that ensued. They were the Holocaust and the continuing consequences of the African diaspora.

Diasporic journeys were of course central to the Jewish and African experiences; migration and a variety of displacements common to that of all colonised peoples. The Holocaust itself involved a matrix of journeys, dragging their travellers inwards towards the extermination centres. They were enforced journeys but in many details reminiscent of familiar excursions and vacations: train journeys in family groups, suitcases, favourite dolls, the normal confusion of new arrivals, lost property and the camp gates, which for many summoned up in their minds a holiday camp, and no doubt expressed another turn of the regime's nihilistic cynicism. At Buchenwald Lee Miller translated her rage at Germans who protested their ignorance of such places into an ironic evocation of tourism:

> My fine Baedecker tour of Germany includes many such places as Buchenwald which were not mentioned in my 1913 edition, and if there is a later one, I doubt if they were mentioned in there either, because nobody in Germany has ever heard of a Concentration Camp and I guess they didn't want any tourist business. Visitors took one-way tickets only. (Quoted in Williams 1994: 36)

In this anti-universe it was the hosts – the camp functionaries – who took the travel photographs. They showed the startled looks from the freight wagons; the now dead tracks leading up to the gates of the crematorium at Birkenau; the crowds on the *Eisenbahnrampe* at Birkenau – the platform at the end of the line – these days its last few feet of track ending in a sudden cut; mediocre souvenir snaps taken by a guard in which we see naked people holding their clothes; naked people queuing up for something.

And now, the journeys of return – to witness against forgetting or denial, to stand among the dead. Perhaps photographs are not needed for these journeys. Like a pilgrim the physical presence of the survivors or their descendants is what matters – the physical touching of the place of evil, the touching of its victims' traces, the attempt to fill the enormous absence with a living body. Jacob Bronowski stood barefoot for the television cameras in the pond at Auschwitz where his murdered family's ashes had been thrown (BBC series *The Ascent of Man*). Dan Jacobson visited, for the first time, Lithuania, where many of his relatives had been killed. He was 'shaken' by standing at the actual sites of their persecution. He'd gone there, he said, to demonstrate the limits of the imagination (BBC Radio 4 discussion programme, *Start the Week*, 23 February 1998, see also his book *Heshel's Kingdom*, 1998).

If this bodily presence is essential then the Holocaust is beyond the limits of the contemporary photograph. Perhaps only those taken at the time are necessary – for documentation and remembrance.

However, some camps have become tourist sites and are therefore served by photographic images. Yet the more directly the camps are looked at the more completely their truth disappears. In terms of photographic style and colour, the packs of colour photographs the visitor can buy at Auschwitz–Birkenau are almost continuous with those of any other tourist site in spite of their funereal religiosity – memorial flames flickering, a rose wilting on the barbed wire. In them Auschwitz looks neat, bright and banal – and well cared for (plate 15).

As if some force field is active in them, photographic representation fails at the places where modernity, humanism, the Enlightenment – the projects photography was born out of – failed; where the direction of all the roads was backwards. It is not only a rabbi's advice and comfort that Herbert's Mr Cogito has lost. In the Shoa a moral and intellectual order extending far beyond that of its Jewish victims vanished, and with it, perhaps, the basis for giving what has happened any meaning at all.

Photography is a medium of appearances. The camps are the sites of disappearances; among the most empty places on the planet. If they have a function in our culture as new destinations of pilgrimage, as the ends of moral journeys, it is to represent the likelihood of the human project's self-termination, the principle of the post-human. Against this all future attempts to redefine the human project are measured. If they are sites of pilgrimage, they are secular and deeply ambiguous ones – ground zero, the source of, or the necessity for, the lonely creation of new values – the postwar Declaration of Human Rights for example – and at the same time their killing ground.

But what kind of photographic imagery might such journeys produce? The contemporary photography of the Holocaust views its subject indirectly, with the most serious irony.

Ania Bien's *Hotel Polen* is a house ruined by melancholy. In a number of large photographs the eponymous hotel's silver menu holder carries a series of images which bring to mind a comfortable middle-class world of central European travel and vacation from before the Second World War. There are postcards, family snaps, a map, a leather luggage tag. We know this world is doomed; and, as with Lee Miller's language of sinister resemblances, the signs of innocent travel contain their monstrous other. What unnamed destinations lie hidden in that map? What address will eventually be written on the luggage tag? And besides, the menu holder also carries different images infiltrating the well-being: a man in striped camp pyjamas, a last (?) letter, a (bad?) chess move, a darkened landscape seen, perhaps, from a train, two beautiful children surely lost for ever somewhere in the hotel. And there *is* one place-name faintly legible on the map – *Oswiecim, Auschwitz*.

The dark travelling of the Final Solution is present in a work by Shimon Attie which projected the faces of deported Berlin Jews taken in the 1930s on to buildings or locations as close to where they were originally photographed as he was able (Shimon Attie 1993). Around them are the cranes and bright building sites of the reconstructing city. But Attie's Berlin is haunted space. These migrating dead, illegal immigrants from the past, linger in its bright, brash and distracting modernity. It is what Bataille might have called 'tragic space', the space of a city as desperate to concrete over and forget history as it is to make it (see Lefebvre 1991: 20).

For at least the inheritors of Europe's traditions, the Holocaust has blighted the optimism of the journey, has diminished moral space. But there is a photography of journeys and places that has internalised it. One example of this is Paul Graham's *New Europe* of 1993 with its accompanying essay titled 'The Thoughtful Traveller'. In Graham's dystopic gallery the multinational continent's soiled, banal things, its small sad moments, its loneliness, its infected and abject corners, its bored and tacky postmodernity, its traces and metaphors of a Fascist past still seeping into the present, are all exhibited like gloomy pathologies, manifestations of something bad and long repressed.

Other dystopic spaces and journeys are to be found in Linda Devlin's presentation of the United States as an archipelago of execution chambers, a serial arrangement of killing sites which counters Ruscha's social neutralism.

There are the outside interiors of those travellers with neither place nor destination, the homeless and their self-made shelters documented in Los Angeles by Anthony Hernandez; or Richard Misrach's trips into the radiation-rotten deserts of America's nuclear test sites. Misrach revives the picturesque to display with a cool grandeur a wasted, abandoned planet from the perspective of a human subject who is no longer there. Misrach only half jokingly proposes these places as future sites for some kind of post-human tourism. One can imagine the guides being authored by Baudrillard.

In the 1960s Derrida was writing of the dislocation of European culture – 'driven from its locus, and forced to stop considering itself as the culture of reference' (Derrida 1978: 282). Deriving itself from such destabilising insights, post-colonial theory has identified the association made between travelling and freedom or play in its various senses as being peculiarly Western, reflecting narrowly shared metropolitan privileges and meanings and still carrying an excess of imperial baggage (see also Pratt 1992; Wolff 1993: 224–39; Schwarz 1987; Beezer 1994). 'Imperialist nostalgia' is the phrase cited by bell hooks in order to describe this sort of travelling. Hooks maintains that, for many, the most likely encounter in travelling is one with terror (hooks 1992: 343–4).

Feminist writers on these questions have sought broader, more multiple conceptions, more specified descriptions of the traveller. Adrienne Rich, for example, argues that the traveller needs to develop 'a dynamic awareness of discrepant attachments', which in her case she registers as 'a woman, a white middle-class writer, a lesbian, a Jew' (quoted in Smith and Katz in Keith and Pile 1993: 78).

For the enslaved, bonded or colonised, the journey had always driven the subject towards new identities at whose core the loss of, the tearing away of, the old selves persisted. The loss was both the emptiness of a wound that refuses to heal and at the same time a space of possibility – the openness of an undecided self, one dispersed across space and time, lost and found, unmade and remade in a permanent condition of travelling. It was the basis of a freedom and creativity that were never, of course, sought and never undergone painlessly. Travelling is at the heart of this kind of being-in-the-world, as both quality and

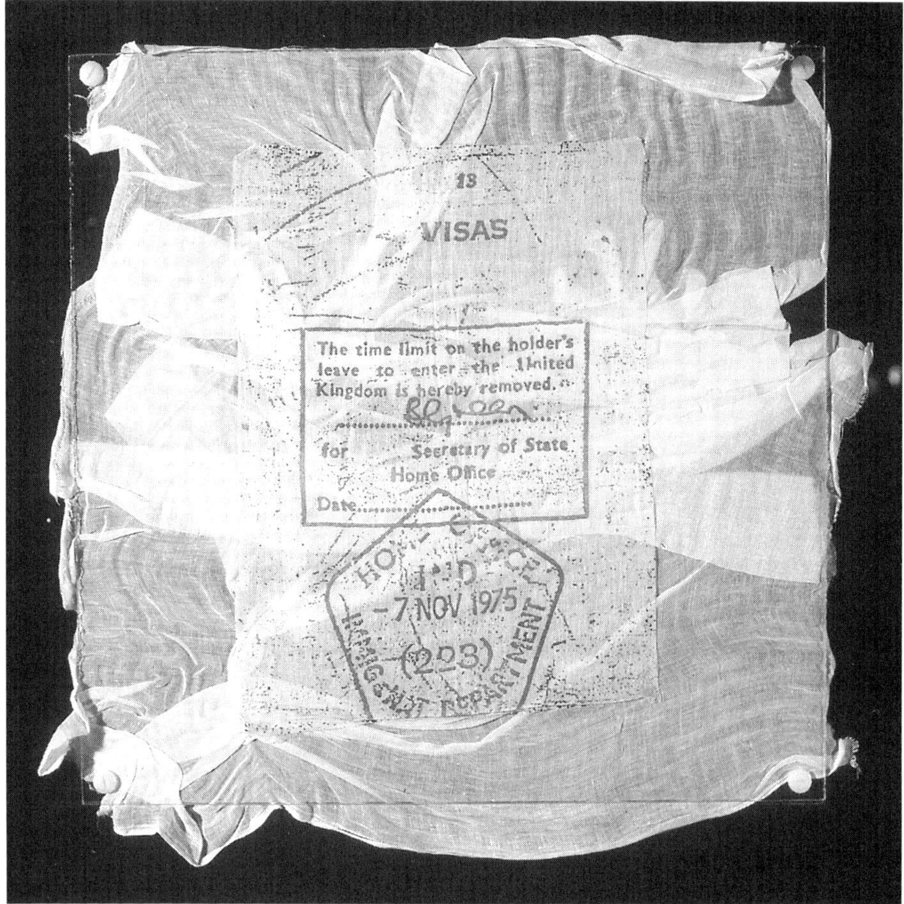

Fig. 48 Zarina Bhimji, from *She Loved to Breathe – Pure Silence*, 1987.

material consequence.

In the work of Zarina Bhimji travelling carries the marks of trauma. Bhimji, whose Muslim Asian family emigrated from Uganda to Britain during the class and ethnic terror of the Idi Amin years, is the inheritor of three dislocations: the colonisation of India, the Indian migrations to British East Africa and the eventual expulsion from Africa to life in the United Kingdom. Each removal entailed the falling away and the acquisition of identities. For this reason travelling is viewed in her work with ambivalence. Her installation piece from 1987, *She Loved to Breathe – Pure Silence*, which incorporated objects, cloth material and photographic images, pairs in one photograph an empty slipper and a small bird whose markings rhyme with the patterns on the slipper.

Both objects can be associated with movement, with walking or flying, with mobility, even with freedom. But the bird is dead; and not only is the slipper more ornamental than practical, it is a shoe designed for men to walk in. The woman can try it on, can play with it, but as signifier in the language of gender it signifies more her domestication than her travelling.

Another panel (figure 48) is wreathed in muslin, a word which slides with ease into *Muslim* (In fact it derives from the Iraqi place-name, *Mosul*). The material resembles translucent skin, the physical surface and border of the self, and a poorly wrapped package. It covers an interior form or entity, an identity crushed by a journey. On one side the muslin/Muslim has been stamped with a British immigration entry permit – a stamp and a brand. It is authorised by the Home Office. *Home Office*: the words form an oxymoron which in its compression of domestic and bureaucratic, state and individual, subject and object, expresses the breaking of borders between areas of existence, by state power in particular. On one panel a rubber glove lies beneath the muslin suggesting to one commentator the gloves used in the physical examination of would-be immigrant women by officials checking their claims to virginity (Haworth-Booth in Bhimji 1992).

These are analogues of self; of a female self traditionally either denied the right to travel or exchanged and dispatched by the needs and conflicts of patriarchal institutions, translated from one place of submission to another. In Bhimji's work the journey is a rite of passage which requires sacrifice – a death, an injury, the giving-up of part of the body, the surrender of the interior, the imposition of a reduced identity. Its territory includes the female body. This theme resonates through other work by Bhimji. It demonstrates that all the territories we travel through are in part psychic and that all maps are in some degree dreamed. For the migrant the dreaming can be so often the symptom of an incurable displacement, the dream of no return – another disappearance.

The African diaspora differs from comparable migrations and violent dispersals not only in its enormity but also through its foundation in the slave system's remorseless project of eradicating the memories and traces of African cultures and identities. Yet out of fracturing and negation new identities emerged. Diasporic identity stands outlined against an 'Africa' which is a place and a principle of origin lost though ever-present. It remains what Stuart Hall has called 'the missing term, the great aporia, which lies at the centre of our cultural identity and gives it a meaning' (Hall in Rutherford 1990: 224). Many diasporic identities have formed in the countless journeyings and cultural spaces produced by the various slave, colonial and wage-labour systems that emerged from the sixteenth century. Hall argues that, while everyone in the diaspora shares the same slave origin and invariably faces the same rejections, identity is based not on an unchanging essence but on 'positioning', on where the subject is placed within shifting histories, geographies and cultures. Identities within the African diaspora then stand in relation to each other in terms of both continuity and difference (Hall in Rutherford 1990: 226–30).

Along with the lines of the great slave and migration routes, Paul Gilroy identifies this pattern of 'unity and differentiation' as one of the most formative oppositions of the African diaspora. It accounts for the versatility and extemporising flair, the active modernity of so many black cultures over the past four centuries as they negotiate 'the unforeseen detours and circuits which mark new journeys and new arrivals that in turn release new political and cultural possibilities'. They adapt, transform and yet somehow reproduce the African refrain time after time, place after place (Gilroy 1993: 86 and 120).

In recent years a number of cultural theorists, generally modernist and anti-essentialist in inclination, have read the formal language of much Black aesthetic practice as the inscription of the most pressing terms of Black experience since slavery; diasporic actualities translated into what has come to be called 'diasporic aesthetics'. This category embraces the arts of discontinuity and improvisation, the poetics of travelling, the unorthodox mix of forms both received and invented, aesthetic devices such as the break, the cut, the recurrent or repeating figure, and the celebration of openness and the acceptance of accident (Hall in Rutherford 1990; Hesse in Keith and Pile 1993; Hebdige 1987; Gilroy 1993).

Joy Gregory's *Memory and Skin* (1998–9) is an example of work readable in these terms. It is a sizeable and complex piece exploring, in her words, 'the issues of fragmentation, layering, dichotomy and contradiction that form the relationship between Europe and the Caribbean' (Gregory in Sand and McNeill 1998: 101). Filling a medium-sized gallery space it comprises sound, spoken narratives, projected video and photographs. In the version exhibited at the Royal Photographic Society Gallery in 1999, the central area of the space is taken up with a series of museum-style cabinets containing items of material and symbolic culture. Each cabinet is devoted to a theme – Memory, Trade, Food, Women, Tobacco & Sugar, Yard, Skin, Land; and displaying foodstuffs, jewellery, popular and promotional images, found photographs, tokens, charms, natural objects, commodities, tools and so on.

While the multiple elements in *Memory and Skin* are clearly bonded thematically, the work appears devoid of ultimate aesthetic cohesion. But this apparent absence of resolution is itself an aesthetic move which reproduces formally the features of the thing it seeks to configure. Thus the system appears as a great scattering of people and cultural fragments around the littorals of a great interior sea and across three continents and indicates the great absence at its centre – the ocean and the oceans of loss. And yet we understand that these fragments have formed the necessary parts of a unitary system, in some ways a kind of nation, albeit one of peripheries and of movements between – more 'outer' than 'inter' national, as Paul Gilroy has phrased it.

The theme is reinforced by large photographs mounted in the centre of clear perspex screens suspended from the gallery ceiling. They show a variety of locations – a garden in Havana, Seville cathedral, Rotterdam port, figures in a Guayanan field, sugar cane, the coast of Haiti among others.

The mode of exposition introduces important complexities into the meanings of these images. Their isolation in individual frames suggests disconnection between the places they depict. However, through each screen other images can be seen and others through them. The images float over and into each other recalling the layering to which Gregory refers. Photographic reference to real histories and places is combined with the use of the exhibition space as an aesthetic device to give reality to a conceptual principle – namely, the coexistence of distance and presence, of separation and interdependence in a system formed historically by both explosive and implosive energies.

And the relative grandeur of the suspended photographs returns importance to 'obscure' places, or places whose historical meanings have grown invisible. For example, one shows the windows of a merchant's house in Nantes. From them European eyes once looked out on to the slave ships, the basis of their wealth, their *position*, and literally, of their *point of view* – the place from where they looked.

The projected video runs continuously. Its sounds and images play through the translucent screens and across the whole space. The images fade in and out like dreams: churches and outlandish European monuments of the tropical Baroque; a neo-Classical gazebo by a hot lake; the British Houses of Parliament (no less bizarre), the roofs and washing line of poor districts. Women laugh, women sing; a cataract of sugar cascades, dissolves to sunlight on waves; sailing ships slip past; trains pull out of stations. There are harbours and fields, faces and working hands – and the sea, always the sea, the Ocean of the Middle-Passage, the slipstreams of ships, the sunlight on the waves. Sounds drift across the room, mixing with the still images as the viewer moves through the exhibition: voices, snatches of song, the sound of waves and currents; and, like a linchpin holding the scattered pieces together, the repeating movement of a hand driving a royal-crested teaspoon into a bowl of white sugar. It is an image at once familiar and violent that shows the ordinary substance as producer of extraordinary wealth and pain, as maker of an ocean of extraordinary narratives.

Displaying items of Caribbean material culture, the cabinets appear to function as parts of a familiar ethnographic curatorial practice. The adoption by a Black artist of a procedure so resonant with its earlier colonialist applications might be thought surprising. However, like the Native American artist Jimmy Durham, the maker of subversive pastiches of American Indian museums, Gregory is an artist not a museum curator. And the space in which she has placed these items is that of the aesthetic not the ethnographic. Rather than laying out the spent objects of immobilised cultures comprehended solely through the museum's categories, the cabinets represent a syncretism of materials and things. In the aesthetic space the display becomes the collage whose combinations and recombinations signify the possibility of new associations and new meanings. What might have been the object of a social science has become the poetic object, the sign-object, a potential source or conductor of cultural energies, an object redeemed from evil determinations.

But unlike collage, the items in the cabinets retain a degree of separation from each other and from the other elements in the overall work. In the gallery space, in the principles governing her aesthetic space, in the distinctions between the individualised portraits along the exhibition's walls and the locations and groups on the screens; in the use of video and display cabinets, sounds and images; and in all the distinct social and historical spaces indicated by her representations Gregory preserves the distances and separations and particularities so characteristic of the diasporic world. Paul Gilroy identifies this celebration of the gap between elements, of their relative autonomy within a work, as a crucial principle of diasporic aesthetics. It represents, he claims, the figuring of Black travelling cultures, vividly apparent in the 'cut 'n' mix' principle of certain kinds of Black musical composition and performance (Gilroy 1993: 104). It exemplifies how, against the habitual assumptions made about Black cultural practices as intuitive, spontaneous or 'authentic', more often than not they are notably analytical, intellectual or synthetic. In *Memory and Skin* the aesthetic organisation brings about the displacement of the photograph from its prominent position. Where there is no centre there can be no central medium; where there is no stasis there can be no static point of view. Everything is transformed by the condition of travelling.

Disappearance

> The loss of the traveller's tale. (Paul Virilio, *Open Sky*, 1997)

> What to do ... keep this connection with otherness. (Jean Baudrillard, *The Ecstasy of Photography*, 1997)

What kinds of travel and travel photography are possible when the traveller's old certainties concerning self, art and the old qualities and purposes of journeys are being lost? Even photographer-travellers committed to the aesthetics of difference are not free of what Paul Virilio calls a crisis manifested most dramatically in the 'waning' of reality. Over-represented and converted into repeating conventions, the real coincides with its own image, becomes too well known, too fast. So much so that weary Baudrillardians no longer need to look out of the window 'to follow the journey' (Baudrillard 1990: 205). Few surprises remain for the traveller as global capitalism extends its standard grammar of image and spectacle to all parts. And the digital generation of images without originals is depriving the makers of travel images of their most treasured asset – representations which are the traces of physical, real-time encounters with actual places and people, whose value rests on their authentic connection to a normally distant origin.

And yet even Baudrillard's scepticism towards the traditional possibilities and pleasures of travel does not prevent him from insisting that we still 'have to' do it. What is even more unexpected perhaps is his reassertion of the continuing importance of the photograph and its distinctive effects.

Leaving until later a closer examination of his recent pronouncements on these questions I want, first, to consider the aesthetic responses of some other traveller-photographers to this 'loss of reality' that calls into question their *raison d'être*.

One option is to re-invent the journey, to 'change the object itself'; as did François Maspero and the photographer Anaïk Frantz who in the late 1980s spent a month travelling through untouristic and unnoticed quarters of the Paris suburbs strung along the RER suburban express line – the Roissy Express. What they discovered were invisible communities and the unread marks of histories which obliged the travellers to revise the conventional imagined cultural geography of their own city, a geography whose limitations the trip had uncovered (Maspero 1994).

In a very different response, Sophie Calle created a structure for a journey which originated, like Beau Brummel's opinions and tastes, entirely from outside of herself. In this way she relinquished the burdens of self-expression and the usual definitions of motivation. Her *Suite Vénitienne* of 1983 recounts her shadowing of a strange man, chosen more or less at random, to and around Venice and photographing the following of him, the waiting, the locations. Calle is not interested in knowledge, blackmail, robbery, murder, sex or sexual voyeurism. The only emotions noted are impatience, and apprehension that the man might not appear or that she might be unmasked – and a kind of impersonal ardour as she becomes embroiled in the project's details.

Her monochrome photographs resemble those of the location scout made for a movie which will never be made: an unvisited plaza, alleyways thronged by anonymous figures, a hotel doorway where the man is expected, some shots of him from behind, a visit to a cemetery.

Calle's trip recalls the psychogeographical city plans and photographs and the *dérives* ('playful-constructive' driftings) of the Situationists, who sought to replace objective or instrumentalist descriptions of urban space by city maps, accounts and images drawn additionally out of the affective and imaginary lives of its inhabitants. In 1957 a British member of the Situationist International, Ralph Rumney, was also tracked around Venice by a photographer. The result was a strip of photographs accompanied by Rumney's own commentary. What interested him was the way the city affected his behaviour, his movements and gestures; how he played in it, and how it played with him (in Blazwick 1989: 45–9).

The similarity with Calle's work is striking but not profound. To begin with, Rumney was complicit with the photographer whereas Calle's subject remains unsuspecting. More importantly, Calle's concerns are aesthetic and indifferent to any affective responses. They also direct the viewer towards a reflection on the nature of her medium. In *Suite Vénitienne* the arrangements of another's life are adopted as the basis of aesthetic order. The other's destiny becomes an element determining form rather than an object of psychological attachment. While the notion of the subject being external to itself, even other than itself, echoes a familiar theme in French literature and philosophy from Rimbaud, through Sartre, Lacan and Derrida to Baudrillard (who introduced Calle's catalogue), it also has links with debates concerning the nature of the photographic image.[3]

First, it evokes photography's early and continuing association with detection, even with detective work. Not only has the photograph always been used by the police, journalism and other investigative agencies, a form of detection is one of its basic effects – the detection of details not necessarily sought by the photographer; an impersonal detection, like Calle's project (see Maynard 1997: 119–46).

Second, Calle, photographer and traveller, not only shadows the man and his trip, becomes his shadow, she makes shadows out of him. Calle's photographs are both the mask of her presence and the revelation of her anonymity. But what she does as a photographer is no more than what the average photographer, and indeed the average traveller, must do: surrender to the external world, be its shadower, journey after it and into it. Calle refines this to its minimum – she travels and photographs without interiority, and offers the viewer a world lightened of its weight of meaning and of the projections of personality – pure outside. Calle, for herself, has escaped elsewhere.

No regret at any loss of authenticity or immediacy marks the work of another French photographer, Bernard Faucon. Distinguished by a realism of artifice, an undisguised use of staging, props, painting, dyes, poetic objects, special effects, colour shifts and by a disturbance of the visual field by the installation of writing in three-dimensional form, Faucon's work is comfortable in a world understood as already represented, already theatrical.

Of interest here are those instances of his work where a Baroque playfulness converges on conditions and concepts linked with travel. For example *Les Grandes Vacances 1977–1981* used the mannequins of adolescent boys to stage a series of comic-sinister *tableaux (non) vivants* depicting holiday events. They are in turn ludicrous, arch, hyperbanal, poetic, magical, dark and apocalyptic – like all the best holidays. It is a photography which does not depend on a 'real world' as an alibi for the meanings it has generated, having invented its own. If his photographs can still be regarded as the traces of pro-photographic events, they are the record of aesthetic acts and moments.

And yet the series does make reference to a world we recognise, one governed by the familiar qualities of the holiday – the mythic, the clichéd and the palpably artificial. Faucon infuses them with something like wry enchantment. This he does through an odd coupling of the mannequins' lifeless immobility with the hyperbolic events filled with fictive energy which take place around them – fires in trees, a sky-searing comet, fields of lavender and broken glass, the crucifixion.

Faucon also has ways with words. In *Les Écritures 1991–1993* formal reflexivity is inseparable from reflecting on travel. In the work Faucon introduces large handwritten phrases carved in wood and covered with light-sensitive material into landscapes photographed in different parts of the world (plate 16).

The words have the properties of physical objects. They exist in the landscape, part of the apparently speechless content of the image. At the same time they are abstract signs produced from a different order to those of the visual and the natural and yet it is through them we determine their significance.

By confusing categories such as icon and symbol, signifier and signified, or language and meta-language, Faucon brings to the fore the concealed presence of signification in visual images. Out of a theoretical insight he creates aesthetic form which makes palpable the ambiguous mix of the sensuous and the conceptual in the process of making and responding to visual representations. To cite Allen S. Weiss, writing in another context, Faucon creates an 'equivocation between epistemophilia and scopophilia' (Weiss in Silverman 1990: 167–8).

Faucon's playful and ironic literalness has a serious aim. Faucon, the photographer, who 'writes with light', adds light-sensitive writing to his scene and photographs it; he rewrites it with light. This way of picturing the relationship between the material world and a photographic representation in terms of written language is as old as the medium and as recent as post-structuralism. However, Faucon ranged as far as Vietnam to make his landscapes. Travelling as idea and practice thus formed the context of their production. And it is the way his work bears on issues of travel that makes his use of the relationship between photography and writing distinctive.

Like arrangements of stones, monuments, flags, markings on walls or trees, travel is one of the means of leaving our presence in and on the indifferent surfaces of the world. Travel is often guided by such markers and frequently includes the making of them.

Photography, too, marks our presence in a place, or rather, has the place mark its presence in our images. It is one of the functions of travel photography. As inscriptions, all of these activities might be described as writing. Writing establishes our presence in the world. Unlike speech it remains in the world like an object, or a physical trace, or a mark. It fills the world with human meaning. Susan Stewart writes:

> Writing leaves its trace, a trace beyond the life of the body. Thus, while speech gains authenticity, writing promises immortality ... our terror of the unmarked grave is a terror of the insignificance of a world without writing. (Stewart 1993: 31)

Faucon makes visible how the traveller's look is also a form of writing, an inscribing of self on to the world, the utterance of a desire to absorb it by visual possession and at the same time to saturate it with consciousness and fill the ontological void between self and world. Faucon's photograph is the inscription of this look.

But the photographer's project must fail and for that reason so must the traveller's. The failure is anticipated in Faucon's scripts. The '*peut-être*'/'perhaps' in the vista of Indo-China suggests that a return is unlikely and makes the picture tremble on the lip of the elegiac. Other phrases used in the series deepen the feeling that the world is irrecoverable and that ultimately travelling and picture-making serve to confirm it. In a stony wilderness beneath dark clouds one text reads: '*On a frappé trés fort et la porte s'est ouverte sur le vide*', ('You knocked hard and the door opens on emptiness'). In a warm and fragrant Provençal landscape stand the words: '*Un jour nous aurons connu le bonheur*' ('One day we shall know happiness'). Another text even conveys the anti-Romantic suggestion that travel functions to establish the limits rather than the limitlessness of the world: '*La diversité n'est pas infinie, tout voyage a une fin*' ('Diversity is not infinite, all journeys end').

It is through the same device that sought to resolve the visible world and the meanings we give to it – language photographed as an object – that the failure takes place. In its conceptual dimension writing transcends moment and location. Travellers can carry the meaning of a place away with them. But, while Faucon's photograph (plate 16) made an image from objects, it was also transforming signs into objects, words into things. As things on sticks the letters remain there outside of the traveller, back there in time, wearing-away in the weather, gradually falling apart. The traveller had hoped to see written into the world visited his or her own hopes and meanings, his or her own face. Instead, the letters have been claimed back by the realm of external things unmoved by either the attendance or disappearance of humans – mute objects without significance.

Faucon's work opposes the nostalgia of Romantic travel with stoicism, with a conception of travel as no more and no less than a reflexive pleasure, as an exploration of itself and as the condition for the staging of aesthetic events.

The theme of travelling recurs throughout Victor Burgin's work over the last twenty years, from the image of the American highway in *USA 77* as it parallels away towards the vanishing point in front of the car windscreen to the displaced and layered journeyings of the 1997 book *Venise*. But as with everything else in his work, travelling and its representation are made problematical. The highway image of *USA 77* is effectively a calm parody of the heroic American road photograph. It invokes the image's conventional connotations of a self possessed of endless unobstructed possibilities that are underwritten by a visual practice assuming unmediated entry into continuous space and self-evident truth, only to disrupt them by contaminating the purity of the visual with a theoretical text titled '*False Perspective*' concerned with the impossibility of presence. 'Mankind', it begins, 'never lives entirely in the present' (Burgin in Burgin 1986b: 49).

It could be argued that the whole of Burgin's work is preoccupied by the principle of non-coincidence or non-presence. It is mostly a photography of representations, of intertextuality, filled with already existing images – advertisements, billboards, faces grabbed off the television screen or by studio reconstructions which mimic particular images or image-genres. The Real, which for Lacanians is anyway a function of the Symbolic, is permanently deferred by the very act of attempting to signify it.

Unable to coincide with our own representations, destined to love in the other what we have projected on to them – hence the near obsession with the *Vertigo* texts – Burgin pictures our condition as one of ceaseless travelling without the prospect of arrival. The actual journeys and identifiable places that are invoked in his work function in part as the motifs of the restlessly mobile and image-dense character of contemporary societies, and as the manifest content of journeys whose true topography is that of the unconscious.

Wilhelm Jensen's *Gradiva*, a novella which Freud read as a narration of the work of repression and the process of psychoanalysis, inspired one of Burgin's photo-textual works in 1982. It concerns an archaeologist who becomes fixated on the stone relief image of a young woman 'who steps along', who may have perished at Pompeii. He travels there as if to find her. For Freud, the woman fixed in stone was an analogue of repression. In the story she corresponds to the repressed and forgotten love the man once had for a girl in childhood. By travelling back to Pompeii he travels back to his own buried self. There he disinters the repressed material by not finding the long-dead Gradiva, the manifest form of his desire, but by re-encountering for real the object of his earlier desire, Zoe. She is the latent object who emerges in the same moment from the site at Pompeii and from the other place, the unconscious, like a 'noon-time ghost'.

Burgin's working of the story in seven images traces two converging journeys. Each begins from the edge of the work, from different ends, and moves towards the centre. Gradiva-Zoe's story moves from an over-attachment to a distant Father to the encounter with the man, or with his look. The man's story moves from the fixation on the Gradiva figure to the realisation that a desirable woman may exist in actuality. The woman's story ends in the image of a female face meeting the viewer's gaze which carries a text referring to Zoe's sense of a man watching her. The man's story ends either in the spectator space before the image of the woman looking out or still contained in the previous frame, in the image of a small, distant and indistinct female figure stepping across a city street whose foreground is almost completely filled by an advertisement showing a man embracing, holding or possessing a woman. The text relates the man's shock on seeing the female figure 'moving with Gradiva's unmistakable gait'.

Where Freud's reading suggests the possibility of release from neurosis through the journey coming to an end in the discovery of the desired person, Burgin's figures remain suspended in absence, in the endless failure of desire to meet anything other than its own representations. The two stories, the two figures, never quite meet. The two journeys never quite end. Between each culminating image lies the interval, the nothingness between the frames, the gap between incommensurate representations. In his own reflections on this work Burgin quotes Lacan accordingly: '*Il n'ya pas de rapport sexuelle*', 'There is no sexual relationship'.

Through his inclusion of the system of contemporary advertising and his use of anonymous images gleaned from the visual media Burgin proposes these hopeless, irresistible journeys of desire as the motifs of a whole cultural system.

Clearly, the same condition prevails in the video and book of 1997, *Venise*.

It is divided between Hitchcock's film with its San Francisco settings and the original Marseilles-based 1950s novel *D'entre les morts* (translation Boileau and Narcejac 1997). Already displaced between two texts and two imagined cities, the conception of the journey as linear, proceeding through continuous time and space and formed by the destiny of a single self, is resisted by an understanding that the destination of each journey is another journey. Each is seen to become the signifier of an other made in other spaces and times and in other memories. The journey to Marseilles evokes the journeys of its history which still move through the present – the deportation of Jews, the colonial wars in the Mahgreb, the immigration routes of North Africans, the fictive links with San Francisco which have written into existence Burgin's own journey. The traveller is always on several journeys at the same time, including those towards death and those which seek to disavow it.

These works by Burgin demonstrate that journeys are only ever journeys signified and therefore subject to the deferrals, displacements, turnings back, the diversions of allusion and connotation and the uncertainties of subject location consequent upon all signification. And they reconfirm the lesson that, while the melancholy which haunts his aesthetics may be the price of insight, it is the unconscious, innocent traveller who does most harm. Absence of insight rather than illicit desire make's Hitchcock's Scotty so destructive in *Vertigo*, as it did Sophocles's Oedipus.

Burgin's works on travelling also establish that just as there are no linear journeys there are no straight photographs and that, besides, it's only death that can bring the anguished complexities of movement and signification to an end. Simply put, undecidability and restlessness are the price of consciousness, of being alive.

While there is some consonance between these and other contemporary photographers and the detail or general tenor of his ideas, Baudrillard differs from most of them in the extreme degree to which he insists that there is no beyond that travel can take us to and there is no higher order of experience or material form that aesthetic practice can offer or separate cultural space in which it can dominate. The real, he tells us, now coincides with its image.

And yet he continues to value the use of travel as a method for producing a more emphatic apprehension of the world's independence, its physical otherness that culture never entirely absorbs – the strangeness and ecstasy of things. Baudrillard was hit by this experience in the American deserts, enraptured by what he calls their 'vertiginous' and unhuman space.

Through such encounters the perceptions and the experience of Being itself are intensified and become acutely particularised. They bring forth, in a way reminiscent of Nietzsche, the renewed ardency of an existence that has rediscovered the self-justifying pleasure of living (Baudrillard 1993: 53, 173–6, cited in Zurbrugg 1997a: 155–6). This is not an advocation of escape from the world but a means of moving *into* rather than *past* it, a procedure in which photography has come to play an essential part.

Baudrillard's strategy is full of ironies. For in *America* the desert is on one hand a space of light void of signs, the refuge from a culture dying under the weight of its own messages. On the other, it is the perfect image of the possible future of that culture – the flatness, the silent linear perfection, the nuclear weapons test sites, the white blindness of the desert light, the nuclear flash. 'The inhumanity of our ulterior, asocial, superficial world', he writes, 'immediately finds its aesthetic form here, its ecstatic form. For the desert is simply that: an ecstatic critique of culture, an ecstatic form of disappearance' (Baudrillard 1988: 5). Baudrillard's desert trip takes in the non-social wilderness of mineral and sunlight and at the same time cruises high on the negation it represents, the light of the post-human abstractions that glimmer on the rim of the future.

His approach acknowledges the famous disappearance of all grand narratives and therefore rejects the use of the journey as metaphor for a principle of universal human progress he can no longer accept. Instead, travelling and the associated making of representations are seen as no more than the acts of the curious individual pursuing self-creation or, as Rorty terms it, 'self-enlargement', through encounters with the world and others which take him or her beyond familiar limits. This endeavour Rorty describes as 'the aesthetic search for novel experiences and novel language' (Rorty quoted in Shusterman 1988: 388 – a sceptical critique of Rorty's 'aestheticism').

In recent years Baudrillard has countered though not cancelled his dystopic dandyism with a few utopian touches. Some of his reflections on the possibility of opposition to the order of things, on the retrieval of an experience, if not of authenticity then of particularity, are established around the question of travel and his related interest in and active pursuit of photography.

It is not art that concerns Baudrillard in the photograph but the way it recalls us to the particular thing, to the 'radical exoticism of the object', and the way it compensates us for the 'disappointment of the world' by bringing us before the 'stunning clarity' of its details and challenging a general system of representation with the item that is not a part of it (Zurbrugg (1997b) in Zurbrugg 1997a: 153 and 162). Just as digital imaging and the might of the empire of simulation were about to disable it, photography has evolved a new indispensability out of its silence, its immobility and the quality, that, in recent years, has been most disputed – its objectivity. If true, photography might offer a resistant cultural enclave against the reigning order where the rates of speed of movement, representation and communication are so great and their itineraries and languages so conventionalised that they threaten to destroy any experience of the particular and the different and leave us in a condition akin to unconsciousness. Besides, speed has become a consumerist value – 'faster, better, more'.

For Baudrillard photography forms part of his engagement in travelling. It is typically done, he says, while walking or crossing cities. But it's not merely an aid to travelling for him, rather it is itself, 'a kind of travelling', a process of self-departure, of 'acting-out'. He says in the same interview from which I've been quoting, 'The Ecstasy of Photography':

> It's ... a way of escaping oneself, of being elsewhere, a form of exoticism too ... I'm not really a photographer. It's not really the image that I produce ... rather it's this kind of activity, this kind of exoteric excursion. (Baudrillard in Zurbrugg 1997a: 33–4)

Ecstasy is 'stepping out'. Photography's ecstasy is, he says, 'the projection into the image' which, as noted earlier, means that the photograph transports us into the 'immanent presence of the object, rather than the representation of the subject' (Baudrillard in Zurbrugg 1997a: 37, 33).

Encountering the object in all its unexplained particularity, the viewer is granted release from the familiar limitations of subjectivity, itself shaped by official and consumerist meanings and desires. Given that Baudrillard maintains we now live in a state 'deprived of the other' where 'there is no other any more ... [and] nothing comes from the outside', travel and photography have become in his mind ways of remaining in touch with and inventing otherness. He is speaking not only of the otherness of things but by extension of the alterity in others and in ourselves too – the dimension that is peculiar and, like Barthes's *punctum*, never entirely absorbed by official meanings (Baudrillard in Zurbrugg 1997a: 48 and Zurbrugg 1997b).

As the age of digital imaging advances it would seem that we are wondering less about the speed at which traditional photography is engulfed by it than about the nature of a relationship between digital and abiding traditional photographic imageries in which both will be changed.

Christopher Pinney sees two ways in which photography still offers critical and liberating effects. They impinge on its relationship both to travel and to the concerns of the later Baudrillard. Pinney argues that ethnographic film, with its narrative logic marching everything towards its narrative closure, reduces objects and events in the frame to 'background' or into complete insignificance. Nothing, he insists, is permitted to distract from picturing a certainty that is in reality by no means certain.

The ethnographic photograph on the other hand remains by nature 'open', its meanings unanchored. There is no structured 'ending' to the still image, it remains perpetually available to new interpretations. Sustaining uncertainty in the ethnographer-traveller's understanding of another social world is welcome and appropriate in Pinney's view. To accept uncertainty is to foreground the limits of such knowledge and to celebrate the persistence of the Other's spaces and meanings situated beyond the explanations of outsiders.

Pinney also identifies a future struggle between the photograph and virtual reality (VR) which touches on the experience and function of travelling. As complete immersion experience, VR abolishes the frames which organise our sense of the real and of self and, for that reason, our apprehension of the Other. Pinney suggests that, as there is no narrative in VR, everything in it is 'experience'. Story structure is lost. With its subject and object, its inside and outside, here and there, the story form gives the self its framework. Its disappearance entails the end of selfhood and the death of the traveller. As Pinney writes: 'If I can arrive without ever having to set out, that self-same "I" ceases to exist' (Pinney in Taylor 1994: 424).

For Pinney and Baudrillard the struggle for the object, for the actualities 'out there', is a struggle to maintain 'the connection with otherness'. For neither is this merely a question of serving a taste for that postmodern sublime, the 'shock of heterogeneity' (Scott Lasch). Through, among other things, travelling and the production of photographic images, the struggle represents a defence and a celebration of the unsettling forces and objective mysteries that make the world worth living in, worth travelling through and worth making photographs of.

In Britain during the Second World War official posters carried the interrogation: 'Is Your Journey Really Necessary?' Whatever the answer was then, for the photographer now it must be an unhesitating 'Yes'. For art photographers at least, travelling and creative practice are frequently inseparable. Aaron Siskind, for one, has travelled continuously in order not simply to find images but to arrive in the right perceptual state to recognise them (Traub in Siskind 1989: Introduction). And even a 'photographer' like Victor Burgin, whose scepticism towards the real and photographic realism is profound, remains absorbed by the meanings and consequences of actual as well as imaginary journeys. Indeed, Nietzsche thought the impulse to make art was always the expression of the desire to be elsewhere. If creative photographic practice retains its importance, then so, it seems, must travelling.

But the power of travel to induce the production of images holds a significance that goes beyond the concerns of art photography and its public. The photographic image continues to play the part in the extension and reinforcement of the global economy and culture it was given at its inception. Yet, in alliance with types of travelling, it remains one of the means of challenging this order. In a world squeezed into the cliché journeys and images which disregard conventional itineraries and resemblances, which endlessly reinvent strangeness and explore new territories of human connection, become indispensable for the continuance of autonomous experience. In the traditions of modernism the traveller-photographer may seek to emphasise the shocking and 'irreducible otherness' of the world and confront viewers with the particularity of their own responses (Porter 1991: 321). Or their practices may resemble those of the ethnographer in hoping to bring the viewer closer to other cultural worlds while they exist; in 'making the strange familiar' and opposing the deadness of the familiar with the enlivening challenge of cultural difference.

More than this, unless the real and photographic modes which remain committed to the referent are consigned to the status of cottage crafts, travelling and photography continue to offer types of experience and visualisation in which the conditions of a certain conception of human existence are clarified. They are delivered through a magnified apprehension of the world of objects;

the blinding focus on *things* – on things as they are. This is to accept Baudrillard's adherence to the object, with its singularity and otherness. But it also contains Czeslaw Milosz's conviction that to travel the world and celebrate the existence of things, by which he means objects and phenomena in which gods no longer reside, is to confirm and celebrate a free and autonomous human existence passed in a material world indifferent to humans. To embrace things is to embrace one's humanity. 'To glorify things just because they are' he writes in his poem 'The Blacksmith Shop', and restates in 'Conversation with Jeanne': 'Untranslatable into words, I chose my home in what is now, / In things of this world, which exist and for that reason delight us' (Milosz 1993: 1, 40).

The monadic loneliness at the core of the Renaissance way of seeing survived its subsequent transformations. The Dutch 'northern eye' never lost it and it remains intact in Cowper's Alexander Selkirk/Robinson Crusoe figure – the 'monarch of all I survey' – a creation of the second half of the eighteenth century. The marooned Selkirk owns everything stretched out before his vision. But the price of absolute sovereignty over his island is absolute solitude: 'Better dwell in the midst of alarms, / Than reign in this horrible place' ('Verses, supposed to be written by Alexander Selkirk, during his solitary abode in the island of Juan Fernandez').

Visual and poetic practices from Romanticism to Modernism and much of contemporary visual and cultural theory have opposed this one-eyed, one-sided mode of seeing. In contemporary visual theory and practice attempts have been made to go beyond the spaces and subjectivities of those objectified in the image. This has involved the inclusion of visual grammars from different cultural traditions; or the introduction into an image of the limits and blindnesses in the seer's visual field and perceptual assumptions (Bryson in Foster 1988: 87–114; Levin in Levin 1993: 186–217). For example, since the post-colonial era some Magnum photographers have featured in their imagery non-Western subjects who block or resist the penetration of the photographer's look: painted eyes which outstare the viewer; or events and signs which defy cultural translation (Harry Gruyaert, Micha Bar-Am, Bruno Barbey, Gilles Peress).

And yet the distant, isolated and all-knowing consciousness persists undiminished in the still influential reflections of theorists such as the mandarin, disengaged Barthes of *The Empire of Signs* or the blanked-out egotist that is the Baudrillard of *America*. Both, of course, were white, male Europeans. Perhaps for that reason I want to bring the study to a close by returning to Wim Wenders's film *Alice in the Cities*, a narrative concerning another male isolate, but one where journeys and photographs which bring about separation also represent the means of escaping it, the ways of helping us 'be at home in the world'.

Throughout his trip across a United States pictured as an infinite loop of traffic, windscreens streaming with neon messages, radio ads and motel televisions which nobody watches, the anomic European protagonist is unable to inhabit the places or moments he arrives in. On the beach by Coney Island, both traumatised and fascinated by America, he makes repetitious polaroids of the sea as though they might bring him closer to his own experience. Voicing lines from The Drifters' 'Under the Board Walk', he stares into the reduced likenesses of what had been in front of him seconds before but has already vanished. 'With my baby on a blanket, that's where I want to be', he warbles, as though he dreams of passing into the perfection of the image. The journeys and the polaroids have simply deepened his displacement, confirmed his remoteness. In his America, images merely generate more images, evolve an ecology of images signifying the redundancy of viewers.

In New York he becomes saddled with the responsibility of helping a small German girl return to Europe and find her grandparents by means of the photograph of their house she carries with her. It is only then that he begins to connect or, rather, coincide with places and people beyond himself. When he and the girl finally stand before the house, he holds the photograph up to it expressing quiet amazement at the precise resemblance as though he'd never fully believed that photographs did this. What makes the journey, the image and his travelling meaningful is the fact of the child's need, her need for his help and his ultimate acceptance of it. Reality, space and mobility are not after all abstractions or entities standing outside of human experience. Rather, they are the products of human activity and engagement – modes of lived existence. And whether or not photographs produce truths is dependent on the kind of contracts we negociate and renegociate with them. Nobody quite finds home in *Alice in the Cities*; but when Wenders's traveller-photographer is able to close the distance between himself and another human being photographs work and journeys begin to lead somewhere.

Notes

1 See also John Schott's work on motels along Route 66.

2 Dimendberg notes how Albert Renger-Patzsch's photography of the Third Reich's autobahn system paired the 'industrialized gaze' with the 'automobilized gaze', one that is moving but at the same time disciplined by the structure and landscape of the road (Dimendberg 1995: 110–11).

3 An impersonality comparable to that in Calle's piece can be found in an account of a return trip from Paris to London by the photographer Bernard Plossu and the writer Michel Butor which replicates the obviousness and banality of an unmomentous rail trip without any attempt at style or sophistication. The approach is described in the book as 'hyperbanalisme'. See Bernard Plossu and Michel Butor, *Paris – Londres – Paris*, Mission Photographique Transmanche Cahier 1, Éditions de la Différence, Centre Régional de la Photographie, Nord Pas-de-Calais, 1988. Calle's work also seems to anticipate the use of the Webcam to follow the lives of strangers in all their insignificances.

References

Abrams, M. H. (1971) *Natural Supernaturalism: Tradition and Revolution in Romantic Literature*, New York, W. W. Norton and Co. Ltd.

Alloula, Malek (1987) *The Colonial Harem*, Manchester, Manchester University Press.

Alpers, Svetlana (1989) *The Art of Describing: Dutch Art in the Seventeenth Century*, Harmondsworth, Penguin.

Adler, Judith (1989) 'Origins of sightseeing', *Annals of Tourism Research*, 16–1.

Amelunxen, Hubertus V., Stefan Iglhaut and Florian Rötzer (eds), in collaboration with Alexis Cassell and Nilolaus G. Schneider (1996) *Photography After Photography: Memory and Representation in the Digital Age*, Munich, G+B Arts, OPA (Overseas Publishers Association).

Anders, Günther (1980) *Die Antiquiertheit des Menschen*, 5th edition, München, C. H. Beck.

Anderson, Patricia (1991) *The Printed Image and the Transformation of Popular Culture 1790–1860*, Oxford, Clarendon Press.

Arditti, Benjamin, 'Una gramática postmoderna para pensar lo social', in Lechner (1987) and Colas (1994).

Ariès, Philippe and Georges Duby (eds) (1990) *A History of Private Life Volume 3*, Cambridge, Massachusetts and London, Belknap Press.

Arshi, Sunpreet, Carmen Kirstein, Riaz Naqui and Falk Pankow, 'Why Travel?', in Robertson et al. (1994).

Attie, Shimon (1993) *The Writing on the Wall: Projections in Berlin's Jewish Quarter*, Heidelberg: Editions Braus.

Augé, Marc (1995) *Non-places: An Introduction to an Anthropology of Supermodernity*, London, Verso.

Bakhtin, Mikhail (1973) *Problems of Dostoyevsky's Poetics*, trans. R. W. Potsel, New York, Ardis.

Barthes, Roland (1972) *Mythologies*, London, Jonathan Cape.

Barthes, Roland (1977) *Image, Music, Text: Essays*, selected and translated by Stephen Heath, London, Fontana.

Barthes, Roland (1982) *Camera Lucida: Reflections on Photography*, London, Jonathan Cape.

Barthes, Roland (1984) *The Empire of Signs*, New York, Hill and Wang.

Barthes, Roland (1995) *Roland Barthes on Roland Barthes*, London, Papermac Macmillan.

Bartkowski, Frances (1995) *Travellers, Immigrants, Inmates: Essays in Estrangement*, Minneapolis and London, University of Minnesota Press.

Bate, David (1992) 'The Occidental Tourist: Photography and Colonizing Vision', *Afterimage*, summer: 11–13.

Bates, H. W. (ed.), (n.d.: late nineteenth century) *Illustrated Travels: A Record of Discovery, Geography and Adventure*, 2 volumes, London and New York, Cassell Petter and Galpin.

Baudrillard, Jean (1988a) *America*, London, Verso.

Baudrillard, Jean (1988b) 'Consumer Society', in Poster (ed.) (1988).

Baudrillard, Jean (1988c) 'Simulacrum and Simulation', in Poster (ed.) (1988).

Baudrillard, Jean (1990) *Cool Memories*, London, Verso.

Baudrillard, Jean (1993) *The Transparency of Evil: Essays in Extreme Phenomena*, London, Verso.

Baudrillard, Jean, 'The System of Collecting', in Elsner (1994).

Bauman, Zygmunt, 'From Pilgrim to Tourist – a Short History of Identity', in Hall and du Gay (1996).

Beezer, Annie (1994) 'Women and "Adventure Travel" Tourism', *New Formations*, 21 (winter).

Benjamin, Walter (1973) *Charles Baudelaire: A Lyric Poet in the Era of High Capitalism*, London, Verso.

Bennington, Geoffrey (1991) 'Postal Politics and the Institution of the Nation', in Bhabha (1991).

Berger, John (1972) *Ways of Seeing*, London and Harmondsworth, BBC with Penguin.

Berger, John (1980) *About Looking*, London, Writers and Readers.

Berger, John (1984) *And Our Faces, My Heart, Brief as Photographs*, London, Granta Books in association with Penguin.

Berger, John and Jean Mohr (1982) *Another Way of Telling*, London, Readers and Writers.

Beverley, John, José Oviedo and Michael Aronna (eds) (1995) *The Postmodernism Debate in Latin America*, Durham and London, Duke University Press.

Bhabha, Homi K. (ed.) (1991) *Nation and Narration*, London and New York, Routledge.

Bhabha, Homi K. (1994) *The Location of Culture*, London and New York, Routledge.

Bhimji, Zarina (1992) *I Will Always Be Here*, introduction by Mark Haworth-Booth, Birmingham, Ikon Gallery.

Bien, Ania, 'Hotel Polen', *Creative Camera, I* (1989).

Bird, Jon, Barry Curtis, Tim Putnam and Lisa Tickner (eds) (1993) *Mapping the Futures: Local Cultures, Global Change*, London, Routledge.

Blazwick, Iwona (ed.) (1989) *An Endless Adventure – An Endless Passion – An Endless Banquet: A Situationist Scrapbook*, London, ICA and Verso.

Boileau, Pierre and Thomas Narcejac (1997) *Vertigo*, translated by Geoffrey Sainsbury, London, Bloomsbury.

Bolton, Richard (ed.) (1992) *The Contest of Meaning: Critical Histories of Photography*, Cambridge, Massachusetts and London, MIT Press.

Boorstin, Daniel (1963) 'The Pseudo Event', in *The Image*, Harmondsworth, Penguin.

Boorstin, Daniel (1985) *The Discoverers: A History of Man's Search to Know His World and Himself*, New York, Random House.

Bourdieu, Pierre (1990) *Photography, A Middle-brow Art*, Oxford, Whiteside Polity Press in Association with Basil Blackwell.

Bourne, Samuel (Correspondence from India):
(1863a) *Journal of the Photographic Society*, 1 July.
(1863b) *Journal of the Photographic Society*, 1 September.
(1864a) *Journal of the Photographic Society*, 1 February.
(1864b) *Journal of the Photographic Society*, 15 February.
(1869a) *Journal of the Photographic Society*, 1 September.
(1869b) *Journal of the Photographic Society*, 26 November.
(1870a) *Journal of the Photographic Society*, 28 March.
(1870b) *Journal of the Photographic Society*, 4 March.

Bragaglia, Antonio and Giulio Bragaglia, 'Futurist Photodynamism', excerpt in Philips (1989).

Brett, Guy (1990) 'Preface', in *Transcontinental: Nine Latin American Artists*, London and New York, Verso.

Bronfen, Elisabeth (1992) *Over Her Dead Body*, Manchester, Manchester University Press.

Browne, Janet (1995) *Charles Darwin: Voyaging*, London, Jonathan Cape.

Brunfield, John (1982) 'The "Americans" and the *Americans*', *Afterimage*, summer: 1–2.

Bryson, Norman, 'The Gaze in the Expanded Field', in Foster (1988).

Buck-Morss, Susan (1989) *The Dialectics of Seeing: Walter Benjamin and the Arcades Project*, Cambridge, Massachusetts and London, MIT Press.

Buck-Morss, Susan, 'The Dream World of Mass Culture – Walter Benjamin's Theory of Modernity and the Dialectics of Seeing', in Levin (1993).

Burgin, Victor (1982) 'Victor Burgin', *Creative Camera*, 215 (November).

Burgin, Victor (1986a) *Between*, London, Basil Blackwell and ICA.

Burgin, Victor (1986b) *The End of Art Theory: Criticism and Modernity*, London, Macmillan.
Burgin, Victor, 'Geometry and Abjection', in Burgin (1986b).
Burgin, Victor, 'Paranoiac Space', in Taylor (1994).
Burgin, Victor (1997) *Venise*, EU, Black Dog Publishing Ltd.
Burke, Edmund (1988) *A Philosophical Enquiry into the Origins of Our Ideas of the Sublime and the Beautiful*, edited by Adam Phillips, Oxford, Oxford University Press.
Cairncross, Frances (1988) *The Death of Distance: How the Communications Revolution Will Change Our Lives*, London, Orion.
Calvino, Italo (1992) *Six Memos for the Next Millennium*, London, Jonathan Cape.
Campbell, C. (1987) *The Romantic Ethic and the Spirit of Modern Consumerism*, Oxford, Basil Blackwell.
Cardinal, Roger, 'Romantic Travel', in Porter (1997).
Carter, Paul (1987) *The Road to Botany Bay: An Essay in Spatial History*, London and Boston, Faber and Faber.
Carter, Paul (1992) *Living in a New Country: Travelling and Language*, London and Boston, Faber and Faber.
Certeau, Michel de (1984) *The Practice of Everyday Life*, Berkeley and Los Angeles, University of California Press.
Charlton, D. G. (1984) *New Images of the Natural in France*, Cambridge, Cambridge University Press.
Clark, Katerina and Michael Holquist (1984) *Mikhail Bakhtin*, Cambridge, Massachusetts and London, Belknap Press, Harvard University Press.
Clifford, James (1988) *The Predicament of Culture*, Cambridge, Massachusetts and London, Harvard University Press.
Cockburn, Claude (1972) *Bestsellers*, London, Sidgwick and Jackson.
Coghill, Sir J. J. (1859) 'Spanish Journey', *Journal of the Photographic Society*, 5, 82 (9 April).
Cohen, Eric (1974) 'Who is a Tourist? – a Conceptual Classification', *The Sociological Review*, 22, 4.
Cohen-Salal, Annie (1993) *Sartre – a Life*, London, Minerva.
Cohn, Bernard S., 'Representing Authority in Victorian India', in Hobsbawm and Ranger (1984).
Colas, Santiago (1994) *Postmodernity in Latin America: The Argentine Paradigm*, Durham and London, Duke University Press.
Coleman, Simon and John Elsner (1995) *Pilgrimage – Past and Present in the World Religions*, London, British Museum Press.
Colomina, Beatriz (ed.) (1992) *Sexuality and Space*, Princeton and New York, Princeton Architectural Press.
Cook, Jno (1982) 'Robert Frank's America', *Afterimage*, 9, 8, March.
Corbin, Alain, 'The Secret of the Individual', in Ariès and Duby (1990).
Coward, Rosalind (1996) 'Sun, Sand and the Encounter with Otherness',

Guardian, 27 May.
Crary, Jonathan (1990) *Techniques of the Observer: On Vision and Modernity in the Nineteenth Century*, Cambridge, Massachusetts and London, MIT Press.
Crick, Malcolm (1984) 'Sun, Sex, Sights, Savings and Servility', *Criticism, Heresy and Interpretation*, 1.
Crimp, Douglas, 'The Photographic Activity of Postmodernism', *October* 15 (winter).
Culler, Jonathan (1989) *Framing the Sign: Criticism and its Institutions*, Oklahoma City, Oklahoma University Press.
Dagognet, François (1992) *Etienne-Jules Marey: A Passion for the Trace*, New York, Zone Books.
Davies, Paul, 'The Face and The Caress', in Levin (1993).
Davis, John (1996) *The Landscape of Belief: Encountering the Holy Land in Nineteenth-century American Art and Culture*, Princeton, Princeton University Press.
Deleuze, Gilles (1988) *Foucault*, Minneapolis, University of Minnesota Press.
Deleuze, Gilles and Félix Guattari (1978) *Anti-Oedipus*, New York, Viking.
Delpire, Robert (1988) 'Josef Koudelka – Discussion', *Camera International* (Paris), 15 (Mai/Juin).
Derrida, Jacques (1973) *Speech and Phenomena and Other Essays on Husserl's Theory of Signs*, Evanston, Northwestern University Press.
Derrida, Jacques (1978) 'Structure, Sign and Play in the Discourse of the Human Sciences', in *Writing and Difference*, London, Routledge.
Descartes, René (1965) *Discourse on Method, Optics, Geometry and Meteorology*, Indianapolis, Bobbs Merrill.
Desnoes, Edmundo (1987) 'Six Stations on the Latin America Via Crucis', *Aperture*, 109 (winter).
Dewan, Janet (1992) 'Delineating Antiquities and Remarkable Tribes: Photographs for the Bombay and Madras Governments 1855–70', *History of Photography*, 16, 4 (winter).
Dews, Peter (1987) *Logics of Disintegration: Post-structuralist Thought and the Claims of Critical Theory*, London, Verso.
Dimendberg, Edward (1995) 'The Will to Motorization', *October*, 73 (summer).
Dittborn, Eugenio (1993) *Mappa – Eugenio Dittborn Airmail Paintings*, London, ICA and Wittede With.
Dittborn, Eugenio and Roberto Merino, 'Signs of Travel – Conversation with Eugenio Dittborn', in Dittborn (1993).
Dufferin and Ava, the Marchioness of (1889) *My Viceregal Life in India*, 2 volumes, London, John Murray.
Durand, Régis, 'How to See Photographically', in Petro (1995).
Eco, Umberto (1997) *The Search for the Perfect Language*, London, Fontana Press (Harper Collins).

Elsner, Jás and Joan-Pau Rubiés (1999) *Voyages and Visions – Towards a Cultural History of Travel*, London, Reaktion Books.

Elsner, John and Roger Cardinal (eds) (1994) *The Cultures of Collecting*, London, Reaktion Books.

Emerson, Ralph Waldo (1994) *Nature and Other Writings*, edited by Peter Turner, Boston and London, Shambhala Pocket Classics.

Enzensberger, Hans Magnus (1973) 'Une théorie du tourisme', in *Culture ou mise en condition?: essais traduit par Bernard Lortholary*, Paris, 10/18, Les Lettres Nouvelles.

Ferguson, Russell, Martha Gever, Trinh T. Minh-ha and Cornel West (eds) (1990) *Out There: Marginalisation and Contemporary Culture*, Cambridge, Massachusetts and London, MIT Press.

Flaubert, Gustave (1976) *Bouvard and Pécuchet and Dictionary of Received Ideas*, Harmondsworth, Penguin.

Foster, Hal (ed.) (1988) *Vision and Visuality*, Seattle, Bay Press.

Foucault, Michel (1974) *The Order of Things: An Archaeology of the Human Sciences*, London, Tavistock Publications.

Foucault, Michel (1988) 'Technologies of the Self', in Martin et al. (1988).

Frank, Robert (1993) *The Americans*, introduced by Jack Kerouac, Manchester, Cornerhouse Publications in association with the National Gallery of Art, Washington.

Frazer, Sir James (1993) *The Golden Bough: A Study in Magic and Religion*, Ware, Wordsworth Reference, Wordsworth Editions Ltd.

Freedberg, David (1989) *The Power of the Image*, Chicago and London, University of Chicago Press.

Freud, Sigmund (1953–) *Standard Edition of the Works of Sigmund Freud*, London, Hogarth Press.

Freund, Gisèlle (1980) *Photography and Society*, London, Gordon Fraser.

Galassi, Peter Henri (1987) *Cartier-Bresson: The Early Work*, New York, Museum of Modern Art New York City.

García Márquez, Gabriel (1987) *One Hundred Years of Solitude*, translated by Gregory Rabassa, London, Picador.

Gay, Peter (1985) *The Education of the Senses – The Bourgeois Experience*, volume 1, Oxford, Oxford University Press.

Geary, Christraud M. and Virginia-Lee Webb (1998) *Delivering Views: Distant Cultures in Early Postcards*, Washington and London, Smithsonian Institute Press.

Gernsheim, Helmut (1988) *The Rise of Photography 1850–80*, London, Thames and Hudson.

Gifford, Don (1990) *The Farther Shore: A Natural History of Perception 1798–1984*, London and Boston, Faber and Faber.

Gilroy, Paul (1993) *Black Atlantic: Modernity and Double Consciousness*, London, Verso.

Glasser, Martin (1992) 'Histories of Photography 1839–1939', *History of*

Photography, 16, 1.
Golding, John (1968) *Cubism – A History and an Analysis 1907–1914*, 2nd edition, London, Faber and Faber.
Graburn, Nelson H., 'Tourism: The Sacred Journey', in Smith (1989).
Green, Jonathan (1984) *A Critical History of American Photography*, New York, Harry N. Abrams Inc.
Greenblatt, Stephen (1980) *Renaissance Self-fashioning*, Chicago, University of Chicago Press.
Greenblatt, Stephen (1991) *Marvellous Possessions – The Wonder of the New World*, Oxford, Clarendon Press.
Greenwood, Davydd J., 'Culture by the Pound: An Anthropological Perspective on Tourism as Cultural Commodification', in Smith (1989).
Gregory, David (1994) *Imagined Geographies*, Oxford, Basil Blackwell.
Grossberg, Lawrence, Cary Nelson and Paula A. Treichler (eds) (1992) *Cultural Studies*, London and New York, Routledge.
Grosz, Elizabeth (1988) 'Space, Time and Bodies', *On the Beach* (Sydney) 13 April.
Grove, Richard H. (1995) *Green Imperialism: Colonial Expansion, Tropical Island Edens and the Origins of Environmentalism 1600–1866*, Cambridge, Cambridge University Press.
Grundberg, Andy (1990) *Crisis of the Real – Writings on Photography 1974–1989*, New York, Aperture Press.
Hale, John (1994) *The Civilisation of Europe in the Renaissance*, London, Fontana.
Hall, Stuart, 'Cultural Identity and Diaspora', in Rutherford (1990).
Hall, Stuart and Paul Du Gay (1996) *Questions of Cultural Identity*, London, Sage.
Hand, Seán (ed.) (1989) *The Levinas Reader: Emmanuel Levinas*, Oxford, Basil Blackwell.
Haraway, Donna (1991) *Simians, Cyborgs and Women – The Re-invention of Nature*, London and New York, Routledge.
Harper, Marjory (ed.) (1994) 'Introduction' to *Through Canada with a Kodak – The Countess of Aberdeen*, Toronto, Buffalo and London, University of Toronto Press.
Hartman, M. and Lois Banner (eds) (1974) *Clio's Consciousness Raised*, New York, Harper Colophon Books.
Harvey, David (1989) *The Condition of Postmodernity*, Oxford, Basil Blackwell.
Harvey, David, 'From Space to Place and Back Again: Reflections on the Condition of Postmodernity', in Bird et al. (1993).
Hebdige, Dick (1987) *Cut 'n' Mix*, London, Routledge.
Heidegger, Martin (1977) 'The Age of the World Picture', in *The Question Concerning Technology and Other Essays*, New York, Harper Torchbooks, Harper and Row.

Henisch, B. A. and H. K. Henisch (1990) 'James Roberton of Constantinople: A Chronology', *History of Photography*, 14, 1 (January/March).

Hesse, Barnor, 'Black to Front and Black Again: Racialization through Contested Times and Space', in Keith and Pile (1993).

Hinde (Ltd), John (1993), *Hindesight: Photographs and Postcards by John Hinde Ltd 1935–1971*, Derry and Manchester, Irish Museum of Modern Art Dublin in Association with Orchard Gallery Derry and Cornerhouse Gallery Manchester.

Hobsbawm, Eric (1992) *The Age of Capital 1848–1875*, London, Abacus Press.

Hobsbawm, Eric and Terence Ranger (1984) *The Invention of Tradition*, Cambridge, Cambridge University Press.

Hockney, David (1988) *Hockney on Photography: Conversations with Paul Joyce*, London, Jonathan Cape.

Holmes, Oliver Wendell (1859) 'The Stereoscope and the Stereograph', in Newhall (1981).

hooks, bell, 'Representing Whiteness in the Black Imagination', in Grossberg et al. (1992).

Horne, Donald (1984) *The Great Museum: The Re-presentation of History*, London and Sydney, Pluto.

Huysmans, J.-K. (1959) *Against Nature*, translated by Robert Baldick, Harmondsworth, Penguin.

Ikko, Narahara (1975) *Where Time Has Vanished*, Tokyo, Asahi Shimbun-sha.

Ikko, Narahara (1978), *Creative Camera International Year Book 1978.*

ICA (Institute of Contemporary Arts) (1986) *ICA Documents 5: Postmodernism*, London, ICA.

Irigaray, Luce (1985) *Speculum, or the Other Woman*, Ithaca, Cornell University Press.

Jameson, Fredric (1994) *The Seeds of Time*, New York, Columbia University Press.

Jay, Martin, 'Scopic Régimes of Modernity', in Foster (1988).

Jay, Martin, 'In the Empire of the Gaze: Foucault and the Denigration of Vision in Twentieth Century French Thought', in ICA (1986).

Jenks, Chris (ed.) (1995) *Visual Culture*, London, Routledge.

Jussim, Estelle (1989) *The Eternal Moment: Essays on the Photographic Image*, New York, Aperture Press.

Jussim, Estelle and Elizabeth Lindquist-Cock (1985) *Landscape as Photograph*, New Haven and London, Yale University Press.

Kant, Immanuel (1960) *Observations of the Beautiful and the Sublime*, reprinted 1991, Berkeley, Los Angeles and London, University of California Press.

Kaplan, Caren (1996) *Questions of Travel*, Durham and London, Duke University Press.

Kay, Ronald and Nelly Richard, 'Metaphors of the Photographic Negative', in

Merewether (1987).

Kearney, Richard (1991) *Poetics of Imagining*, London, Harper Collins Academic.

Keith, Michael and Steve Pile (eds) (1993) *Place and Space and the Politics of Identity*, London and New York, Routledge.

Kermode, Frank (1968) *The Sense of an Ending: Studies in a Theory of Fiction*, Oxford, Oxford University Press.

Kermode, Frank (1979) *The Genesis of Secrecy – On the Interpretation of Narrative*, Cambridge, Massachusetts and London, Harvard University Press.

Kern, Stephen (1983) *The Culture of Time and Space 1880–1918*, Cambridge, Massachusetts and London, Harvard University Press.

Koudelka, Josef (1984) *Josef Koudelka* (Hayward Gallery exhibition catalogue), introduction by Bernard Cau, Paris and London, Centre National de la Photographie in association with the Arts Council of Great Britain and the Hayward Gallery.

Koudelka, Josef (1988) *Exiles*, foreword by Czeslav Milosz, London, Thames and Hudson.

Kozloff, Max (1988) 'Josef Koudelka's Theater of Exile', *Artforum*, September.

Krauss, Rosalind, 'Photography in the Service of Surrealism', in Krauss, Rosalind and Jane Livingstone (1986) *L'Amour fou: Photography and Surrealism* (Hayward Gallery exhibition catalogue), London, Arts Council of Great Britain and the Hayward Gallery.

Kristeva, Julia (1976) 'Signifying Practice and Mode of Production', in *Edinburgh '76 Magazine*, 1, edited by Phil Hardy, Claire Johnson, Paul Willemen, Edinburgh, British Film Institute Assisted Publication.

Kyro, Ado (1966) *L'Age d'or de la carte postale*, Paris, André Ballard.

Lawrence, Karen (1994) *Penelope Voyages: Women and Travel in the British Literary Tradition*, Ithaca, New York and London, Cornell University Press.

Lechner, Norbert (ed.) (1987) *Cultura, politica y democratización*, Santiago de Chile, FLACSO.

Lee, David, 'Introduction to *Hindesight*', in Hinde (1993).

Lefebvre, Henri (1991) *The Production of Space*, reprinted 1993, Oxford, Blackwell.

Léger, Ferdinand (1973) *The Functions of Painting*, New York, Viking.

Lemagny, Jean-Claude and André Rouillé (eds) (1987) *A History of Photography – Social and Cultural Perspectives*, Cambridge, Cambridge University Press.

Lencek, Lena and Gideon Bosker (1998) *The Beach: The History of Paradise on Earth*, London, Secker and Warburg.

Levin, David Michael (ed.) (1993) *Modernity and the Hegemony of Vision*, Berkeley, Los Angeles and London, University of California Press.

Levin, David Michael, 'Decline and Fall: Ocularcentrism in Heidegger's

Reading of the History of Metaphysics', in Levin (1993).
Lèvinas, Emmanuel (1989) *Ethics as First Philosophy,* in Hand (1989).
Linkman, A. E. (1990) 'The Itinerant Photographer in Britain 1850–1880', *History of Photography,* 14, 1 (January–March).
Lister, Raymond (1973) *British Romantic Art*, London, G. Bell and Sons.
Lukács, György (1971) *History and Class Consciousness*, London, The Merlin Press.
Lury, Celia (1998) *Prosthetic Culture: Photography Memory and Identity*, London, Routledge.
Lutz, Catherine A. and Jane L. Collins (1993) *Reading National Geographic*, Chicago and London, Chicago University Press.
Macauley, Rose (1964) *Pleasure of Ruins*, London, Thames and Hudson.
MacCannell, Dean (1976) *The Tourist: A New Theory of the Leisure Class*, New York, Shocken Books.
MacCannell, Dean (1992) *Empty Meeting Grounds: The Tourist Papers*, London and New York, Routledge.
Mackenzie, Ray (1987) 'The Laboratory of Mankind: John McCosh and the Beginnings of Photography in British India', *History of Photography*, 11, 2 (April–June).
Magnum (1996) *Magnum Landscape*, foreword by Ian Jeffrey, London, The Phaidon Press.
Mahr, Mari (1989) 'Mari Mahr: Finding a New Language, Interview with John Stathos', *Creative Camera*, 6.
Manchester, William (1989) *In Our Time: The World as Seen by Magnum Photographers*, London, The South Bank Centre and Andre Deutsch.
Marbot, Patrick, 'Towards the Discovery', in Lemagny and Rouillé (1987).
Marcorelles, Louis (1973) *Living Cinema: New Directions in Contemporary Filmmaking*, London, George Allen and Unwin.
Markus, John (1986) 'Out of Darkness, a Vision of Grace', *American Photographer*, January.
Martin, Luther H, Huck Gutman and Patrick H. Hutton (eds) (1988) *Technologies of the Self: A Seminar with Michel Foucault*, London, Tavistock Publications.
Maspero, Jean (1994) *Roissy Express – A Journey Through the Paris Suburbs*, photographs by Anaïk Frantz, London, Verso.
Maynard, Patrick (1997) *The Engine of Visualization: Thinking Through Photography*, Ithaca and London, Cornell University Press.
McGrane, Bernard (1989) *Beyond Anthropology*, New York, Columbia University Press.
McQuire, Scott (1998) *Visions of Modernity*, London, Sage.
Merewether, Charles (ed.) (1987), *A Marginal Body – The Photographic Image in Latin America / Un Cuerpo Marginal – La Imagen Fotográfica en América Latina*, Sydney, Australian Centre for Photography.
Metz, Christian 'Photography and Fetish', in Squiers (1990).

Metzinger, Jean (1911) *Du Cubisme*, 6th edition, Paris, Eugene Fuguiere.

Mill, John Stuart (1968) 'On Liberty', in *Mill – Selected Writings*, edited by Maurice Cowling, London, Mentor Book – New English Library.

Miller, David Philip and Peter Hanns Reill (eds) (1996) *Visions of Empire: Voyages, Botany, and Representations of Nature*, Cambridge, Cambridge University Press.

Miller, Michael B. (1981) *The Bon Marché: Bourgeois Culture and The Department Store 1869–1920*, London, George Allen and Unwin.

Mills, Sara (1991) *Discourses of Difference: An Analysis of Women's Travel Writing and Colonialism*, London and New York, Routledge.

Milosz, Czeslaw (1993) *Provinces, Poems 1987–1991*, Manchester, Carcanet.

Minh-ha, Trinh T., 'Other than Myself/My Other Self', in Robertson et al. (1994).

Mitchell, Timothy (1991) *Colonising Egypt*, Berkeley, Los Angeles and London, University of California Press.

Mitchell, W. J. T. (1994) *Picture Theory: Essays on Verbal and Visual Representation*, Chicago and London, University of Chicago Press.

Moholy-Nagy, Laszlo (1922) 'Dynamic-constructive System of Forces 1922', in Passuth (1985).

Moholy-Nagy, Laszlo (1943) 'Space-time and the Photographer', in Passuth (1985).

Moretti, Franco, 'The Spell of Indecision', in Nelson and Grossberg (1988).

Morris, James (Jan) (1979a) *Pax Britannica: The Climax of Empire*, volume 1 of *Pax Britannica*, Harmondsworth, Penguin.

Morris, James (Jan) (1979b) *Heaven's Command: An Imperial Progress*, volume 2 of *Pax Britannica*, Harmondsworth, Penguin.

Morris, James (Jan) (1979c) *Farewell the Trumpet – An Imperial Retreat*, volume 3 of *Pax Britannica*, Harmondsworth, Penguin.

Mouffe, Chantal, 'For a Politics of Nomadic Identity', in Robertson et al. (1994).

Nadeau, Maurice (1973) *The History of Surrealism*, Harmondsworth, Penguin.

Nash, Dennison (1981) 'Tourism as an Anthropological Subject', *Current Anthropology*, 22, 5.

National Portrait Gallery (1996) *David Livingstone and the Encounter with Africa*, London, National Portrait Gallery.

Nead, Lynda, 'Gender, Space and Modernity in Mid-Victorian London', in Porter (1997).

Nelson, Cary and Grossberg, Lawrence (eds) (1988) *Marxism and the Interpretation of Culture*, Urbana, University of Illinois.

Newhall, Beaumont (ed.) (1981) *Photography – Essays and Images: Illustrated Readings in the History of Photography*, London, Secker and Warburg.

Nir, Yeshayahu (1985) *The Bible of the Image: The History of Photography in the Holy Land, 1839–1899*, Philadelphia, University of Pennsylvania Press.

O'Connor, Steven (1997) *Postmodernist Culture – An Introduction to Theories of the Contemporary*, 2nd edition, Oxford, Blackwell.

Ollman, Arthur (1983) *Samuel Bourne – Images of India*, Carmel, California, Untitled 33, Friends of Photography.

Oppenheimer, Paul (1997) *An Intelligent Person's Guide to Modern Guilt*, London, Duckworth.

Osman, Colin (1997) *Egypt caught in time*, Reading, Garnet Publishing Ltd.

Papastergiadis, Nicos (1993) *Modernity as Exile – the Stranger in John Berger's Writing*, Manchester, Manchester University Press.

Parr, Martin (1993) *Home and Abroad*, introduction by Ian McEwan, London, Jonathan Cape.

Parr, Martin (1995) *Small World*, with a text by Simon Winchester, Stockport, Dewi Lewis Publishing.

Parr, Martin and Nicholas Barker (1994) *From A to B: Tales of Modern Motoring*, London, BBC Books.

Passuth, Kristina (1985) *Moholy-Nagy*, London, Thames and Hudson.

Perez, Nissan N. (1988) *Focus East: Early Photography in the Near East 1839–1885*, New York, Harry N. Abrams Inc.

Petro, Patrice, 'After Shock/ Boredom and History', in Patrice Petro (ed.) (1995) *Fugitive Images: From Photography to Video*, Bloomington and Indianapolis, Indiana University Press.

Philips, Christopher (1989) *Photography in the Modern Era: European Documents and Critical Writings 1913–1940*, New York, Metropolitan Museum of Modern Art and Aperture Press.

Pinney, Christopher, 'Future Travel', in Taylor (1994).

Porter, Dennis (1991) *Haunted Journeys: Desire and Transgression in European Travel Writing*, Princeton, Princeton University Press.

Porter, Roy (ed.) (1997) *Rewriting the Self: Histories from the Renaissance to the Present*, London and New York, Routledge.

Poster, Mark (ed.) (1988) *Jean Baudrillard Selected Writings*, Oxford, Polity Press, Blackwell.

Pratt, Mary Louise (1992) *Imperial Eyes: Travel Writing and Transculturalism*, London and New York, Routledge.

Raby, Peter (1996) *Bright Paradise: Victorian Scientific Travellers*, London, Chatto and Windus.

Rancière, Jacques, 'Discovering New Worlds: Politics of Travel and Metaphors of Space', in Robertson et al. (1994).

Richard, Nelly (1986) *Margins and Institutions: Art in Chile Since 1973*, *Art and Text*, 21, Special Issue, May–June.

Richard, Nelly, 'Metaphors of the Photographic Negative', in Merewether (1987).

Richard, Nelly, 'Cultural Peripheries: Latin America and Postmodernist De-centering', in Beverley (1995).

Richards, Thomas (1991) *The Commodity Culture of Victorian England:*

Advertising and Spectacle 1851–1914, London, Verso.

Robertson, George, Melinda Mash, Lisa Tickner, John Bird, Barry Curtis and Tim Putnam (eds) (1994) *Travellers' Tales: Narratives of Home and Displacement*, London and New York, Routledge.

Robinson, Jane (1996) *Angels of Albion: Women of the Indian Mutiny*, Harmondsworth, Viking, Penguin.

Rojeck, Chris and John Urry (eds) (1997) *Tourism Cultures: Transformations of Travel and Theory*, London and New York, Routledge.

Rorty, Richard (1989) *Contingency, Irony and Solidarity*, Cambridge, Cambridge University Press.

Rose, Gillian (1993) *Feminism and Geography – The Limits of Geographical Knowledge*, Oxford, Polity Press.

Rosler, Martha (1981) *Marthe Rosler, Three Works*, Halifax, Canada, Nova Scotia Pamphlet Press (Nova Scotia College of Art and Design).

Rushdie, Salman (1995) *The Moor's Last Sigh*, London, Jonathan Cape.

Rushdie, Salman (1992) 'On Gunther Grass', in *Imaginary Homelands: Essays and Criticism 1981–1991*, Harmondsworth, Penguin (Granta).

Rutherford, Jonathan (ed.) (1990) *Identity: Community, Culture, Difference*, London, Lawrence and Wishart.

Said, Edward (1986) *After the Last Sky – Palestinian Lives*, with photographs by Jean Mohr, London and Boston, Faber and Faber.

Said, Edward, 'Reflections on Exile', in Ferguson et al. (1990).

Said, Edward (1991) *Orientalism*, Harmondsworth, Penguin Books.

Sallenave, Danielle (1979) 'On the Cold Roads of Time', *Camera*, August.

Sampson, Gary (1992) 'The Success of Samuel Bourne in India', *History of Photography*, 16, 4 (winter).

Sand, Michael L. and Anne McNeill (eds) (1998) *Continental Drift: Europe Approaching the Millennium – 10 Photographic Commissions*, Munich and New York, Prestel.

Santa Barbara Museum of Art (1997) *Revealing the Holy Land: The Photographic Exploration of Palestine*, Santa Barbara, Los Angeles, Berkeley and London, University of California Press.

Sartre, Jean-Paul (1972) *Psychology of Imagination*, London, Methuen.

Sayre, Nora (1997) *Previous Convictions: A Journey Through the Fifties*, New York, Rutgers.

Scharf, Aaron (1974) *Art and Photography*, revised edition, Harmondsworth, Penguin.

Schivelbusch, Wolfgang (1987) *The Railway Journey: The Industrialisation of Time and Space in the Nineteenth Century*, Berkeley, University of California Press.

Schwarz, Bill (1987) 'Travelling Stars', *New Formations*, 3.

Sennett, Richard (1986) *The Fall of Public Man*, London and Boston, Faber and Faber.

Sharma, Brij Bhushar (1987) 'James Ricalton – an American photographer in

India', *History of Photography*, 11, 1 (January–March).
Shields, Rob (1991) *Places on the Margin: Alternative Geographies of Modernity*, London and New York, Routledge.
Shusterman, Richard (1988) 'Postmodern Aestheticism: A New Moral Philosophy?', *Theory, Culture and Society*, 5, 2/3 (June), special issue on postmodernism.
Silverman, Hugh J. (ed.) (1990) *Postmodernism – Philosophy and the Arts*, London, Routledge.
Simmel, Georg (1950) *The Sociology of Georg Simmel*, London, Collier Macmillan.
Siskind, Aaron (1989) *Road Trip*, San Francisco, Friends of Photography.
Slater, Don, 'Photography and Modern Vision', in Jenks (1995).
Slater, Michael (ed.) (1996) *Dickens' Journalism*, Volume 2 *'The Amusements of the People and Other Papers', Reports Essays and Reviews 1834–51*, London, J. M. Dent.
Smith, Daniel Scott, 'Family Limitation, Sexual Control and Domestic Feminism in Victorian America', in Hartman and Banner (1974).
Smith, Neil and Cindi Katz, 'Grounding Metaphor – Towards a Spatial Politics', in Keith and Pile (1993).
Smith, Valene L. (ed.) (1989) *Hosts and Guests: The Anthropology of Tourism*, 2nd edition, Philadelphia, University of Pennsylvania Press.
Sontag, Susan (1978) *On Photography*, Harmondsworth, Penguin.
Spacks, Patricia Meyer (1995) *Boredom*, Chicago, University of Chicago Press.
Squiers, Carol (ed.) (1990) *The Critical Image*, London, Lawrence and Wishart.
Stauth, George and Bryan S. Turner (1988) 'Nostalgia, Postmodernism and the Critique of Mass Culture', *Theory, Culture and Society*, 5, 2/3 (June).
Steiner, George (1971) 'The Language Animal', in *Extraterritorial*, Harmondsworth, Penguin.
Sternfeld, Joel (1994) *American Prospects*, San Francisco, Chronicle Books/Friends of Photography.
Stewart, Susan (1993) *On Longing: Narratives of the Miniature, the Gigantic, the Souvenir, the Collection*, Durham and London, Duke University Press.
Stone, Lawrence (1982) *The Family, Sex and Marriage in England 1500–1800*, abridged edition, Harmondsworth, Penguin.
Tagg, John (1988) *The Burden of Representation: Essays on Photographies and Histories*, Basingstoke and London, Macmillan.
Taylor, Charles (1992) *Sources of the Self: The Making of Modern Identity*, Cambridge, Cambridge University Press.
Taylor, Lucien (ed.) (1994) *Visualising Theory: Selected Essays from V.A.R. 1990–94*, London and New York, Routledge.
Teynard, Félix (1992) *Calotypes of Egypt – A Catalogue Raisonné*, New York and London, Hans B. Krauss Junior and Robert Herschowitz, and the Carmel Gallery, California.

Thoman, Ritchie (1979) 'Bonfils and Son: Egypt, Greece and the Levant 1869–94', *History of Photography*, 3, 1 (January).

Toulimin, Stephen (1990), *Cosmopolis*, Chicago, University of Chicago Press.

Tournier, Michel (1988) *The Golden Droplet*, translated by Barbara Wright, London, Methuen Paperback.

Tournier, Michel (1992) *The Midnight Love Feast*, translated by Barbara Wright, London, Minerva.

Traub, Charles, 'Introduction' to Siskind (1989).

Trevor-Roper, Patrick (1990) *The World Through Blunted Sight: An Enquiry Into the Influence of Defective Vision on Art and Character*, new and revised edition, Harmondsworth, Penguin.

Turner, Bryan S. (1987) 'A Note on Nostalgia', *Theory, Culture and Society*, 4, 1.

Turner, Victor and Turner, Edith (1978) *Image and Pilgrimage in Christian Culture*, New York, Columbia University Press.

Urry, John (1990) *The Tourist Gaze: Leisure and Travel in Contemporary Cultures*, London, Sage.

Urry, John (1995) *Consuming Places*, London and New York, Routledge.

Van Haaften, Julia (1980) *Egypt and the Holy Land in Historic Photographs – 77 Views by Francis Frith*, New York, Dover.

Victoria and Albert Museum (1984) *The Discovery of the Lake District*, London, Victoria and Albert Museum.

Virilio, Paul (1994) *The Vision Machine*, Bloomington and London, Indiana University Press and the British Film Institute.

Virilio, Paul (1997) *Open Sky*, London and New York, Verso.

Warner, Marina (1992) 'Parlour Made – Victorian Women's Family Albums', *Creative Camera*, 315 (April–May).

Watson, G. Llewellyn and Joseph P. Kopachevsky (1990) 'Interpretation of Tourism as Commodity', *Annals of Tourism Research*, 21, 3.

Wees, William C. (1980) 'The Cinematic Image and the Visualisation of Sight', *Wideangle*, 4, 3.

Weiss, Allen S., 'Lucid intervals – Photography and Postmodernism', in Silverman (1990).

West, Nathanael (1957) *Miss Lonelyhearts* (1931), reprinted 1968, London, Secker and Warburg.

Wheelock, Arthur K. Junior (1977) *Perspective, Optics and Delft Artists Around 1650*, New York and London, Garland Publications Inc.

White, John (1987) *The Birth and Rebirth of Pictorial Space*, 3rd edition, London and Boston, Faber and Faber.

Whitford, Margaret (1991) *Luce Irigaray: Philosophy in the Feminine*, London and New York, Routledge.

Wigley, Mark, 'Untitled: The Housing of Gender', in Colomina (1992).

Wilden, Anthony (1968) 'The Discourse of the Other', in *The Language of the Self*, Baltimore, Johns Hopkins.

Williams, Raymond (1975) *The Country and the City*, St Albans, Paladin.

Williams, Val (1994) *Warworks – Women, Photography and the Iconography of War*, London, Virago Press.

Wilton, Andrew and Ilaria Bignamini (eds) (1997) *Grand Tour: The Lure of Italy in the Eighteenth Century*, London, Tate Gallery.

Wittkower, Rudolf (1987) *Allegory and the Migration of Symbols*, London, Thames and Hudson.

Wolff, Janet (1993) 'On the Road Again: Metaphors of Travel in Cultural Criticism', *Cultural Studies*, 7, 2 (May).

Wollen, Peter (1984) *Fire and Ice – Photographies*, 4.

Wombell, Paul (ed.) (1989) *The Globe: Presenting the World*, York, Impressions Gallery.

Wood, James (1995) Review of Gavin Young, *From Sea to Shining Sea*, *Guardian*, 28 February.

Woodruff, Philip (1954) *The Guardians – The Men who Ruled India*, London, Jonathan Cape.

Woody, Howard, 'International Postcards: Their History, Production and Distribution (circa 1895–1915)', in Geary and Webb (1998).

Zurbrugg, Nicholas (ed.) (1997a) *Jean Baudrillard: Art and Artefact*, London, Sage.

Zurbrugg, Nicholas (1997b) 'Barthes, Burroughs and "Absolute Photography"', in Zurbrugg (1997a).

Zurbrugg, Nicholas (1997c) 'The Ecstasy of Photography – interview with Jean Baudrillard', in Zurbrugg (1997a).

Index

Note: 'n.' after a page reference indicates a note number on that page.